Health and Social Relationships

Health and Social Relationships

Social Relationships

The Good, the Bad, and the Complicated

Edited by Matthew L. Newman and Nicole A. Roberts

American Psychological Association • Washington, DC

Published by
American Psychological Association
750 First Street, NE
Washington, DC 20002
www.apa.org

To order
APA Order Department
P.O. Box 92984
Washington, DC 20090-2984
Tel: (800) 374-2721; Direct: (202) 336-5510
Fax: (202) 336-5502; TDD/TTY: (202) 336-6123
Online: www.apa.org/pubs/books
E-mail: order@apa.org

In the U.K., Europe, Africa, and the Middle East, copies may be ordered from
American Psychological Association
3 Henrietta Street
Covent Garden, London
WC2E 8LU England

Typeset in Goudy by Circle Graphics, Inc., Columbia, MD

Printer: United Book Press, Baltimore, MD
Cover Designer: Naylor Design, Washington, DC

The opinions and statements published are the responsibility of the authors, and such opinions and statements do not necessarily represent the policies of the American Psychological Association.

Library of Congress Cataloging-in-Publication Data

Health and social relationships : the good, the bad, and the complicated / edited by Matthew L. Newman and Nicole A. Roberts. — 1st ed.
       p. cm.
   Includes bibliographical references and index.
   ISBN 978-1-4338-1222-4 — ISBN 1-4338-1222-3 1. Social networks—Health aspects.
2. Interpersonal relations—Health aspects. 3. Social interaction—Health aspects.
4. Health—Social aspects. I. Newman, Matthew L. II. Roberts, Nicole A.
   RA418.H43 2013
   613—dc23
                                    2012019789

British Library Cataloguing-in-Publication Data
A CIP record is available from the British Library.

Printed in the United States of America
First Edition

DOI: 10.1037/14036-000

CONTENTS

CONTRIBUTORS

Anne Arewasikporn, MA, Department of Psychology, Arizona State University, Tempe

Stephanie Brown, PhD, Stony Brook University Medical Center, New York, NY; Institute for Social Research, University of Michigan, Ann Arbor

Kathleen S. Bryan, MS, School of Social and Behavioral Sciences, Arizona State University, Phoenix

Mary H. Burleson, PhD, School of Social and Behavioral Sciences, Arizona State University, Phoenix

Emily A. Butler, PhD, Family Studies and Human Development, University of Arizona, Tucson

Yulia Chentsova-Dutton, PhD, Department of Psychology, Georgetown University, Washington, DC

Mary C. Davis, PhD, Department of Psychology, Arizona State University, Tempe

Sally S. Dickerson, PhD, Department of Psychology and Social Behavior, University of California, Irvine

Xin Guan, MS, School of Social and Behavioral Sciences, Arizona State University, Phoenix

Anya V. Kogan, MA, Department of Psychology, University of Arizona, Tucson

Sara Konrath, PhD, Institute for Social Research, University of Michigan, Ann Arbor; Department of Psychiatry, University of Rochester Medical Center, Rochester, NY

Suman Lam, PhD, Department of Psychology and Social Behavior, University of California, Irvine

Elizabeth A. Lee, PhD, Department of Psychology, The Pennsylvania State University, University Park

Ashley E. Mason, MA, Department of Psychology, University of Arizona, Tucson

Matthew L. Newman, PhD, School of Social and Behavioral Sciences, Arizona State University, Glendale

Sarah A. Novak, PhD, Department of Psychology, Hofstra University, Hempstead, NY

Yesmina N. Puckett, MS, School of Social and Behavioral Sciences, Arizona State University, Phoenix

Nicole A. Roberts, PhD, School of Social and Behavioral Sciences, Arizona State University, Phoenix

Theodore F. Robles, PhD, Department of Psychology, University of California, Los Angeles

David A. Sbarra, PhD, Department of Psychology, University of Arizona, Tucson

Jane A. Skoyen, MA, Department of Psychology, University of Arizona, Tucson

Richard B. Slatcher, PhD, Department of Psychology, Wayne State University, Detroit, MI

José A. Soto, PhD, Department of Psychology, The Pennsylvania State University, University Park

Erin T. Tobin, MA, Department of Psychology, Wayne State University, Detroit, MI

Tara M. Vincelette, MS, School of Social and Behavioral Sciences, Arizona State University, Phoenix

Alex Zautra, PhD, Department of Psychology, Arizona State University, Tempe

ACKNOWLEDGMENTS

The initial idea for this book grew out of a seminar course developed by Matthew Newman. We are grateful to the students and colleagues who helped shape our thinking on the topic of health and social relationships over the years—particularly the students who suggested that we "should write a book on this stuff."

We would like to thank Maureen Adams, senior acquisitions editor at American Psychological Association Books, for her support throughout the process of transforming an idea into a book. We also would like to thank the volume's contributors, who brought their research on health and social relationships to life to create this important resource for our field.

Preparation of this manuscript was partially supported by an internal grant from the New College of Interdisciplinary Arts and Sciences at Arizona State University, through the Scholarship, Research, and Creative Activities program.

Last but not least, we are grateful to our families for their patience and support during the writing and editing process and for the positive role they undoubtedly play in promoting good health.

Health and Social Relationships

INTRODUCTION

MATTHEW L. NEWMAN

Social support—the physical and emotional comfort given to us by our friends, family, and romantic partners—can lower blood pressure, strengthen the immune system, and even prolong life among those who are terminally ill. At the other end of the spectrum, a sense of social isolation is associated with psychological maladjustment and poor health and can double the risk of mortality. Between these extremes, variations in real and perceived relationship quality are both cause and effect of variations in mental and physical health. Bad marriages are bad for our health, and stressful life events can be bad for our marriages. Stigmatizing illnesses can make us feel isolated, and isolation makes it harder to heal from illness. Our religious communities can provide valuable coping resources, but rejection by these communities can pose a significant threat to mental and physical health.

Relationships are such a pervasive aspect of our lives that we may not even think about them until there is a problem. Similarly, until we experience

DOI: 10.1037/14036-001
Health and Social Relationships: The Good, the Bad, and the Complicated, Matthew L. Newman and Nicole A. Roberts (Editors)

ailments, we may take for granted being in good health. Researchers have grappled with defining and measuring constructs such as *social support* and *health* and have made great strides in understanding the links between them. But how might something as seemingly intangible as social relationships have such a profound impact on something as concrete as mental and physical health outcomes? One answer involves broadening our conceptualization of health and illness, including why people get sick in the first place. The field of health psychology has adopted a general definition of *health* from the World Health Organization (1948) as "a complete state of physical, mental, or social wellbeing, and not merely the absence of disease or infirmity" (p. 100). This definition hints at two facts: that physical and emotional health are closely intertwined and that perceptions or subjective experience of health may or may not be associated with "objective" markers.

The research reviewed in this volume reflects the *biopsychosocial model* (e.g., Borrell-Carrió, Suchman, & Epstein, 2004; Engel, 1977), whereby health and illness are shaped by multiple influences, including biological factors (e.g., genetic predisposition), behavioral factors (e.g., lifestyle), and social factors (e.g., relationships). For example, imagine Joe has the misfortune to be sneezed on by Bob, who has a nasty case of the flu. The sneeze will no doubt increase Joe's odds of contracting the flu, but the course of this disease will also depend on the quality of Joe's marriage, the frequency of his workouts, and the amount of stress he is facing at work (cf. Cohen, Tyrell, & Smith, 1991).

As alluded to by this example, social psychological models of health, illness, and relationships draw on a "stress and coping" perspective by considering how physical illness (e.g., the common cold) is exacerbated or mitigated by social factors and intervening cognitive processes. Similarly, in the mental health field the *diathesis–stress model* suggests that genetic predispositions plus environmental stress yields mental illness (e.g., depression). More recent models of health and illness have expanded both of these perspectives by developing a greater understanding of cognitive, emotional, and physiological mechanisms (mediators) and mitigating factors such as age, gender, and context (moderators).

FROM STRESS TO ILLNESS

The concept of stress plays a key role in the biopsychosocial model (Kemeny, 2003). Researchers in the field of health psychology tend to make a distinction between *stressors*, or potentially threatening life events that impinge on an important goal, and *stress*, or the physiological correlates and psychological feeling of being overwhelmed by these events. Stressors can be things that threaten our physical well-being (e.g., hunger, fire) or challenge our sense of control and psychological well-being (e.g., loud neighbors, fear of bankruptcy).

The pathway from stress to illness involves an unfortunate paradox: The same finely tuned system that helps the body adapt and respond to threats has negative consequences in the long run. Broadly speaking, the physiological stress response involves both a neural component and a hormonal component (for an in-depth discussion of these processes, see Kemeny, 2007). The neural component involves activation of the sympathetic nervous system, which increases heart rate, inhibits digestion, and stimulates the release of epinephrine from the adrenal glands. This "fight-or-flight" response serves to shift resources to systems that are more essential in the face of a threat. The slower hormonal component involves a chain reaction from the hypothalamus to the pituitary gland to the adrenal glands (the HPA axis), triggering the release of cortisol into the bloodstream. Cortisol serves to sustain the body's responses to stress and aids in adaptations to long-term stressors.

Exposure to stressful events, both acute and chronic, has an impact on the body's immune system, with implications for health and disease outcomes (Kemeny, 2007). The manifestation of these outcomes depends on a wide range of variables, including genetics, personality differences, and the nature of the stressor itself. The initial sympathetic response to acute trauma or stress activates several immune functions—including the immediate production and release of white blood cells to attack disease organisms and an increase in natural killer cells—to help prepare the body for dealing with wounds and infections that may result from fighting or fleeing.

This picture becomes more complicated in cases of chronic stress exposure. Several researchers have suggested that the effort required to respond and adapt to a chronic stressor can have negative consequences (e.g., Berntson & Cacioppo, 2000; McEwen, 2004). In the short term, the process of adapting to environmental stress helps to maintain a balance in the various physiological systems that promote survival. Yet, in the long term, repeated adaptations can take a toll on the body and eventually lead to maladaptive responses to stress. In McEwen's (2004) view, the "adaptive effects of [maintaining] homeostasis are, when mismanaged or overused, also involved in the cumulative wear and tear effects of daily life" (p. 43). The "wear and tear" of chronic stress is often referred to as *allostatic load* and can result in conditions such as decreases in immune function, elevated blood pressure, chronic high levels of cortisol, increased storage of abdominal fat, and problems with memory resulting from shrinking of the hippocampus (Seeman, McEwen, Rowe, & Singer, 2001).

In the case of the immune system, specialized T cells become desensitized by long-term exposure to cortisol and are no longer inhibited by its release. The result of this desensitization is an increase in inflammatory responses, paired with an increase in cortisol. This physiological profile has been associated with an increased risk of several major health problems, including cardio-vascular disease, diabetes, and hypertension (e.g., Kemeny, 2007; McEwen, 2004). These inflammatory processes have also been implicated in the development of depression (e.g., Schiepers, Wichers, & Maes, 2005), highlighting a potential pathway connecting stress with both physical and mental health.

Perhaps most interesting is that the body's physiological stress response makes only minor distinctions between physical and social threats. Encountering a mugger in a dark alley and worrying about paying one's bills can lead to a similar cascade of biological responses. Because the brain's highly developed frontal lobes allow us to plan for the future and anticipate stressors, we are capable of being "stressed" by things that might happen in the future. If Joe is constantly worried that his marriage is failing, this will increase his level of stress and make him more susceptible to Bob's flu virus.

In summary, the connection between stress and illness involves a cascade of physiological responses to social–environmental triggers, which ultimately has implications for disease. Researchers working in the field of health psychology have studied every step of the process, including hormonal and cardiovascular responses to stress, biomarkers of immune system function, healthy and unhealthy behaviors, and the connection of each of these to mental and physical health outcomes. In studying these health outcomes, researchers in health psychology have cast a wide net. In some cases, the focus is on the predictors of a particular mental or physical disease, such as cancer, heart disease, or depression. In other cases, the focus is on a state of overall health or wellness, which, as noted previously, represents a complete state of well-being, rather than merely the absence of disease. And in still other cases, psychologists have focused on the predictors of *subjective well-being,* which encompasses individuals' perceptions of their happiness, quality of life, and positive affect (e.g., Diener, 1984).

Regardless of which particular outcome is under study, the stress and coping literature has devoted much attention to the origins and moderators of stress responses. Indeed, stressful events seem less so if we can predict their occurrence and if we believe we have some control over them—even if this belief is false (e.g., Langer & Rodin, 1976; Mineka & Hendersen, 1985). As described as follows, one of the most influential moderators turns out to be our relationships with other people.

STRESS AND RELATIONSHIPS

Supportive relationships have long been known to reduce the impact of daily stress and improve both physical and emotional well-being. Indeed, these connections were the subject of empirical reviews as early as the 1970s (e.g., Cobb, 1976, 1979; Mitchell, Billings, & Moos, 1982; see Taylor, 2007, for an updated review). But social support as a moderator really gained prominence in 1988, when a review of five separate prospective studies established a causal link between social connections and decreased mortality rates (House, Landis, & Umberson, 1988). Even after controlling for a host of factors, including overall health, socioeconomic status, and drug use, higher levels of social integration were associated with a 50% reduction in mortality. In addition, as House et al. (1988) pointed out, many of these control variables are themselves likely related to social support, making the 50% estimate likely to be a conservative one.

Following the publication of House et al.'s (1988) review, research on the benefits of social relationships exploded in the social sciences, with a focus on both the mechanisms and the moderators of these effects (cf. Holt-Lunstad, Smith, & Layton, 2010). In general, social support is thought to have both direct and buffering effects on health outcomes. First, social support can affect our health directly, by encouraging healthier (or less unhealthy) behaviors (Taylor, 2007; see also Chapter 5, this volume) and/or by providing a sense of purpose and meaning (Baumeister & Vohs, 2002; Park, 2010).

In addition to these direct effects, social support is thought to buffer the impact of stressful events (Cohen, Doyle, Skoner, Rabin, & Gwaltney, 1997; Taylor, 2007) by providing resources to reduce the magnitude of the stress response. In a 1996 review, Uchino, Cacioppo, and Kiecolt-Glaser identified three physiological systems that were positively affected by the presence of social support. These included the cardiovascular system (better regulation of stress responses), the endocrine system (diminished HPA axis responses), and the immune system (more efficient activity of natural killer cells). Uchino et al. suggested that these physiological systems reflect an overall dampening of the body's fight-or-flight response as a result of supportive social relationships. (For further discussion of the physiological benefits of close relationships, see Chapter 3, this volume.)

In a recent meta-analysis, Holt-Lunstad et al. (2010) reviewed 148 studies on the link between social support and mortality risk, with a focus on the moderators of these connections. Across all studies, and consistent with the House et al. (1988) review, the authors reported a 50% reduction in mortality among those with the strongest social relationships. However, their analyses also revealed a striking amount of variation, depending on how social support was measured. The simplest "binary" indicators (e.g., living with another person rather than alone) were associated with only a 19% reduction in mortality, whereas the most complex assessments of "social integration" were associated with a 91% reduction—a greater reduction in mortality rates than that of smoking cessation. Beyond making a methodological point about the need for complex assessment, this variability suggests that the quality of relationships is a critical moderator of their benefits. Consistent with this idea, recent work has suggested that social support is beneficial only if the recipient perceives it as responsive to his or her needs (Maisel & Gable, 2009).

Another way to appreciate the value of relationships is to examine the consequences of their real and perceived absence. Research by Cacioppo, Hawkley, and their colleagues has highlighted the cumulative health risks of isolation and loneliness. Individuals with the lowest level of social ties are more than twice as likely to die prematurely as those with the highest levels (Berkman & Syme, 1979). In a pair of studies exploring the potential mechanisms for these effects, Cacioppo et al. (2002) found that lonely individuals had poorer sleep quality and increased blood pressure responses to laboratory stressors. The overall picture suggests that loneliness leads people to experience both everyday events and interactions with other people as more stressful and also interferes with the body's healing processes (Hawkley, Burleson, Berntson, & Cacioppo, 2003; see also Cacioppo & Patrick, 2008).

Of course, not all relationships are positive. In the flurry of studies following early reviews of the social support literature, researchers had a tendency to equate social relationships with supportive relationships—assuming that merely having social ties was good for one's health. In an attempt to correct this assumption, Rook (1984) assessed both positive and negative aspects of relationships using structured interviews with a sample of elderly widowed women. Rook measured these constructs by asking about people who provided both supportive ties (e.g., through emotional and instrumental support) and problematic ties (e.g., through breaking promises and provoking conflict). Her analyses revealed that subjective well-being was consistently better predicted by the negative aspects of relationships than the positive ones (cf. Okun, Melichar, & Hill, 1990). That is, the social problems that participants reported were significantly negatively correlated with subjective well-being, whereas reports of "social supports" were unrelated to well-being. In other words, the impact of bad perceptions on subjective well-being is typically stronger than the impact of good perceptions. This general pattern—that "bad is stronger than good"—is one that occurs consistently across numerous domains in psychology (Baumeister, Bratslavksy, Finkenaur, & Vohs, 2001).

A large body of research has documented the costs of bad relationships and of recurring conflict in otherwise "good" relationships. Children raised in "risky" families—those characterized by neglect, conflict, and lack of warmth—tend to have poorer self-reported health later in life and heightened cortisol responses to stress (e.g., Repetti, Taylor, & Seeman, 2002; Taylor, Lerner, Sage, Lehman, & Seeman, 2004; see also Chapter 6, this volume). Children and adolescents who are bullied or otherwise mistreated by their peers show lasting changes in stress and emotion processes (Hamilton, Newman, Delville, & Delville, 2008; Newman, Holden, & Delville, 2011). Marriages characterized by higher levels of conflict lead to more health problems in both partners and are more likely to end in divorce (e.g., Gottman, 1994; Gottman & Levenson, 1992). In addition, unsupportive partners of patients who have cancer can even exacerbate poor health outcomes (e.g., Manne, Taylor, Dougherty, & Kemeny, 1997). In fact, even brief laboratory experiences of social threat or conflict can produce heightened emotional, physiological, and behavioral responses (e.g., Cacioppo, Berntson, Sheridan, & McClintock, 2000; Dickerson, Gruenewald, & Kemeny, 2004; see also Chapter 1, this volume).

There is one additional layer of complexity: Many of our social relationships are both positive and negative—that is, they are complicated. Uchino, Holt-Lunstad, Uno, and Flinders (2001) offered a framework for thinking about the varieties of relationships, suggesting that positivity and negativity are orthogonal dimensions in our connections to others. Thus, relationships can be *supportive* (high positivity, low negativity), *aversive* (low positivity, high negativity), *indifferent* (low positivity, low negativity), or *ambivalent* (high positivity, high negativity). Ambivalent relationships include, for example, a loving spouse with whom one fights constantly. In several studies, ambivalent relationships have been consistently associated with the worst outcomes, including greater perceived stress, more cardiovascular arousal, and increased risk of depression (Birmingham, Uchino, Smith, Light, & Sandonmatsu, 2009; Holt-Lunstand, Uchino, Smith, & Hicks, 2007; Uchino et al., 2001). In summarizing this work, Birmingham et al. (2009) suggested that "a network tie that is a source of both positivity and negativity may be considerably less predictable and thus may be associated with greater emotional responses, and, therefore reactivity" (p. 114).

OVERVIEW OF THE BOOK

In short, our relationships with other people are complex, but they matter a great deal. In this edited volume, we review recent perspectives on the connections between social relationships and physical and mental health. Although the potential for psychological events and emotions to affect health is no longer novel, our understanding of their intricacies—from physiological processes to cultural mechanisms—is constantly evolving.

The individual chapters in this book explore the myriad connections between stress and illness and how these connections are shaped by the quality of our relationships with other people. Relationships, as examined in this volume, span the full continuum—from social support to social isolation—as do their benefits and costs. Throughout the volume, we emphasize two key themes. First, for all the reasons mentioned previously, the chapters emphasize the fact that relationships matter. The quality and quantity of our connections with other people predict outcomes ranging from happiness to heart disease, from adjustment to maladjustment, and from mortality to longevity. The chapters in this volume are designed to explore the scope of and the mechanisms for these associations, as well as their implications for improving both health and relationships.

Second, the chapters emphasize the fact that perceptions matter. One of the most robust conclusions from the stress literature (if not all psychological literature) is that people's perceptions are dramatic and important moderators of emotional, behavioral, and physiological responses. Both actual support (e.g., Cohen, 2004) and perceived support (e.g., Lakey & Cassady, 1990) are predictive of better health; both physical isolation (e.g., Berkman & Syme, 1979) and perceived loneliness (e.g., Hawkley et al., 2003) are predictive of poorer health. A host of individual differences likewise moderate the impact of social threat (see Chapter 1), caregiver stress (Chapter 2), romantic loss (Chapter 4), and exposure to risky families (Chapter 6). Each of the chapters in this volume highlights the importance of perceptions and individual differences and examines the reasons that these play such an important role.

The chapters discuss a number of related constructs under the general umbrella of *health*, including physical and mental health outcomes, as well as the emotional and physiological mechanisms that may act as precursors to these outcomes. In many cases, these chapters examine moderators of the link between health and relationships—for example, the impact of a romantic loss depends in part on the personality and gender of the person experiencing the loss (see Chapter 4). In other cases, where the mechanisms are understood, the chapters focus on mediators of the link between health and relationships—for example, physical affection appears to be the mediating mechanism for the health benefits of marriage (see Chapter 2).

The volume is organized into four parts. Part I offers an overview of "the big picture," with two chapters highlighting the complexity of our social relationships. In Chapter 1, Suman Lam and Sally S. Dickerson provide an overview of the pathways linking social relationships with health outcomes. They begin with an overview of the physiological systems involved in stress reactivity and spend the bulk of the chapter summarizing the literature on responses to acute social threat. They then review how these responses can be moderated and attenuated by both personality characteristics and by the presence of supportive others and conclude with a discussion of the implications of acute social threat processes for health and disease outcomes.

In Chapter 2, Sara Konrath and Stephanie Brown highlight the complexity of social support, by reviewing research on the health outcomes associated with both giving and receiving social support. Although both giving and receiving are associated with positive outcomes overall, both also have the potential to backfire, undermining the attempt to help and leaving one or both relationship partners feeling worse off. In their review of the literature, Konrath and Brown discuss the moderators of successful and less successful support giving and offer a theoretical model for integrating these outcomes. This chapter is included in "The Big Picture" section of the book because it highlights the complex, bidirectional connections between relationships and health and the possible mechanisms of these connections.

Part II is focused on romantic relationships, with three chapters covering the health impact of spousal-type relationships and affectionate touch; loss due to separation, divorce, or widowhood; and the day-to-day dyadic regulation of health behaviors. Part II opens with Chapter 3, by Mary H. Burleson, Nicole A. Roberts, Tara M. Vincelette, and Xin Guan, on the connections between marriage and physical health. Married people appear to live longer and remain healthier than unmarried people, and this finding is robust across different societies and time periods. However, the specific mechanisms accounting for the benefits of marriage have not been fully explored. In this chapter, Burleson et al. provide a comprehensive review of recent literature on the health benefits of marriage and present evidence suggesting that physical affection and intimacy may be a key mediator of these effects.

In Chapter 4, Ashley E. Mason and David A. Sbarra focus on the consequences of romantic loss, including the loss of a partner through separation, divorce, or death. One's risk of morbidity and mortality increases following the loss of a romantic partner, particularly over the first 6 months following the loss. In this chapter, Mason and Sbarra provide an interdisciplinary review of variables that moderate the impact of romantic loss, including personality, social ties, and ethnocultural background.

In Chapter 5, Jane A. Skoyen, Anya V. Kogan, Sarah A. Novak, and Emily A. Butler offer an in-depth look at the dyadic processes of health behavior and emotion regulation in romantic couples. Romantic partners can encourage health-enhancing (e.g., healthy eating, exercising) or health-compromising (e.g., smoking, drinking alcohol) behaviors, but sometimes these "compromising" behaviors can play a key role in emotion regulation and relationship maintenance (e.g., sharing a cigarette after an argument). In this chapter, Skoyen et al. review the complex pathways linking health behaviors with dyadic emotion regulation.

Part III broadens the focus beyond romantic dyads, with three chapters examining family relationships, peer relationships, and cultural norms regarding health and support. Part III opens with Chapter 6, by Erin T. Tobin, Richard B. Slatcher, and Theodore F. Robles, on the connections between family relationships and physical health. Family relationships early in life can have a dramatic impact on health outcomes in adulthood—supportive families can protect health and teach coping resources, whereas risky families can lead to emotional and behavioral problems and chronic illness. In this chapter, Tobin et al. review both the damaging and beneficial influences of family relationships, with a focus on the biological mediators linking these relationships to children's current and future health.

In Chapter 7, Kathleen S. Bryan, Yesmina N. Puckett, and I review the research linking peer relationships to health outcomes. Peers can be a valuable source of support, setting positive examples and providing shoulders to cry on in times of need. However, peers can also be bad for our health, encouraging bad habits and passing judgment on stigmatizing conditions. In this chapter, we review the mediating mechanisms behind the costs and the benefits of peer relationships and highlight the unique role that peer relationships play during childhood, adolescence, and adulthood.

In Chapter 8, José A. Soto, Yulia Chentsova-Dutton, and Elizabeth A. Lee add a valuable additional layer to the discussion, emphasizing the fact that social relationships and their links to health are embedded in a cultural context. For example, receiving support from others is beneficial only if this support is viewed as normal by one's culture; this echoes Konrath and Brown's argument from Chapter 2 that support is helpful only if it is done in the "right" way. In this chapter, Soto et al. summarize two areas of research—social support and emotion regulation—that highlight the importance of fit between an individual's behavior and cultural standards regarding that behavior.

Finally, the two chapters in Part IV examine the practical implications of this research, with chapters on resilience and clinical applications. Part IV opens with Chapter 9, by Anne Arewasikporn, Mary C. Davis, and Alex Zautra, on the social nature of resilience. Following decades of a "risk" focus in the field of psychology, there is growing awareness of the fact that people can recover and even thrive in the face of traumatic events. That is, the focus is shifting toward psychological assets—such as resilience—rather than risk factors. Resilient responses to trauma are those involving successful adaptation to the experience, and much of this adaptation involves support from others. In this chapter, Arewasikporn et al. summarize recent work on resilience, with a focus on the importance of social connections.

In the final chapter, Chapter 10, Nicole A. Roberts revisits the key themes in the book, with a focus on their practical application. By this point, it is clear that good, high-quality relationships are good for one's health. However, how does one go about finding and cultivating these relationships in the first place? Roberts suggests several ways in which the therapeutic relationship can serve as a model for promoting healthy interpersonal relationships and draws lessons from the chapters in this volume regarding healthier ways of relating.

The topic of health and social relationships spans multiple perspectives within psychology and related fields, and we have attempted to capture this diversity in this volume. As can be seen from these brief sketches, the chapters herein draw on social psychology, clinical psychology, developmental psychology, family and dynamic systems, psychophysiology, and culture. This approach also reflects the diverse background of the contributors—and the coeditors, a social and a clinical psychologist, who both rely on psychophysiological methods in our work. Accordingly, we have compiled this volume with a wide range of researchers and practitioners in mind. Although the primary intended audience is academic psychologists, we believe that many of the chapters will be of interest to health care professionals and therapists who focus on relationship issues. We also anticipate this volume can be an excellent companion to graduate and advanced undergraduate courses on the topics of stress, health, emotion, and relationships.

One common thread through all of these chapters is an emphasis on the complexity of social relationships. This field of study has gradually evolved from an early focus on the benefits of relationships, through a brief emphasis on the costs of relationships, to a current appreciation of the incredible complexity of social relationships and their connections to health. Research on the connections between relationships and health is growing at a rapid pace and includes new methods for measuring biobehavioral processes and new statistical techniques for quantifying these processes. This volume attempts to integrate these new developments and includes a combination of foundational and cutting-edge research in the field. Thus, our hope is that the volume will serve as a valuable resource to all scientists and practitioners interested in relationships and health.

REFERENCES

Baumeister, R. F., Bratslavksy, E., Finkenaur, C., & Vohs, K. D. (2001). Bad is stronger than good. *Review of General Psychology, 5*, 323–370. doi:10.1037/1089-2680.5.4.323

Baumeister, R. F., & Vohs, K. D. (2002). The pursuit of meaningfulness in life. In C. R. Snyder & S. J. Lopez (Eds.), *Handbook of positive psychology* (pp. 608–618). New York, NY: Oxford University Press.

Berkman, L. F., & Syme, S. L. (1979). Social networks, host resistance, and mortality: A nine-year follow-up study of Alameda County residents. *American Journal of Epidemiology, 109*, 186–204.

Berntson, G. G., & Cacioppo, J. T. (2000). From homeostasis to allodynamic regulation. In J. T. Cacioppo, L. G. Tassinary, & G. G. Berntson (Eds.), *Handbook of psychophysiology* (pp. 459–481). Cambridge, England: Cambridge University Press.

Birmingham, W., Uchino, B. N., Smith, T. W., Light, K. C. & Sandonmatsu, D. M. (2009). Social ties and cardiovascular function: An examination of relationship positivity and negativity during stress. *International Journal of Psychophysiology*, *74*, 114–119.

Borrell-Carrió, F., Suchman, A. L., & Epstein, R. M. (2004). The biopsychosocial model 25 years later: Principles, practice, and scientific inquiry. *Annals of Family Medicine*, *2*, 576–582. doi:10.1370/afm.245

Cacioppo, J. T., Berntson, G., Sheridan, J. F., & McClintock, M. K. (2000). Multi-level integrative analysis of human behavior: Social neuroscience and the complementing nature of social and biological approaches. *Psychological Bulletin*, *126*, 829–843. doi:10.1037/0033-2909.126.6.829

Cacioppo, J. T., Hawkley, L. C., Crawford, L. E., Ernst, J. M., Burleson, M. H., Kowaleski, R. B., . . . Berntson, G. G. (2002). Loneliness and health: Potential mechanisms. *Psychosomatic Medicine*, *64*, 407–417.

Cacioppo, J. T., & Patrick, W. (2008). *Loneliness: Human nature and the need for social connection*. New York, NY: Norton.

Cobb, S. (1976). Social support as a moderator of life stress. *Psychosomatic Medicine*, *38*, 300–314.

Cobb, S. (1979). Social support and health through the life course. In M. W. Riley (Ed.), *Aging from birth to death: Interdisciplinary perspectives* (pp. 93–106). Boulder, CO: Westview Press.

Cohen, S. (2004). Social relationships and health. *American Psychologist*, *59*, 676–684. doi:10.1037/0003-066X.59.8.676

Cohen, S., Doyle, W. J., Skoner, D. P., Rabin, B. S., & Gwaltney, J. M. Jr. (1997, June 25). Social ties and susceptibility to the common cold. *JAMA*, *277*, 1940–1944. doi:10.1001/jama.277.24.1940

Cohen, S., Tyrell, D. A. J., & Smith, A. P. (1991, August 29). Psychological stress and susceptibility to the common cold. *The New England Journal of Medicine*, *325*, 606–612. doi:10.1056/NEJM199108293250903

Dickerson, S. S., Gruenewald, T. L., & Kemeny, M. E. (2004). When the social self is threatened: Shame, physiology, and health. *Journal of Personality*, *72*, 1191–1216. doi:10.1111/j.1467-6494.2004.00295.x

Diener, E. (1984). Subjective well-being. *Psychological Bulletin*, *95*, 542–575. doi:10.1037/0033-2909.95.3.542

Engel, G. L. (1977, April 8). The need for a new medical model: A challenge for biomedicine. *Science*, *196*, 129–136. doi:10.1126/science.847460

Gottman, J. M. (1994). *Why marriages succeed or fail*. New York, NY: Simon & Schuster.

Gottman, J. M., & Levenson, R. W. (1992). Marital processes predictive of later dissolution: Behavior, physiology, and health. *Journal of Personality and Social Psychology*, *63*, 221–233. doi:10.1037/0022-3514.63.2.221

Hamilton, L. D., Newman, M. L., Delville, C., & Delville, Y. (2008). Physiological stress response of young adults exposed to bullying during adolescence. *Physiology & Behavior, 95,* 617–624. doi:10.1016/j.physbeh.2008.09.001

Hawkley, L. C., Burleson, M. H., Berntson, G. G., & Cacioppo, J. T. (2003). Loneliness in everyday life: Cardiovascular activity, psychosocial context, and health behaviors. *Journal of Personality and Social Psychology, 85,* 105–120. doi:10.1037/0022-3514.85.1.105

Holt-Lunstad, J., Smith, T. W., & Layton, J. B. (2010). Social relationships and mortality risk: A meta-analytic review. *PLoS Medicine, 7,* e1000316. doi:10.1371/journal.pmed.1000316

Holt-Lunstad, J. L., Uchino, B. N., Smith, T. W., & Hicks, A. (2007). On the importance of relationship quality: The impact of ambivalence in friendships on cardiovascular functioning. *Annals of Behavioral Medicine, 33,* 278–290. doi:10.1007/BF02879910

House, J. S., Landis, K. R., & Umberson, D. (1988, July 29). Social relationships and health. *Science, 241,* 540–545. doi:10.1126/science.3399889

Kemeny, M. E. (2003). The psychobiology of stress. *Current Directions in Psychological Science, 12,* 124–129. doi:10.1111/1467-8721.01246

Kemeny, M. E. (2007). Psychoneuroimmunology. In H. S. Friedman & R. C. Silver (Eds.), *Foundations of health psychology* (pp. 92–116). New York, NY: Oxford University Press.

Lakey, B., & Cassady, P. B. (1990). Cognitive processes in perceived social support. *Journal of Personality and Social Psychology, 59,* 337–343.

Langer, E. J., & Rodin, J. (1976). Effects of choice and enhanced personal responsibility for the aged: A field experiment in an institutional setting. *Journal of Personality and Social Psychology, 34,* 191–198. doi:10.1037/0022-3514.34.2.191

Maisel, N. C., & Gable, S. L. (2009). The paradox of received support: The importance of responsiveness. *Psychological Science, 20,* 928–932. doi:10.1111/j.1467-9280.2009.02388.x

Manne, S. L, Taylor, K. L., Dougherty, J., & Kemeny, N. (1997). Supportive and negative responses in the partner relationship: Their association with psychological adjustment among individuals with cancer. *Journal of Behavioral Medicine, 20,* 101–125.

McEwen, B. S. (2004). Protective and damaging effects of stress mediators. In J. T. Cacioppo & G. G. Berntson (Eds.), *Essays in social neuroscience* (pp. 41–51). Cambridge, MA: MIT Press.

Mineka, S., & Hendersen, R. W. (1985). Controllability and predictability in acquired motivation. *Annual Review of Psychology, 36,* 495–529. doi:10.1146/annurev.ps.36.020185.002431

Mitchell, R. E., Billings, A. G., & Moos, R. H. (1982). Social support and well-being: Implications for prevention programs. *The Journal of Primary Prevention, 3,* 77–98. doi:10.1007/BF01324668

Newman, M. L., Holden, G. W., & Delville, Y. (2011). Coping with the stress of being bullied: Consequences of coping strategies among college students. *Social Psychological and Personality Science, 2*, 205–211. doi:10.1177/1948550610386388

Okun, M. A., Melichar, J. F., & Hill, M. D. (1990). Negative daily events, positive and negative social ties, and psychological distress among older adults. *The Gerontologist, 30*, 193–199. doi:10.1093/geront/30.2.193

Park, C. L. (2010). Making sense of the meaning literature: An integrative review of meaning making and its effects on adjustment to stressful life events. *Psychological Bulletin, 136*, 257–301. doi:10.1037/a0018301

Repetti, R. L., Taylor, S. E., & Seeman, T. E. (2002). Risky families: Family social environments and the mental and physical health of offspring. *Psychological Bulletin, 128*, 330–366. doi:10.1037/0033-2909.128.2.330

Rook, K. S. (1984). The negative side of social interaction: Impact on psychological well-being. *Journal of Personality and Social Psychology, 46*, 1097–1108. doi:10.1037/0022-3514.46.5.1097

Schiepers, O. J. G., Wichers, M. C., & Maes, M. (2005). Cytokines and major depression. *Progress in Neuro-Psychopharmacology & Biological Psychiatry, 29*, 201–217. doi:10.1016/j.pnpbp.2004.11.003

Seeman, T. E., McEwen, B. S., Rowe, J. W., & Singer, B. H. (2001). Allostatic load as a marker of cumulative biological risk: MacArthur studies of successful aging. *Proceedings of the National Academy of Sciences of the United States of America, 98*, 4770–4775. doi:10.1073/pnas.081072698

Taylor, S. E. (2007). Social support. In H. S. Friedman & R. Cohen Silver (Eds.), *Foundations of health psychology* (pp. 145–171). New York, NY: Oxford University Press.

Taylor, S. E., Lerner, J. S., Sage, R. M., Lehman, B. J., & Seeman, T. E. (2004). Early environment, emotions, responses to stress, and health. *Journal of Personality, 72*, 1365–1393. doi:10.1111/j.1467-6494.2004.00300.x

Uchino, B. N., Cacioppo, J. T., & Kiecolt-Glaser, J. K. (1996). The relationship between social support and physiological processes: A review with emphasis on underlying mechanisms and implications for health. *Psychological Bulletin, 119*, 488–531. doi:10.1037/0033-2909.119.3.488

Uchino, B. N., Holt-Lunstad, J., Uno, D., & Flinders, J. B. (2001). Heterogeneity in the social networks of young and older adults: Prediction of mental health and cardiovascular reactivity during acute stress. *Journal of Behavioral Medicine, 24*, 361–382. doi:10.1023/A:1010634902498

World Health Organization. (1948). *Constitution of the World Health Organization*. Geneva, Switzerland: Author.

I

THE BIG PICTURE

1

SOCIAL RELATIONSHIPS, SOCIAL THREAT, AND HEALTH

SUMAN LAM AND SALLY S. DICKERSON

Positive social relationships can confer beneficial effects on health. A large body of literature has shown that the presence of strong social ties is associated with reduced morbidity and mortality (e.g., Berkman & Syme, 1979; House, Landis, & Umberson, 1988). For example, several seminal studies have demonstrated that those who have fewer social and community ties have higher mortality rates than those with many connections (Berkman & Syme, 1979). These associations exist even after controlling for self-reported physical health, socioeconomic status, health behaviors, and use of medical services, suggesting a direct effect of social ties on health outcomes. It is not only that possessing social ties is beneficial but also that the provision of support to others has also been associated with positive health outcomes. Specifically, those who offer encouragement, help, or assistance to friends, family, and spouses exhibit reduced mortality rates compared with those who do not provide support, even when controlling for personality and demographic

DOI: 10.1037/14036-002
Health and Social Relationships: The Good, the Bad, and the Complicated, Matthew L. Newman and Nicole A. Roberts (Editors)

characteristics (Brown, Nesse, Vinokur, & Smith, 2003; see also Chapter 2, this volume). Taken together, this research has demonstrated that the presence of social ties, as well as receiving and providing support, can have positive effects on health.

Although social relationships are associated with health benefits, relationships can come with costs. At times, social interactions can be characterized by negative exchanges, criticism, or rejection. These types of evaluative and rejecting interactions can be profoundly threatening, because they jeopardize the fundamental need to belong or to be socially accepted by others (Baumeister & Leary, 1995). These social threats can elicit emotional, physiological, and behavioral responses (e.g., Cacioppo, Berntson, Sheridan, & McClintock, 2000; Dickerson, Gruenewald, & Kemeny, 2004), which in turn can have implications for health (e.g., McEwen, 2000; Sapolsky, 2005).

A burgeoning area of research has examined the effects of acute and chronic social threats on physiological functioning. Understanding these effects helps to shed light on the broader connections between social relationships and health. In this chapter, we give an overview of the research on pathways linking social relationships to health. First, we examine some of the physiological systems implicated in stress reactivity, followed by a summary of the literature on acute responses to social threat. Next, we review personality characteristics that may affect one's perception of social threat and physiological reactivity in these contexts. We also present research on the general benefits of social support on health and how different sources of support can buffer the effects of social threat on physiological reactivity. Finally, we close with implications of these processes for health and disease.

STRESS PHYSIOLOGY

Threats to physical self-preservation, such as threats to safety or survival, can trigger a wide range of physiological responses. These changes are thought to be adaptive in the short term because they can facilitate changes in energy mobilization that help organisms adjust to the demands of the situation. This can include increases in sympathetic adrenal medullary activity (leading to the release of the hormones epinephrine and norepinephrine) and resulting changes in cardiovascular activity, such as increases in systolic blood pressure (SBP), diastolic blood pressure (DBP), and heart rate. These changes can help prepare and facilitate immediate behavioral responses—for example, to fight or flee from a physical threat. However, chronic sympathetic activation has been associated with health risks. For example, higher heart rates are associated with higher incidence of heart attacks and cardiovascular-related mortality (Fox et al., 2008), and risk of cardiovascular disease is associated with elevated and prolonged SBP and DBP responses (Franklin, Khan, Wong, Larson, & Levy, 1999).

Another important stress-responsive system is the hypothalamic–pituitary–adrenal (HPA) axis. In the face of a stressor, brain regions central to appraising, processing, and generating emotions associated with the threat send signals to the hypothalamus. This leads the paraventricular nucleus of the hypothalamus to stimulate and release corticotropin-releasing hormone (CRH). CRH then triggers the release of adrenocorticotropin hormone (ACTH) from the anterior pituitary. ACTH is transported through the blood and stimulates the adrenal cortex to release cortisol into the bloodstream. Cortisol is involved in the regulation of many important biological processes (for a review, see Sapolsky, Romero, & Munck, 2000). For example, it is integral in maintaining metabolic processes and function; cortisol can release glucose energy stores to provide "fuel" for the central nervous system and peripheral systems. In turn, cortisol can regulate other physiological processes, including sympathetic nervous system (SNS) activity and immune function.

Short-term activation of the HPA axis is considered adaptive because cortisol released during a threat can release energy stores and redirect energy to cope with the stressor. However, long-term or chronic activation of the HPA axis can cause dysregulation of the system, leading to blunted or heightened cortisol responses—either of which could be harmful for long-term health (McEwen, 2000). Dysregulated cortisol response patterns have also been shown in a number of clinical populations. For example, those with depression have exhibited heightened cortisol responses to stressors (Burke, Davis, Otte, & Mohr, 2005); depression following a trauma has also been associated with increased cortisol responses (Kaufman et al., 1997). In contrast, those who present with posttraumatic stress disorder typically exhibit blunted cortisol output (Miller, Chen, & Zhou, 2007; Yehuda, 2002). Numerous theories have suggested that HPA activation exerts its effects on health and disease by exposing bodily tissues and organs to increased levels of stress hormones. Furthermore, other research posits that declines in cortisol output (i.e., hypocortisolism) can also contribute to the development and progression of disease (e.g., Heim, Ehlert, & Hellhammer, 2000). Therefore, chronic dysregulation of HPA parameters may have long-term health effects.

RESPONSES TO SOCIAL-EVALUATIVE THREAT

Although threats to physical self-preservation are the prototypical contexts in which stress-responsive systems are activated, threats to other central goals may trigger these physiological changes as well. The need to belong to a social group is a fundamental necessity in humans (Baumeister & Leary,

1995). Therefore, threats to the "social self," such as contexts characterized by rejection or negative social evaluation, may elicit emotional, physiological, and behavioral responses (Dickerson et al., 2004). Threats to the social self are situations that could lead to the loss of social status, acceptance, or esteem, where others may negatively judge an important aspect of the self (i.e., *social-evaluative threat;* Dickerson & Kemeny, 2004). Social-evaluative contexts include those in which one's abilities and attributes (e.g., intelligence, expertise) could be on display for others to critique (e.g., during job interviews, performances, or competitions) or in which uncontrollable or stigmatized characteristics or identities (e.g., age, race, gender) are made salient. Research in this area has suggested that humans are motivated to protect the self against this loss of social esteem and status, which could activate a coordinated set of responses to the threat, including SNS and HPA responses. We review literature on these two systems next.

Cortisol Responses

A meta-analytic review of 208 studies revealed that stressors with an element of social evaluation (e.g., presence of an evaluative audience, social comparison, or video camera during the task) were associated with greater cortisol responses compared with stressors without this characteristic (Dickerson & Kemeny, 2004). This effect was highly significant even when controlling for other methodological factors that influence cortisol responses (e.g., time of day, timing of assessment). Furthermore, this effect was heightened when the stressor was also uncontrollable. A task can be categorized as relatively uncontrollable when failure is a likely outcome. For example, an uncontrollable laboratory task could include trying to solve math problems with unrealistic time constraints so that it is impossible to do well. Tasks with both uncontrollable and social-evaluative elements were associated with cortisol responses more than three times the size of either component alone. With these types of stressors, participants are likely to not perform well (the uncontrollable element), and this failure occurs in front of others (the social-evaluative element); this combination is a potent elicitor of cortisol reactivity.

These meta-analytic results mirror findings from nonhuman animal models that uncontrollable social threat is associated with elevations in cortisol (e.g., Sapolsky, 2005). Animals that are more socially stressed show greater basal levels of glucocorticoids and impaired sensitivity to the negative feedback regulation associated with this response system. However, both dominant and subordinate animals can exhibit this stress-response profile, depending on the social organization of their species and whether they have control over others and/or their environment. Thus, the social milieu of different primate populations dictates which social ranks are more stressful.

A number of studies have experimentally manipulated social-evaluative threat in the laboratory to examine its effects on cortisol responses. For example, Gruenewald, Kemeny, Aziz, and Fahey (2004) randomly assigned participants to complete a modified version of the Trier Social Stress Test (TSST; Kirschbaum, Pirke, & Hellhammer, 1993). In the TSST, participants are asked to give a speech and perform difficult arithmetic problems. Gruenewald et al. manipulated the social context of the stressor by having participants complete the task in one of two conditions: alone in a room (non-social-evaluative threat condition; non-SET) or in front of a negative two-member evaluative audience and video camera (social-evaluative threat condition; SET). Only the participants in the SET condition showed increases in cortisol; those performing the exact same task alone in a room showed no changes in this parameter. These findings again demonstrate that social-evaluative threat can elicit increases in cortisol, particularly when compared with otherwise equivalent stressors without SET. Subsequent studies have replicated and extended this basic finding using different types of stressors and different methodologies (e.g., Dickerson, Mycek, & Zaldivar, 2008; Het, Rohleder, Schoofs, Kirschbaum, & Wolf, 2009; Schwabe, Haddad, & Schachinger, 2008), as well as examining potential moderators of the social-evaluative effect.

Research on the SET phenomenon has more recently concentrated on the contextual moderators of SET effects. That is, although early studies documented that social-evaluative threat provides one set of conditions capable of eliciting cortisol responses, it was unclear what particular element of the social-evaluative context is responsible for increases in this parameter. For example, is it that other people are simply present, or is it that they are in an explicitly evaluative situation? To test this question, Dickerson et al. (2008) had participants deliver a speech in one of three conditions: alone in a room (non-SET), in front of an evaluative audience (SET), or in the presence of an inattentive confederate (PRES). Participants in the PRES and non-SET conditions did not show increases in cortisol, whereas those in the SET condition demonstrated a significant cortisol response to the speech task. Results from this study indicated that explicit social evaluation, and not merely social presence alone, is a critical component for eliciting increases in cortisol.

Several follow-up studies examined whether physical presence is a key component of SET-related cortisol increases. These studies found that remote evaluation during a stressor task (e.g., through an intercom or one-way mirror) can also lead to increased cortisol levels (e.g., Andrews et al., 2007; Kelly, Matheson, Martinez, Merali, & Anisman, 2007). However, increases in cortisol were generally larger in studies where an evaluative panel was present in the same room as the participant rather than at a different location (Kelly et al., 2007). These studies suggest that having a visibly present evaluative panel elicits greater reactivity compared with being evaluated by a remote audience.

Other studies have tested whether the number of evaluative audience members influences the magnitude of cortisol responses. Bosch et al. (2009) asked participants to deliver two speeches in one of three conditions: a no audience condition, or one- or four-audience-member conditions. There was little to no reactivity among those performing the task alone in a room. Both audience conditions elicited cortisol responses; however, the four-audience-member condition was associated with greater increases in reactivity compared with the one-audience-member condition. Other studies manipulated audience size by asking participants to deliver a speech in front of one or two audience members and found no differences between the conditions (Andrews et al., 2007). Taken together, these studies suggest that the mere presence of one evaluative audience member is sufficient to elicit cortisol reactivity, with larger audiences potentially eliciting larger responses.

Another important question is whether the valence of the evaluation from a panel influences the magnitude of the cortisol responses. Taylor et al. (2010) randomly assigned participants to perform a speech and math stressor in front of an unsupportive audience, a supportive audience, or no audience. Contrary to hypotheses, there were no differences in cortisol reactivity between the supportive and nonsupportive audiences; both elicited the same increases in cortisol. This suggests that the valence of feedback from the audience members may play less of a role than the overall evaluative context in triggering cortisol responses. The physical presence of an evaluative panel, whether supportive or nonsupportive, can be enough to elicit cortisol responses.

Although laboratory manipulations of social threat can delineate the specific factors that influence cortisol responses, it is also important to investigate how social threat affects physiology in everyday life. To observe whether social-evaluative threat elicits cortisol in response to naturally occurring stressors, Rohleder, Beulen, Chen, Wolf, and Kirschbaum (2007) examined competitive ballroom dancers. These competitions contain many of the characteristics needed to evoke SET in naturally occurring situations (i.e., threat to important goals, social evaluation, uncontrollability). On days of competitive ballroom dancing, participants exhibited much larger diurnal cortisol output than they did on days without a competition. Furthermore, when comparing the cortisol responses to SET in real life and in response to laboratory stressors, this sample showed cortisol increases that were almost twice as high following a ballroom dancing competition than those typically seen following a social-evaluative stressor in the laboratory. This suggests that, perhaps not surprisingly, social evaluation in everyday life may actually have greater consequences for physiological functioning, and laboratory studies may underestimate the effects of some forms of social-evaluative threat in naturally occurring situations.

Taken together, these studies have demonstrated that social-evaluative threat provides one set of conditions that can markedly increase cortisol levels. This is particularly likely when the conditions are also uncontrollable or when social evaluation is highlighted or salient. Moreover, the effects of social-evaluative threat on cortisol responses can be observed in both laboratory and real-life stressor conditions.

Cardiovascular Responses

Social threat can also elicit cardiovascular responses; for example, social-evaluative and uncontrollable stressors such as the TSST reliably increase SBP, DBP, and heart rate (Kirschbaum et al., 1993). As described previously, experimental studies have manipulated the social-evaluative context by increasing or decreasing the importance of the evaluative nature of the experiment, asking confederates to exhibit socially supportive or nonsupportive behaviors during the task or manipulating the number of evaluators present in the audience panels. Studies using manipulations with social-evaluative components have resulted in greater cardiovascular responses compared with nonevaluative comparison conditions (e.g., Christian & Stoney, 2006; Gruenewald et al., 2004; Lepore, Allen, & Evans, 1993; Smith, Nealey, Kircher, & Limon, 1997).

How one appraises social stressors can have implications for the pattern and magnitude of cardiovascular responses. *Challenge appraisals* result when an individual feels that he or she has the necessary resources to cope with the demands of the situation; in contrast, *threat appraisals* result when resources are not present to overcome the demands. These stress appraisals have been associated with different patterns of cardiovascular reactivity (for a review, see Blascovich & Mendes, 2000). In a series of studies, Tomaka, Blascovich, Kelsey, and Leitten (1993) asked participants to perform mental arithmetic tasks quickly and without error, making the task difficult and demanding. Participants' threat appraisals of the upcoming tasks were significantly associated with their self-reported stress. That is, participants who found the tasks to be more threatening also reported feeling more stress. Cardiovascular reactivity was assessed with impedance cardiography, which allows one to test whether cardiovascular responses are due to myocardial (e.g., faster or stronger heartbeats) or vascular (i.e., blood vessel constriction) changes. Those who appraised the stressor as a threat exhibited increases in both cardiac output and peripheral resistance. Challenge appraisals, in contrast, were associated with increases in cardiac output but decreases in peripheral resistance.

The latter pattern represents an "efficient" use of cardiovascular resources and parallels physiological changes during exercise. Thus, the ways in which one appraises a social stressor (i.e., as a challenge or threat) has predicted different cardiovascular profiles.

One's expectations of a social situation may also modulate cardiovascular responses. Social interactions with others, whether threatening or benign, can be stressful, depending on one's expectations of the situations. People who violate expectations during social interactions can increase ambiguity or uncertainty, which can contribute to stress. A series of three studies was conducted to examine whether expectancy violation predicted psychological and cardiovascular threat responses in participants (Mendes, Blascovich, Hunter, Lickel, & Jost, 2007). Measures of cardiovascular reactivity (i.e., cardiac output, total peripheral resistance, and ventricular contractility) were collected. In the first two experiments, participants interacted with Caucasian or Latino confederates who varied in their socioeconomic status (i.e., high or low). In the third experiment, participants interacted with Caucasian or Asian confederates who spoke with Southern accents or accents expected of their ethnicity. Across these studies, participants who interacted with expectancy-violating confederates had cardiovascular responses indicative of threat (e.g., greater total peripheral resistance). These results suggest that social interactions that elicit perceptions of threat in the form of expectancy violation can also predict patterns of cardiovascular reactivity.

A socially threatening situation can intensify the importance of performing well under evaluation, which could subsequently affect physiological responses. In one study (Smith et al., 1997), participants were randomly assigned to a condition in which they were told they would be given $5 to prepare and deliver a speech in front of an evaluator, or a condition in which participants were told that receiving the money was contingent on the evaluator's assessment. Participants were also randomly assigned to a low or high evaluative threat condition; those in the low evaluative threat condition were told that their speech would be evaluated for clarity or "how well your words are pronounced," whereas those in the high evaluative threat condition were told their speech would be rated for verbal intelligence. These manipulations heightened the importance of performing well in front of an evaluator because accomplishment of their goal hinged on their presentation. The results indicated that those who were not guaranteed money had significantly higher SBP reactivity, with those who were not guaranteed money and in the high evaluative threat condition demonstrating the greatest SBP reactivity. These results lend further support to the idea that contexts that amplify the importance of social evaluation can have profound effects on cardiovascular responses.

The presence of social evaluation can also influence how individuals adapt to recurrent stressors. Kelsey et al. (1999) asked participants to complete a set of three mental arithmetic tasks, with the presence of social evaluation (i.e., a video camera) varied within participants (Kelsey et al., 1999). This approach permitted the researchers to investigate whether adding and removing the evaluative component allowed their cardiovascular responses to return to baseline levels. It also allowed the researchers to examine how participants responded if the evaluative component was not removed. Participants were told that their performance on the tasks would be reviewed and scored by evaluators. Physiological measurements such as preejection period (PEP; i.e., the time interval from the beginning of the electrical stimulation of the heart ventricles to the opening of the aortic valve to release blood) and blood pressure were taken. Those who completed the task alone in a room had lower PEP reactivity (indicating lower sympathetic activity) compared with those who had the evaluative audience introduced while they completed their second and third tasks. Specifically, those who completed the tasks in front of the camera for the second and third tasks did not exhibit PEP adaptation, whereas those who had the audience removed for the third task showed lower levels of PEP reactivity (Kelsey et al., 1999). These results suggest that the potential for evaluation elicits greater cardiovascular reactivity, whereas having the evaluative component removed allows participants to acclimate to the task.

Only a handful of the experimental studies looked at both HPA and cardiovascular responses to social-evaluative threat. Some results indicate that greater HPA and cardiovascular reactivity occur together under social-evaluative threat, whereas other studies show that HPA and cardiovascular responses may not be elicited in concert. Further studies incorporating both systems need to be conducted to further examine this question. These studies clearly document that social threat can lead to substantial cardiovascular reactivity; factors that heighten the appraisals of threat in the social context (e.g., increasing uncertainty, ambiguity, importance of the performance) can heighten these responses.

INDIVIDUAL DIFFERENCES IN PERCEPTIONS OF THREAT

Personality and individual difference factors can influence how one perceives and responds to social threats, which in turn can affect physiological responses. Individual differences may also play a role in how one regulates or copes with social threats, which could have subsequent consequences on stress reactivity. In the following section, we review several individual differences that may contribute to the perception of threat and moderate its effects on physiology.

Self-Esteem

Individual differences in self-esteem may predict how one responds to social threats. *Self-esteem* can be defined as the value that one places on oneself. Those with high self-esteem have favorable self-evaluations, whereas those with low self-esteem typically have less positive self-evaluations. Thus, self-esteem is a perception or appraisal of the self rather than being an objective measure of worth (Baumeister, Campbell, Krueger, & Vohs, 2003). Self-esteem may moderate physiological responses to social threat, particularly because it may affect the detection or perception of negative social evaluation; those with high self-esteem may appraise a socially threatening situation as more positive (or less negative).

Ford and Collins (2010) examined how self-esteem affects psychological and physiological responses to social rejection. Participants were invited to the lab to participate in a 10-minute online chat with an opposite gender partner. Participants were asked to review a packet about the opposite gender partner that included his or her photo and were told their partner was doing the same. To manipulate social rejection, participants were told either that there would be no online chat because the other partner "chose not to continue with the experiment (rejection condition)" or that the other participant could not continue with the experiment because he or she was feeling sick (control condition). Those with low self-esteem in the rejection condition appraised themselves more negatively and made more self-blaming attributions than those with high self-esteem. In addition, individuals with low self-esteem showed higher cortisol levels following rejection than those with high self-esteem. Further analyses indicated that the relationship between low self-esteem and cortisol levels after rejection was mediated by blame attributions; that is, those low on self-esteem made more attributions of self-blame, which in turn were linked with higher cortisol levels in an interpersonal rejection context (Ford & Collins, 2010).

Other studies have found relationships between self-esteem and cardiovascular parameters. For example, Hughes (2007) asked participants to complete a picture-masking task. Participants were given performance feedback, which was randomly assigned to either be positive, negative, or neutral, compared with average scores. For those with low self-esteem, negative feedback was associated with greater cardiovascular reactivity.

Hostility

Another individual difference that may influence how one reacts to social threat is hostility. Smith (1994) defined *trait hostility* as "a negative attitude towards others, consisting of enmity, denigration, and ill will" (p. 26).

Hostility may be particularly relevant in contexts of social threat; in social situations, those who are hostile may attempt to influence others in a domineering and controlling manner. Because of these types of behaviors, hostile people tend to report greater levels of stress and conflict with others (Smith, 1992). Hostile individuals typically respond to interpersonal stressors with heightened physiological reactivity compared with those who are lower on hostility (Smith, 1992; Smith & Gallo, 1999). For example, in one study, participants high and low in hostility were recruited to participate in a roleplay study of interpersonal conflict. Those high in hostility had greater DBP reactivity to the conflict task than those low in hostility (Hardy & Smith, 1988).

The links between social threat, hostility, and greater cardiovascular reactivity have also been found in studies with married couples. In a study on individual differences in hostility, married couples participated in two experimental manipulations of social stressors (Smith & Gallo, 1999). First, participants completed a battery of questionnaires including measures of trait hostility. They were then asked to complete discussion tasks under high or low evaluative threat conditions. Hostility predicted greater SBP reactivity for the men in the high evaluative threat condition. Women's hostility scores were not associated with cardiovascular reactivity (Smith & Gallo, 1999). This study demonstrates the importance of the social-evaluative context for elucidating the relationship between hostility and physiological reactivity and suggests that there could be important gender differences in these effects.

Social Identity Threat

Other individual differences related to how one responds to social identity threat (i.e., stereotype threat) could also predict physiological reactivity in a social-evaluative context. Under *social identity threat,* an individual feels that a group to which he or she belongs is being evaluated negatively. This could be particularly likely in situations with social-evaluative components in which an uncontrollable aspect of the self (i.e., race, gender) is highlighted and could be potentially judged negatively. For example, in one experiment, female participants who varied in their chronic perceptions of sexism interacted with a male confederate (Townsend, Major, Gangi, & Mendes, 2011). In one condition, participants learned that this male confederate held sexist attitudes, while in another condition his attitudes were not known. Participants were told they would interact with a male on a cognitive task and then receive feedback on their desirability as a coworker and supervisor. Participants who held chronically higher perceptions of sexism had greater cortisol reactivity to the task regardless of the experimental condition. These results showed that individual differences in the perception of threat, specifically based on potential gender discrimination, were associated with cortisol responses (Townsend et al., 2011).

Taken together, these studies demonstrate that many of the individual differences that influence one's perception of threat may also predict heightened cardiovascular and cortisol responses to stress. These studies suggest that, in addition to the social-evaluative context, one's perceptions or construals of the environment can affect physiological responses, which in turn may be associated with downstream health effects. However, more longitudinal studies on the effects of repeated or chronic experiences of social-evaluative threat (and concomitant perceptions, appraisals, or construals) are needed to delineate the potential long-term effects on health. These findings also highlight individual differences that may be particularly tied to exaggerated reactivity; this could lead to targeted interventions for the most vulnerable.

BUFFERING SOCIAL THREAT

Experiencing social threats is inevitable in everyday life, and these threats can affect physiological stress responses. However, as we review in this section, several factors such as self-resources (e.g., self-affirmation) and social support have been shown to buffer the effect of these threats on physiological outcomes.

Self-Affirmation

Self-affirmation can be defined as acknowledging and asserting important aspects of self-worth, such as central values, personality characteristics, or relationships. Self-affirmation theory hypothesizes that affirming important aspects of the self can help buffer against social threats to the self and reduce the impact of the threats on physiological responses (Sherman & Cohen, 2006). Everyday stressors such as being judged or criticized at work can threaten aspects of the self, and this threat can be attenuated with the affirmation of other important aspects of the self.

Several studies have examined whether self-affirmation can buffer the physiological effects of social threat. Prior to completing set of stressful tasks, participants were asked to rank their preferences for a list of values (Creswell et al., 2005). Those randomly assigned to the control condition answered a list of questions on their fifth ranked value, whereas those in the value affirmation condition answered questions on their top ranked value. Participants in the value affirmation condition had significantly lower cortisol responses to stress compared with those in the control condition (Creswell et al., 2005). In addition, trait self-esteem and optimism moderated the relationship between value affirmation and psychological stress responses, with those who had high self-esteem and optimism and who affirmed their values reporting the least psychological stress. This demonstrates that self-affirmation, in combination with existing personal strengths (i.e., trait self-esteem and optimism), may be an effective buffer in the face of social threat.

Sherman, Bunyan, Creswell, and Jaremka (2009) examined self-affirmation in the context of a naturally occurring stressor. Undergraduate participants provided urine samples 2 weeks prior to a stressful examination and again on the morning of an exam. The urine samples were assayed for epinephrine and norepinephrine, hormones reflecting SNS activity. In the self-affirmation condition, participants were asked to write essays on their own important values over the 2-week period, while those in the control condition wrote essays on general values. As hypothesized, epinephrine levels increased from baseline to the exam for participants in the control condition, whereas there was no change in this hormone for those in the self-affirmation condition. This buffering effect was strongest among those who were most worried about negative evaluations. These results indicated that self-affirmation can attenuate SNS responses to naturalistic stressors.

Social Support

Being socially supported by others or perceiving that one is supported can also have an effect on physiological responses to social threat. A voluminous literature has demonstrated that social support can have wide-ranging health benefits. In several seminal studies, the presence of social ties has been associated with lower mortality rates. For example, Berkman and Syme's (1979) examination of the effects of social ties on mortality rates in Alameda County, California, showed that those who reported fewer social ties at baseline were more likely to die after the 9-year follow-up period. These ties included marriage, contact with friends and family members, and membership in organizations, suggesting that those who are more socially integrated also live longer. These findings have been replicated and generalized to other populations as well (see Berkman, 1995; House et al., 1988). The effects that social support has on health may be potentially due to buffering responses to stress. Several key studies that have investigated whether social support can mitigate reactivity to social-evaluative threat are reviewed next.

In a typical study, participants are randomly assigned to undergo a laboratory stressor under conditions that differ in the amount of social support available. For example, Lepore, Allen, and Evans (1993) had participants give a speech in one of three conditions: alone in a room, in the presence of a nonsupportive evaluator, or in front of a supportive evaluator. Participants who gave their speech in the nonsupportive (social-evaluative) condition showed the largest increases in SBP, whereas those in the supportive condition showed the smallest increases in SBP. This demonstrates that social support can buffer, and social evaluation can exacerbate, cardiovascular responses to social threat.

Other studies have examined whether the effects of social support on cardiovascular reactivity depend on the relationship between a support provider and the participant (Christenfeld et al., 1997). All participants delivered a speech in front of an audience member; in one condition, the observer was a friend who was brought in by the participant and was trained to be supportive during the stressor. In the other conditions, participants gave the speech in front of a confederate who was a stranger and who behaved in either a supportive or neutral manner. Although both supportive conditions produced significantly smaller increases in cardiovascular parameters than the confederate-neutral condition, the smallest increases of all were observed in the friend-supportive condition. Thus, social support from a friend attenuated cardiovascular reactivity in a laboratory setting to a greater degree than social support from a stranger. The results showed that participants' appraisal of socially supportive behaviors can have an effect on cardiovascular responses to a stress task beyond the effects of the supportive behaviors themselves.

Other studies have examined social support as a moderator of cortisol responses to social threat. One study found that individuals who reported more supportive interactions with others during a 10-day period before a social-evaluative laboratory stressor showed reduced cortisol reactivity compared with those who reported less supportive ties (Eisenberger, Taylor, Gable, Hilmert, & Lieberman, 2007). Studies that have manipulated social support in the laboratory have shown that men randomly assigned to go through a social-evaluative stressor with a friend or partner present show reduced cortisol responses compared with those in conditions in which a source of social support is not present (e.g., Heinrichs et al., 2003; Kirschbaum, Klauer, Filipp, & Hellhammer, 1995).

Other research has shown that supportive individuals might not even need to be present to have beneficial effects; internal representations of supportive ties may buffer physiological responses to stress tasks (Smith, Ruiz, & Uchino, 2004). Smith et al. (2004) asked undergraduates to write about either their supportive ties or casual acquaintances before undergoing a social threat experience. Those who wrote about supportive ties had reductions in negative affect as well as reduced heart rate and blood pressure responses during a subsequent speech task stressor compared with those writing about casual acquaintances. Thus, these results show that merely thinking about a close friend can reduce cardiovascular responses during a stress task. Thus, in some contexts, simply thinking about social support can activate the benefits of support.

Although the existence of personal resources and social support can have stress-buffering effects, some individuals may not have these means available to them. Several studies have explored the moderating effects of nonhuman forms of support, namely, pet ownership, on autonomic reactivity. In one study of the benefits of pet ownership, participants were asked to complete math tasks either in front of an experimenter, in the presence of a friend, or in the presence of their dog. Participants in the pet condition showed lower autonomic reactivity than participants in the other two conditions. These results suggest that support from a pet may appear less evaluative than the presence of a friend or experimenter (Allen, Blascovich, Tomaka, & Kelsey, 1991).

Taken together, these studies suggest that factors such as self-resources and actual and perceived social support may have stress-buffering properties. There is evidence that the availability of self-resources such as self-affirmation can help buffer sympathetic and HPA axis responses to stressful tasks, which may be associated with downstream effects on health. Self-affirmation may be a useful resource that is affordable and easy to administer for reducing stress in normal and patient populations.

Further, there is a large body of literature showing that those who are well integrated in their social groups are mentally and physically healthier than their counterparts who lack these social contacts. It can be argued that the presence of social support helps buffer against physiological stress responses by lessening the impact of social threat, which could be a pathway through which social support affects health. Future research should consider whether interventions that focus on the use of self-resources or social support in times of stress will reduce physiological responses, particularly in populations of individuals susceptible to disease.

CHRONIC SOCIAL THREAT AND HEALTH

Acute social threats may lead to short-term physiological changes that could be adaptive when confronting these situations. These types of short-term alterations of physiological parameters would be unlikely—in and of themselves—to lead to negative effects on health. However, under certain circumstances, experiencing these threats could have detrimental consequences. This could include contexts involving chronic or enduring forms of social threat. For example, the experience of repeated interpersonal stressors such as racial discrimination or growing up in a critical or rejection-laden family can be viewed as a chronic social threat (for a discussion of family relationships and health, see Chapter 6, this volume). These social interactions may be burdened with conflict and criticism, which can be threatening to the social self. In turn, these contexts may influence how one perceives threat in the social environment and may lead to physiological dysregulation that could have health consequences. Across a number of studies, social threats have been associated with heightened cardiovascular and HPA activity. If the social threats are recurrent or prolonged, these systems could be overactivated or turned on for too long; this type of chronically heightened activation can have negative effects on health (McEwen & Stellar, 1993). For example, this could result in altered basal levels of hormones and immune parameters. Further, the functioning of the cardiovascular or HPA systems may be altered, resulting in blunted or exaggerated reactivity; both are indicative of dysregulation.

These physiological consequences of repeated exposure to stressors have been termed *allostatic load* (McEwen, 2000). Frequent activation of these physiological systems, in conjunction with preexisting personality and environmental factors, may lead to cumulative strain on the body (McEwen, 2000). Several conditions may lead to allostatic load, including the failure to habituate to a recurring stressor, longer recovery times in response to stressors or failure to turn off the hormonal stress response, dampened physiological responses leading to compensatory hormonal activity of other physiological parameters, and repeated exposure to novel stressors (McEwen, 2000). Social threat—which can potently activate the stress responsive systems—may be one set of conditions that could lead to allostatic load if experienced persistently over time. The research that has elucidated the factors and conditions under which social threat can elicit these biological responses can therefore help us understand the conditions that could lead to allostatic load. Individual differences, self- and social resources, and other factors that could exacerbate or buffer physiological responses could also moderate effects on health. Clearly, longitudinal studies will be critical for examining how social threat can lead to physiological dysregulation and effects on health.

CONCLUSION

Acute threats to the social self have been associated with heightened cardiovascular and HPA activity; personal resources, social support, and the presence of close ties have been linked with stress-buffering effects, and the presence of social connections has been associated with more adaptive physiological responding. Future research should further examine the mechanisms and pathways through which social threats "get under the skin" to affect health, and how positive social relationships can buffers these effects.

REFERENCES

Allen, K. M., Blascovich, J., Tomaka, J., & Kelsey, R. M. (1991). Presence of human friends and pet dogs as moderators of autonomic responses to stress in women. *Journal of Personality and Social Psychology, 61*, 582–589. doi:10.1037/0022-3514.61.4.582

Andrews, J., Wadiwalla, M., Juster, R. P., Lord, C., Lupien, S. J., & Pruessner, J. C. (2007). Effects of manipulating the amount of social-evaluative threat on the cortisol stress response in young healthy men. *Behavioral Neuroscience, 121*, 871–876. doi:10.1037/0735-7044.121.5.871

Baumeister, R. F., Campbell, J. D., Krueger, J. I., & Vohs, K. D. (2003). Does high self-esteem cause better performance, interpersonal success, happiness, or healthier lifestyles? *Psychological Science in the Public Interest, 4*, 1–44. doi:10.1111/1529-1006.01431

Baumeister, R. F., & Leary, M. R. (1995). The need to belong: Desire for interpersonal attachments as a fundamental human motivation. *Psychological Bulletin, 117*, 497–529. doi:10.1037/0033-2909.117.3.497

Berkman, L. F. (1995). The role of social relations in health promotion. *Psychosomatic Medicine, 57*, 245–254.

Berkman, L. F., & Syme, S. L. (1979). Social networks, host resistance, and mortality: A nine-year follow-up study of Alameda County residents. *American Journal of Epidemiology, 109*, 186–204.

Blascovich, J., & Mendes, W. B. (2000). Challenge and threat appraisals: The role of affective cues. In J. Forgas (Ed.), *Feeling and thinking: The role of affect in social cognition* (pp. 59–82). Cambridge, England: Cambridge University Press.

Bosch, J. A., de Geus, E. J., Carroll, D., Anane, L. E., Helmerhorst, E. J., Goedhart, A. D., & Edwards, K. E. (2009). A general enhancement of autonomic and cortisol responses during social evaluative threat. *Psychosomatic Medicine, 71*, 877–885. doi:10.1097/PSY.0b013e3181baef05

Brown, S. L., Nesse, R., Vinokur, A. D., & Smith, D. M. (2003). Providing support may be more beneficial than receiving it: Results from a prospective study of mortality. *Psychological Science, 14*, 320–327. doi:10.1111/1467-9280.14461

Burke, H. M., Davis, M. C., Otte, C., & Mohr, D. C. (2005). Depression and cortisol responses to psychological stress: A meta-analysis. *Psychoneuroendocrinology, 30*, 846–856. doi:10.1016/j.psyneuen.2005.02.010

Cacioppo, J. T., Berntson, G., Sheridan, J. F., & McClintock, M. K. (2000). Multilevel integrative analysis of human behavior: Social neuroscience and the complementing nature of social and biological approaches. *Psychological Bulletin, 126*, 829–843. doi:10.1037/0033-2909.126.6.829

Christenfeld, N., Gerin, W., Linden, W., Sanders, M., Mathur, J., Deich, J. D., & Pickering, T. G. (1997). Social support effects on cardiovascular reactivity: Is a stranger as effective as a friend? *Psychosomatic Medicine, 59*, 388–398.

Christian, L. M., & Stoney, C. M. (2006). Social support versus social evaluation: Unique effects on vascular and myocardial response patterns. *Psychosomatic Medicine, 68,* 914–921. doi:10.1097/01.psy.0000244023.20755.cf

Creswell, J. D., Welch, W. T., Taylor, S. E., Sherman, D. K., Gruenewald, T. L., & Mann, T. (2005). Affirmation of personal values buffers neuroendocrine and psychological stress responses. *Psychological Science, 16,* 846–851. doi:10.1111/j.1467-9280.2005.01624.x

Dickerson, S. S., Gruenewald, T. L., & Kemeny, M. E. (2004). When the social self is threatened: Shame, physiology, and health. *Journal of Personality, 72,* 1191–1216. doi:10.1111/j.1467-6494.2004.00295.x

Dickerson, S. S., & Kemeny, M. E. (2004). Acute stressors and cortisol responses: A theoretical integration and synthesis of laboratory research. *Psychological Bulletin, 130,* 355–391. doi:10.1037/0033-2909.130.3.355

Dickerson, S. S., Mycek, P. J., & Zaldivar, F. (2008). Negative social evaluation, but not mere social presence, elicits cortisol responses to a laboratory stressor task. *Health Psychology, 27,* 116–121. doi:10.1037/0278-6133.27.1.116

Eisenberger, N. I., Taylor, S. E., Gable, S. L., Hilmert, C. J., & Lieberman, M. D. (2007). Neural pathways link social support to attenuated neuroendocrine stress responses. *NeuroImage, 35,* 1601–1612. doi:10.1016/j.neuroimage.2007.01.038

Ford, M. B., & Collins, N. L. (2010). Self-esteem moderates neuroendocrine and psychological responses to interpersonal rejection. *Journal of Personality and Social Psychology, 98,* 405–419. doi:10.1037/a0017345

Fox, K., Ford, I., Steg, P. G., Tendera, M., Robertson, M., & Ferrari, R. (2008, September 6). Heart rate as a prognostic risk factor in patients with coronary artery disease and left-ventricular systolic dysfunction (BEAUTIFUL): A subgroup analysis of a randomised controlled trial. *The Lancet, 372,* 817–821. doi:10.1016/S0140-6736(08)61171-X

Franklin, S. S., Khan, S. A., Wong, N. D., Larson, M. G., & Levy, D. (1999). Is pulse pressure useful in predicting risk for coronary heart disease? The Framingham Heart Study. *Circulation, 100,* 354–360.

Gruenewald, T. L., Kemeny, M. E., Aziz, N., & Fahey, J. L. (2004). Acute threat to the social self: Shame, social self-esteem, and cortisol activity. *Psychosomatic Medicine, 66,* 915–924. doi:10.1097/01.psy.0000143639.61693.ef

Hardy, J. D., & Smith, T. W. (1988). Cynical hostility and vulnerability to disease: Social support, life stress, and physiological response to conflict. *Health Psychology, 7,* 447–459. doi:10.1037/0278-6133.7.5.447

Heim, C., Ehlert, U., & Hellhammer, D. H. (2000). The potential role of hypocortisolism in the pathophysiology of stress-related bodily disorders. *Psychoneuroendocrinology, 25,* 1–35. doi:10.1016/S0306-4530(99)00035-9

Heinrichs, M., Baumgartner, T., Kirschbaum, C., & Ehlert, U. (2003). Social support and oxytocin interact to suppress cortisol and subjective responses to psychosocial stress. *Biological Psychiatry, 54,* 1389–1398. doi:10.1016/S0006-3223(03)00465-7

Het, S., Rohleder, N., Schoofs, D., Kirschbaum, C., & Wolf, O. T. (2009). Neuroendocrine and psychometric evaluation of a placebo version of the "Trier Social Stress Test." *Psychoneuroendocrinology, 34*, 1075–1086. doi:10.1016/j.psyneuen.2009.02.008

House, J. S., Landis, K. R., & Umberson, D. (1988, July 29). Social relationships and health. *Science, 241*, 540–545. doi:10.1126/science.3399889

Hughes, B. M. (2007). Self-esteem, performance feedback, and cardiovascular stress reactivity. *Anxiety, Stress, & Coping, 20*, 239–252. doi:10.1080/10615800701330218

Kaufman, J., Birmaher, B., Perel, J., Dahl, R. E., Moreci, P., Nelson, B., . . . Ryan, N. D. (1997). The corticotropin-releasing hormone challenge in depressed abused, depressed nonabused, and normal control children. *Biological Psychiatry, 42*, 669–679. doi:10.1016/S0006-3223(96)00470-2

Kelly, O., Matheson, M., Martinez, A., Merali, Z., & Anisman, H. (2007). Psychosocial stress evoked by a virtual audience: Relation to neuroendocrine activity. *CyberPsychology & Behavior, 10*, 655–662. doi:10.1089/cpb.2007.9973

Kelsey, R. M., Blascovich, J., Tomaka, J., Leitten, C. L., Schneider, T. S., & Wiens, S. (1999). Cardiovascular reactivity and adaptation to recurrent psychological stress: The moderating effects of evaluative observation. *Psychophysiology, 36*, 818–831. doi:10.1111/1469-8986.3660818

Kirschbaum, C., Klauer, T., Filipp, S.-H., & Hellhammer, D. H. (1995). Sex specific effects of social support on cortisol and subjective responses to acute psychological stress. *Psychosomatic Medicine, 57*, 23–31.

Kirschbaum, C., Pirke, K. M., & Hellhammer, D. H. (1993). The "Trier Social Stress Test"—A tool for investigating psychobiological stress responses in a laboratory setting. *Neuropsychobiology, 28*, 76–81. doi:10.1159/000119004

Lepore, S. J., Allen, K. A., & Evans, G. W. (1993). Social support lowers cardiovascular reactivity to an acute stressor. *Psychosomatic Medicine, 55*, 518–524.

McEwen, B. S. (2000). Allostasis and allostatic load: Implications for neuropsychopharmacology. *Neuropsychopharmacology, 22*, 108–124. doi:10.1016/S0893-133X(99)00129-3

McEwen, B. S., & Stellar, E. (1993). Stress and the individual: Mechanisms leading to disease. *Archives of Internal Medicine, 153*, 2093–2101. doi:10.1001/archinte.1993.00410180039004

Mendes, W. B., Blascovich, J., Hunter, S. B., Lickel, B., & Jost, J. T. (2007). Threatened by the unexpected: Physiological responses during social interactions with expectancy-violating partners. *Journal of Personality and Social Psychology, 92*, 698–716. doi:10.1037/0022-3514.92.4.698

Miller, G. E., Chen, E., & Zhou, E. S. (2007). If it goes up, must it come down? Chronic stress and the hypothalamic–pituitary–adrenocortical axis in humans. *Psychological Bulletin, 133*, 25–45. doi:10.1037/0033-2909.133.1.25

Rohleder, N., Beulen, S. E., Chen, E., Wolf, J. M., & Kirschbaum, C. (2007). Stress on the dance floor: The cortisol stress response to social-evaluative threat in competitive ballroom dancers. *Personality and Social Psychology Bulletin, 33,* 69–84. doi:10.1177/0146167206293986

Sapolsky, R. M. (2005, April 29). The influence of social hierarchy on primate health. *Science, 308*(5722), 648–652. doi:10.1126/science.1106477

Sapolsky, R. M., Romero, L. M., & Munck, A. U. (2000). How do glucocorticoids influence stress responses? Integrating permissive, suppressive, stimulatory, and preparative actions. *Endocrine Reviews, 21,* 55–89. doi:10.1210/er.21.1.55

Schwabe, L., Haddad, l., & Schachinger, H. (2008). HPA axis activation by a socially evaluated cold-pressor task. *Psychoneuroendocrinology, 33,* 890–895. doi:10.1016/j.psyneuen.2008.03.001

Sherman, D. K., Bunyan, D. P., Creswell, J. D., & Jaremka, L. M. (2009). Psychological vulnerability and stress: The effects of self-affirmation on sympathetic nervous system responses to naturalistic stressors. *Health Psychology, 28,* 554–562. doi:10.1037/a0014663

Sherman, D. K., & Cohen, G. L. (2006). The psychology of self-defense: Self-affirmation theory. In M. P. Zanna (Ed.), *Advances in experimental social psychology* (Vol. 38, pp. 183–242). San Diego, CA: Academic Press.

Smith, T. W. (1992). Hostility and health: Current status of a psychosomatic hypothesis. *Health Psychology, 11,* 139–150. doi:10.1037/0278-6133.11.3.139

Smith, T. W. (1994). Concepts and methods in the study of anger, hostility, and health. In A. W. Siegman & T. W. Smith (Eds.), *Anger, hostility, and the heart* (pp. 23–42). Hillsdale, NJ: Erlbaum.

Smith, T. W., & Gallo, L. C. (1999). Hostility and cardiovascular reactivity during marital interaction. *Psychosomatic Medicine, 61,* 436–445.

Smith, T. W., Nealey, J. B., Kircher, J. C., & Limon, J. P. (1997). Social determinants of cardiovascular reactivity: Effects of incentive to exert influence and evaluative threat. *Psychophysiology, 34,* 65–73. doi:10.1111/j.1469-8986.1997.tb02417.x

Smith, T. W., Ruiz, J. M., & Uchino, B. M. (2004). Mental activation of supportive ties, hostility, and cardiovascular reactivity to laboratory stress in young men and women. *Health Psychology, 23,* 476–485. doi:10.1037/0278-6133.23.5.476

Taylor, S. E., Seeman, T. E., Eisenberger, N. I., Kozanian, T. A., Moore, A. N., & Moons, W. G. (2010). Effects of a supportive or unsupportive audience on biological and psychological responses to stress. *Journal of Personality and Social Psychology, 98,* 47–56. doi:10.1037/a0016563

Tomaka, J., Blascovich, J., Kelsey, R. M., & Leitten, C. L. (1993). Subjective, physiological and behavioral effects of threat and challenge appraisal. *Journal of Personality and Social Psychology, 65,* 248–260. doi:10.1037//0022-3514.65.2.248

Townsend, S. S. M., Major, B., Gangi, C. E., & Mendes, W. B. (2011). From "in the air" to "under the skin": Cortisol responses to social identity threat. *Personality and Social Psychology Bulletin, 37,* 151–164. doi:10.1177/0146167210392384

Yehuda, R. (2002). Current status of cortisol findings in post-traumatic stress disorder. *Psychiatric Clinics of North America, 25,* 341–368. doi:10.1016/S0193-953X(02)00002-3

2

THE EFFECTS OF GIVING ON GIVERS

SARA KONRATH AND STEPHANIE BROWN

Ever since the groundbreaking study in which House, Landis, and Umberson (1988) argued that social relationships were equally important predictors of health as smoking, blood pressure, obesity, and physical activity, research on the health effects of social processes has exploded. An updated meta-analysis on 148 prospective studies found a 50% increase in survival likelihood for people who have robust social relationships (Holt-Lunstad, Smith, & Layton, 2010). This effect is stable across gender, age, country of origin, and operationalization of social relationships. Being socially connected is good for one's health.

This is a complex issue, however, because social relationships encompass both giving and receiving social support, and it is unclear whether both

The authors were supported by two grants at the time of writing this article. Stephanie Brown was supported by a grant from the National Science Foundation (No. 0820609, Physiological Effects of Helping Others) and Sara Konrath was supported by a grant from Wake Forest University via the John Templeton Foundation (Dispositional Empathy as a Character Trait).

DOI: 10.1037/14036-003
Health and Social Relationships: The Good, the Bad, and the Complicated, Matthew L. Newman and Nicole A. Roberts (Editors)

aspects contribute to health. Here, we summarize research on the health outcomes associated with being a recipient of help versus giving help and offer a theoretical model for integrating this body of research. Most of the studies are cross-sectional (i.e., correlational studies each conducted at a single time point) or longitudinal (i.e., studies each following individuals over time to examine the effect of giving or receiving help on some sort of health outcome), but a few experiments do exist.

Cross-sectional studies are difficult to interpret because the direction of causality between two variables is unclear. For example, a cross-sectional study finding that people who volunteer have improved health outcomes could mean that volunteering leads to health benefits, but it could also mean that people who feel more physically healthy are more likely to volunteer. With cross-sectional studies, there is also the possibility that another variable best explains the relationship. For example, it is possible that people with higher annual incomes are more likely to volunteer and are also in better health. Thus, income could explain the relationship between volunteering and health.

Longitudinal studies can clarify the direction of causality because one variable (e.g., volunteering) clearly comes before another (e.g., health), but the problem of third variables still exists in these types of studies. This does not mean that we should ignore any study that is not experimental but, rather, that we have to be careful in drawing conclusions from them. Much of what we know about more traditional health risk behaviors (e.g., smoking, obesity) is derived from longitudinal studies because it would be unethical and unrealistic to randomly assign people to smoke, for instance. Thus, we see much validity in the longitudinal method, but third variables should always be considered when using it.

THE EFFECTS OF RECEIVING SUPPORT FROM OTHERS

As reviewed next, the majority of the large literature on the topic suggests that there may be minor health benefits from receiving support from others. However, such health effects are complicated by recipient need. It is likely that people with ongoing health problems will be more likely to receive help from others, and this should be taken into account in studies. Being the recipient of help is also complicated by issues of status and power, with lower status individuals more likely to be seen as needing help, regardless of their actual need state. It is also likely that there are issues with respect to recipients' sense of efficacy and personal mastery that need to be considered within this literature.

There is a difference between believing that social support will be available if it is needed and actually being the recipient of social support. Simply believing that one has an available network of supporters is associated with a number of positive mental and physical health outcomes, including better stress regulation and improved recovery from illness (Katz, Monnier, Libet, Shaw, & Beach, 2000; Lindorff, 2000; Monahan & Hooker, 1995). This may be due to the strength of one's social connections, but it may also be explained by something about the individuals themselves, such as holding more optimistic worldviews.

When it comes to actually receiving help, though, the relationship appears to be more complex. On the one hand, correlational studies have shown that receiving social support is associated with increased depression, feelings of guilt, and feelings of dependency (Liang, Krause, & Bennett, 2001; Lu, 1997; Lu & Argyle, 1992). In a 5-year longitudinal study that controlled for a number of potential alternative explanations (e.g., age, gender, physical health, health risk behaviors, personality traits), there was a 30% increase in mortality for individuals who reported receiving practical support from friends and family members at the beginning of the study (S. L. Brown, Nesse, Vinokur, & Smith, 2003).

On the other hand, correlational studies have shown that receiving social support is also linked with better mental and physical health (Schwartz, Keyl, Marcum, & Bode, 2009; Schwartz, Meisenhelder, Ma, & Reed, 2003), and a 5-year longitudinal study found that individuals who reported receiving social support scored lower on measures of depression by the end of the study (S. L. Brown, Brown, House, & Smith, 2008). A meta-analysis examining the overall effect of receiving social support on psychological and physical health outcomes found relatively small effect sizes, ranging from −.02 to .22 (C. Smith, Fernengel, Holcroft, Gerald, & Marien, 1994). These effects depended on the type of health examined and the type of support received but did not differ by gender, age, or type of study (cross-sectional vs. longitudinal). The authors suggested that "a better understanding of an individual's need for and acceptance of social support is necessary before using the commonly recommended interventions of self-help, bereavement, and marital or family therapy groups" (C. Smith et al., 1994, p. 358). Other meta-analyses have found that these small beneficial effects of receiving support are mediated by positive cardiovascular, endocrine, and immune responses (Thorsteinsson & James, 1999; Uchino, 2006; Uchino, Cacioppo, & Kiecolt-Glaser, 1996).

Several factors determine whether receiving support will have a positive effect on the health of recipients. One such factor is the gender of the recipient. Although C. Smith et al. (1994) found that gender did not moderate outcomes, more recent work suggests that researchers must take into account gender norms that make it more difficult for men to accept and benefit from help. For example, one correlational study found that men who received support reported decreased psychological well-being, especially when the support received was for an important problem (Lindorff, 2000). Women did not experience this adverse outcome. A more recent experimental study randomly assigned participants to receive support or not from someone with whom they had just formed a bond or not. Participants were then told that they would give a speech, and salivary cortisol was assessed before and after the speech. The researchers found that cortisol increased dramatically in men who received social support from a close other, and this pattern did not occur after men received support from less close others, or among women (A. M. Smith, Loving, Crockett, & Campbell, 2009).

Personality traits may also determine whether receiving support will be associated with health benefits. For example, one study randomly assigned female participants to receive social support (i.e., positive feedback) or not during a social stress task (e.g., giving a speech). Participants only experienced dampened physiological responses to receiving support if they had a compassionate personality. Participants who were high in compassion and received social support had lower blood pressure, lower cortisol, and higher high frequency heart rate variability (indicating more efficient regulation of physiological arousal). This is likely because compassionate people are more willing to seek out and accept social support when needed (Cosley, McCoy, Saslow, & Epel, 2010). There are probably other traits that would moderate the effect of receiving support (e.g., trust, optimism), and future research should consider this possibility.

Two other factors affect whether receiving support is beneficial to health. One is the blatancy of the support. Some people give support in a direct manner but fail to consider how it might feel to receive such obvious gestures of help. Obvious attempts at helping could affect recipients' sense of autonomy, competence, or self-esteem and therefore undermine any potential psychological health benefits that may have accrued otherwise (Bolger & Amarel, 2007). Effective support givers are cognizant of such issues and try to minimize their support attempts or make them altogether invisible. For example, an effective supporter might realize that his friend is confused about a statistics problem, and rather than try to help directly, he might ask the professor to clarify the question, saying that he himself does not understand it. Strategies such as these have been shown to reduce the negative side effects of being a recipient (Bolger & Amarel, 2007). Finally, there is research suggesting that another way to minimize potential negative outcomes of receiving help is to give support in return. Reciprocity of helping seems to be an important predictor of positive social support experiences (Buunk, Doosje, Jans, & Hopstaken, 1993; Gleason, Iida, Bolger, & Shrout, 2003).

THE EFFECTS OF GIVING SUPPORT TO OTHERS

A generous person will prosper; whoever refreshes others will be refreshed.

—Proverbs 11:25

We next turn to research on the effects of giving on givers, which is the main focus of this chapter. Giving is also complex, with people who are healthier likely finding it easier to give help. Thus, baseline health has to be measured and covaried in studies that are interested in the health effects of giving on the giver. Is it better to give than to receive? As will be seen, there are contradictory findings about the potential health costs versus benefits to giving one's resources (i.e., time, money, and care) to others, with the balance of studies leaning toward the benefits of giving. Although we review the literature extensively next, we are not aware of any meta-analyses to date that would assess this question more quantitatively.

We define *giving* quite broadly to include prosocial attitudes, traits, and behaviors. Behaviors themselves can range widely from informal support and care to formal giving experiences, such as volunteering. What each of these has in common is that they are all focused on increasing others' well-being, whether simply in desire (e.g., concern for others) or in reality (e.g., by providing tangible assistance). Attempts to understand the mechanisms for giving effects can also be elucidated by studying its flip side, or extreme self-focus. Thus, we also summarize work on the health-related outcomes associated with a higher self-focus.

Giving Time and Money to Organizations

Although the literature on volunteering behavior and health is relatively well-established, intriguing work has also found correlational links between making charitable donations and psychological well-being (Aknin et al., 2010; Dunn, Aknin, & Norton, 2008). These correlations are consistent across many different cultures (Aknin et al., 2010). What remains to be seen is whether giving to others makes people happier, whether happier people simply give more, or whether some third variable best explains this finding.

The majority of studies on volunteering and health are focused on older adults, yet volunteering appears to have a beneficial effect on other populations as well, including younger adults (Musick & Wilson, 2003), doctors (less burnout; C. Campbell et al., 2009), and patients with posttraumatic stress disorder (better treatment outcomes; Warren, 1993). In both correlational and longitudinal studies, volunteers have reported more positive affect, life satisfaction, and psychological well-being, and less depression compared with nonvolunteers, even when considering a variety of covariates (Greenfield &

Marks, 2004; Lum & Lightfoot, 2005; Morrow-Howell, Hinterlong, Rozario, & Tang, 2003; Musick & Wilson, 2003; Piliavin & Siegl, 2007; Sarid, Melzer, Kurz, Shahar, & Ruch, 2010; Thoits & Hewitt, 2001; Van Willigen, 2000; Windsor, Anstey, & Rodgers, 2008). There seems to be evidence for a curvilinear effect of volunteering such that there are mental health benefits associated with moderate levels of volunteering but not extremely high levels (i.e., 800 or more hours per year; Windsor et al., 2008).

Studies on physical health outcomes associated with volunteering have focused almost entirely on older adults, likely because this is a group with an increased risk of health problems, functional limitations, and ultimately, mortality. Longitudinal studies have found that volunteers report being in better health and having fewer functional limitations than nonvolunteers, even when controlling for demographic and socioeconomic variables (Lum & Lightfoot, 2005; Piliavin & Siegl, 2007; Thoits & Hewitt, 2001; Van Willigen, 2000). A number of longitudinal studies have found that older adults who volunteer experience a significantly reduced mortality risk several years later, even when including a host of covariates (Harris & Thoresen, 2005; Konrath, Fuhrel-Forbis, Lou, & Brown, 2012; Luoh & Herzog, 2002; Musick, Herzog, & House, 1999; Oman, Thoresen, & Mcmahon, 1999). Our recent work has found that the reasons people volunteer are important determinants of whether they will experience this mortality risk decrease 4 years later (Konrath et al., 2012). Volunteers who donate their time for other-oriented reasons (e.g., compassion) experience a significant reduction in their mortality risk, but volunteering for more self-oriented reasons (e.g., to learn something new or to feel good about oneself) is not associated with any change in mortality risk. In fact, after considering covariates, self-oriented volunteers are just as likely to die as older adults who do not volunteer.

Although volunteering behavior itself appears to be protective for mental and physical health, there are inconsistencies with regard to the impact of the type and number of organizations to which one volunteers and the duration or frequency of volunteering, with some research suggesting that these factors play no role and others finding that they do matter. A meta-analytic integration of the literature would clarify this, and indeed, one of us is working on exactly this issue (Brown & Okun, in press).

Giving Social Support

Measures of social support given encompass both practical (e.g., money, time, errands) and more emotional types of support given to known others such as friends and family. Several correlational studies have found that giving social support to others is associated with higher psychological

well-being, such as more happiness, increased self-esteem, and less loneliness (De Jong Giefveld & Dykstra, 2008; Dunn et al., 2008; Krause &
Shaw, 2000; Schwartz et al., 2003). These findings have been confirmed in
longitudinal studies (S. L. Brown et al., 2008; Gleason et al., 2003; Ironson,
2007; Schwartz & Sendor, 1999). Experimental and quasi-experimental
studies have found that people who are randomly assigned to perform such
behaviors as caring for plants, giving money to others, or giving massages to
infants experience increased psychological well-being and decreased depression (Aknin et al., 2010; Field, Hernandez-Reif, Quintino, Schanberg, &
Kuhn, 1998; Langer & Rodin, 1976). However, giving is not always related
to more positive mental health outcomes. One study found no relationship between giving social support and depression (Liang, et al., 2001), and
other studies have found that at times giving social support can be associated
with negative outcomes, such as a sense of burden and frustration (Fujiwara,
2009; Lu, 1997; Lu & Argyle, 1992), especially if others make too many
demands, if givers become overwhelmed by others' problems, or if there is
low reciprocity within the interactions (Buunk et al., 1993; Schwartz et al.,
2003; Strazdins & Broom, 2007).

The relationship between giving to others and physical health is more
consistent in the literature. In correlational studies, giving to others has
been shown to be associated with positive health outcomes, including fewer
health conditions among older adults and longer term survival among people with AIDS (W. M. Brown, Consedine, & Magai, 2005; Ironson et al.,
2002; Schwartz et al., 2003, 2009). Although this effect seems to general-
ize across diverse ethnic and cultural groups (W. M. Brown et al., 2005),
one study found that among teenagers the correlation between giving to
others and physical health only existed in females (Schwartz et al., 2009).
Longitudinal studies again confirmed physical health benefits associated
with giving to others, including signals of good health such as lower blood
pressure and lower viral loads (Ironson, 2007; Piferi & Lawler, 2006) and,
ultimately, a significantly lower risk of mortality in older adults or chronically ill patients (S. L. Brown et al., 2003; McClellan, Stanwyck, & Anson,
1993). These effects appear to be especially strong when the recipients of
giving are close others (e.g., family, friends) rather than more distant others
(e.g., nurses, doctors, other patients; McClellan et al., 1993) and are also
robust to covariates (S. L. Brown et al., 2003; Ironson, 2007; McClellan
et al., 1993). Experimental and quasi-experimental studies that directly
examine the physiological effects of giving in the laboratory point to potential mechanisms within the neuroendocrine system. In particular, giving to
others leads to decreases in cortisol (Field et al., 1998; A. M. Smith et al.,
2009) and increases in progesterone and oxytocin within givers (S. L. Brown,
Konrath, Seng, & Smith, 2011).

Compassionate Attitudes and Traits

A number of studies have examined the relationship between compassionate attitudes and traits, and health. These should be related to better health to the extent that they increase the likelihood that people will engage in behaviors that are intended to benefit others. Indeed, those who score high on other-oriented measures such as compassion, altruism, caring, and empathy seek out more caregiving opportunities (Davis, 1983; K. D. Smith, 1992; Steffen & Masters, 2005). With dispositional empathy declining over the past 30 years in the United States (Konrath, O'Brien, & Hsing, 2011), the issue of how empathy is related to health will likely become more important in the future.

A number of correlational studies have found that people who score high in empathy or compassion have lower stress, anxiety, hopelessness, and depression (Au, Wong, Lai, & Chan, 2011; Ironson et al., 2002; Steffen & Masters, 2005), even when controlling for other traditional predictors of mental health, such as coping and social support, although unknown third variables may still account for such effects (Au et al., 2011). The samples in these studies varied widely and included high school students, college students, community samples, and people with chronic illnesses, yet the results are consistent. Even in jobs that are associated with high stress and potential compassion fatigue, such as health care, individuals who are more compassionate, caring, or prosocially oriented have higher job satisfaction and lower stress and burnout (Burtson & Stichler, 2010; Dyrbye et al., 2010). Of course, it is possible that those experiencing lower stress and burnout simply have more available energy to be compassionate, but a 60-year longitudinal study has suggested that the direction of causality goes in the other direction: Those who had altruistic personalities as adolescents had better mental health outcomes in late adulthood, even when controlling for their initial health and social class (Wink & Dillon, 2002). One potential mechanism of this effect is that compassionate people are more likely to seek, accept, and be satisfied with social support from others (Cosley et al., 2010; Steffen & Masters, 2005). It is important to note the distinction between having an other-oriented compassionate focus (i.e., empathic concern) versus a self-oriented emotional reaction (i.e., personal distress) in response to another person's suffering. The latter is likely to be associated with poor mental health outcomes in contrast to more other-focused feelings (O'Connor, Berry, Weiss, & Gilbert, 2002).

In terms of physical health, correlational studies have found that people with higher empathy participate in fewer health risk behaviors such as drinking and smoking (Adams, 2010; Kalliopuska, 1992). One interesting experiment found that simply showing participants a film clip of an extremely compassionate exemplar (Mother Teresa) increased a biomarker of healthy immune functioning (S-IgA) compared with a control film clip. This effect was especially strong for participants who were high in affiliation motivation, or the desire to connect with others (McClelland & Krishnit, 1988). Longitudinal studies have confirmed that caring and altruistic individuals have better self-reported physical health, more robust immune responses in chronic illnesses, and are even lower in mortality risk several years later (Dillon & Wink, 2007; Ironson, 2007; Konrath & Fuhrel-Forbis, 2011b). However, the role of covariates needs to be clarified, with one study showing that health and social class explained the later health outcomes (Dillon & Wink, 2007) and another finding that the health outcomes were robust to a number of plausible confounds (Konrath & Fuhrel-Forbis, 2011b).

CAREGIVING BEHAVIORS

Caregiving behaviors involve unpaid assistance with activities of daily living (e.g., bathing, dressing, eating) that is given to someone experiencing an illness or functional limitation. For example, the spouse of an older adult who had recently experienced a severe stroke or who has dementia would likely be involved in at least some daily caregiving activities. Similarly, parents of children with disabilities nearly always face additional caregiving responsibilities beyond typical parenting tasks. Caregiving is qualitatively different from other types of giving for a number of reasons: (a) it nearly always involves exposure to a loved one who is in pain or distress; (b) it is often nonvoluntary because of financial or other circumstances; and (c) it often involves considerably more cost to the self in terms of time, energy, and financial contribution compared with other types of giving. As such, caregiving is a considerably more stressful experience for givers than other types of giving. Given this, researchers must tease apart some of the unique features of caregiving contexts (e.g., the effects of seeing loved ones in pain or anticipatory bereavement) from the effects of actually giving help to loved ones, if they want to understand the independent effects of altruistic behavior (S. L. Brown, Smith, et al., 2009).

A meta-analysis of 23 studies that compared caregivers of people with dementia with age- and gender-matched noncaregivers found that caregivers self-reported more health problems, more physical symptoms, and more medication use compared with noncaregivers; they also had higher levels of stress hormones and weaker immune responses, (Vitaliano, Zhang, & Scanlan, 2003). Although the average effect of caregiving on health was statistically significant, the wide range of outcomes in the studies suggests that caregiving does not necessarily lead to poor health outcomes in itself but likely interacts with a number of factors to predict such outcomes. For example, meta-analyses have found that caregiving is associated with more negative physical health outcomes for women (Pinquart & Sörensen, 2006; Vitaliano et al., 2003), older caregivers (Pinquart & Sörensen, 2007; Vitaliano et al., 2003), and people from ethnic minority groups (Pinquart & Sörensen, 2005). It is notable that women, older adults, and people from ethnic minorities also tend to be groups with lower socioeconomic resources relative to men, middle-aged adults, and Caucasians.

Specific features of the caregiving situation also predict health outcomes. Caregivers who provide more hours of care and more caregiving tasks for a more (physically and cognitively) impaired recipient for longer periods of time are more susceptible to psychological and physical health problems, especially if care recipients exhibit behavioral problems (Pinquart & Sörensen, 2007). Protective factors include having access to greater economic resources and social support (Pinquart & Sörensen, 2007). Taken together, these studies on the health effects associated with caregiving suggest that not all caregiving is created equally and that interventions should especially target higher risk groups.

Recent research has highlighted the importance of teasing apart the influence of actual support-giving behaviors from the influence of such risk factors. In a longitudinal study that followed 3,376 older adult caregivers (age 70+) from the Health and Retirement Study, researchers found that hours of care given and spousal impairment both independently predicted mortality status 7 years later (S. L. Brown, Smith, et al., 2009). Providing 14 or more hours of care per week to spouses was associated with a lower mortality risk, and at the same time, caregivers whose spouses had more functional impairments had a higher mortality risk. These effects remained even when controlling for potential demographic (age, gender, race), socioeconomic (education, employment status, net worth), and health-related confounds (health, illnesses, functional status, depression). Another recent study using daily diaries demonstrated the importance of separating time spent actively helping spouses from time being "on call" to provide help if needed (Poulin et al., 2010). The researchers found that the more caregivers actually helped their spouses, the more positive affect they experienced. However, the more time they were on call, the less positive affect they experienced. This effect was moderated by interdependence such that those who reported being in more interdependent relationships experienced more positive affect (and no negative affect) when helping their spouses, whereas those who had less interdependent relationships experienced more negative affect (and no positive affect).

Lee, Brennan, and Daly (2001) found that empathy can be a double-edged sword when it comes to caregiving. On the one hand, caregivers who were high in a more cognitive form of empathy reported lower stress and depression and higher life satisfaction. This is likely because cognitive empathy allows one to consider the perspectives and needs of others but also allows for some emotional distancing to occur. On the other hand, those who scored high in emotional empathy reported lower life satisfaction, with a nonsignificant tendency to score higher in depression. Although perspective taking and emotional empathy are typically positively correlated (Davis, 1983), they are not identical, and their differences may be important when considering extremely high-stress, time-intensive, and unavoidable situations like informal caregiving.

Self-Focus and Health

The majority of this chapter has focused on the health benefits associated with being focused on others. But the flip side of this topic also deserves some attention. Are there negative health outcomes associated with an increase in self-focus? This has been less frequently studied in the literature but will likely become increasingly important with societal rises in individualism, self-esteem, and narcissism over the past few decades (Twenge, 1997; Twenge & Campbell, 2001, 2008; Twenge, Campbell, & Gentile, 2011; Twenge, Konrath, Foster, Campbell, & Bushman, 2008).

Self-esteem and the personality trait narcissism are associated with positive mental health outcomes. For example, people with high self-esteem have high satisfaction with their lives and are less likely to be depressed or anxious (Crandall, 1973; Diener, 1984; Tennen & Herzberger, 1987). It is not surprising that self-esteem is associated with positive mental health outcomes, and indeed, it is sometimes seen as a marker of mental health in itself. Although self-esteem and narcissism are positively correlated, people with high self-esteem have positive views of the self and others, whereas people scoring higher in narcissism see themselves as superior and others as inferior. Surprisingly, those who score high in narcissism also have lower depression, anxiety, and loneliness (Sedikides, Rudich, Gregg, Kumashiro, & Rusbult, 2004; Watson & Biderman, 1993) and increased happiness and subjective well-being compared with those who score lower in narcissism (Watson & Biderman, 1993). This is true despite their documented difficulties in maintaining healthy interpersonal relationships (W. K. Campbell, Foster, & Finkel, 2002). It remains to be seen whether these apparent mental health benefits associated with narcissism run deep, are a result of some sort of defensive self-enhancement, or exist because of narcissism's correlation with self-esteem (Rosenthal & Hooley, 2010).

Narcissism makes individuals susceptible to a host of unrealistic self-views that are difficult and stressful to continuously maintain (Morf & Rhodewalt, 2001). Although at first glance these positive self-views may manifest themselves as high psychological well-being, in the long term having unrealistically positive views about oneself actually leads to declines in psychological well-being (Robins & Beer, 2001). Moreover, attempting to maintain such views may lead to chronic hyperactivation of the physiological stress response system, which could ultimately weaken the body's natural defenses against disease. Thus, examining the physical health outcomes associated with narcissism is as important as examining mental health outcomes associated with it. Although only a few studies have been conducted so far, they have consistently found an overactivation of stress responses among narcissists. Males who score high in narcissism have high levels of stress hormones compared with males who score low in narcissism, especially when under stress (Edelstein, Yim, & Quas, 2010; Reinhard, Konrath, Cameron, & Lopez, 2012). There is no relationship between narcissism and cortisol among women. Among men and women, narcissism is related to increased cardiovascular reactivity when thinking of stressful stimuli (Kelsey, Ornduff, McCann, & Reiff, 2001) or after a stressor (Kelsey, Ornduff, Reiff, & Arthur, 2002). Similarly, thinking of interpersonal rejection leads to increased diastolic blood pressure and heart rate for men and women scoring high on narcissism (Sommer, Kirkland, Newman, Estrella, & Andreassi, 2009).

Our recent work found that it is not necessary to score high in a personality trait such as narcissism to experience some negative health outcomes. Simply focusing on personal benefits that one may receive from volunteering is sufficient. In unadjusted models, more self-oriented reasons for volunteering were associated with increased mortality in older adults; however, this effect was reduced to nonsignificance when covariates were included (Konrath et al., 2012). Note that these reasons were not selfish per se but simply focused on mundane potential benefits that volunteers might experience besides helping others, such as learning new things or feeling needed. In other words, self-focus need not be too extreme to be costly to health.

Another way to conceptualize self-focus is to measure people's first person pronoun use (e.g., I, me, my, mine). This method is useful because, unlike something as chronic as a trait or set of core motives, there are likely changes in pronoun use within individuals depending on situations. Several studies have found that depressed or bipolar individuals use more first person singular pronouns than controls, especially the word *I* (Bucci & Freedman, 1981; Lorenz & Cobb, 1952; Rude, Gortner, & Pennebaker, 2004; Weintraub, 1981). Although the direction of causality is unclear, these studies suggest that excessive self-focus is at the very least a signal of poor mental health. Indeed, other research has confirmed that compared with nonsuicidal poets, poets who later committed suicide made fewer references to other people, used fewer first person plural pronouns (e.g., *we*), and used more first person singular pronouns (Stirman & Pennebaker, 2001).

Excessive first person pronoun use is also associated with physical health outcomes. One program of research examined such use in the context of coronary heart disease (Scherwitz & Canick, 1988; Scherwitz, Graham, & Ornish, 1985). The researchers found that participants who frequently used first person pronouns had higher blood pressure, more occluded arteries, a more severe disease status, more previous myocardial infractions, and a greater risk of mortality in longitudinal studies. These effects remained even when other important risk factors were covaried (e.g., age, smoking, cholesterol).

Taken together, it appears that self-focus might at times be linked to poor mental health, depending on how it is conceptualized. It also seems to be linked to increased physiological indicators of stress and, ultimately, to coronary heart disease. However, the work on this topic has many more gaps than does the topic of altruism and health, and much future research is needed.

THEORETICAL MODEL OF CAREGIVING AND HEALTH

We next present a theoretical model of caregiving (or nurturing) and health that can help to integrate previous research by predicting under which circumstances giving is likely to result in health benefits versus costs. This model can also be a useful tool to inspire future research on the topics discussed previously.

We propose that giving to others can be beneficial to health to the extent that it engages the biological *caregiving system* (see Figure 2.1), which is a physiological (hormonal, neurological) and psychological (cognitions, emotions) system that evolved to facilitate the creation and maintenance of social bonds, including parental caregiving behavior and various kinds of helping and giving behaviors (S. L. Brown & Brown, 2006; S. L. Brown, Brown, & Preston, 2011). This caregiving system has been shown to drive maternal behavior

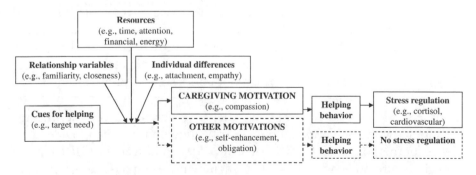

Figure 2.1. A model of caregiving motivation and stress regulation.

in rodents (Numan, 2006) and may facilitate human helping and caregiving behavior by both increasing the desire to help (i.e., approach motivation) and by decreasing the desire to avoid harm or cost to oneself (i.e., avoidance of stress responses; Numan, 2006). This system is hypothesized to interrupt the physiological stress response, which if true, should lead to psychological and physical health benefits over time. There are many nonaltruistic reasons that people help, including that it is required (e.g., service learning as part of a course requirement, community service penalties), that they have no other choice (e.g., cannot afford to pay for a caregiver), or that it can somehow benefit themselves (e.g., advance their career). This model allows for these other reasons and simply argues that these alternative reasons to help will not activate the caregiving system and thus should not lead to health benefits (see Konrath et al., 2012, for an example).

Outcome: Stress Regulation

This model posits that one of the downstream consequences of the activation of caregiving motivations is increased stress regulation. Studies of both human and animal maternal behavior have provided initial evidence for exactly this process, finding that the neuroendocrine system releases hormones such as oxytocin and progesterone during normal maternal–infant interactions (Feldman, Gordon, Schneiderman, Weisman, & Zagoory-Sharon, 2010; Numan, 2006). Interestingly, giving to others can itself be a source of stress (e.g., from exposure to others' pain) and can be costly to the self in terms of having fewer resources (time, money, energy). This model posits that caregiving motivations can help to alleviate givers' stress responses regardless of why they occur, even if they originate from the giving behavior itself.

Relationship Variables

A number of factors make it more likely that caregiving motivation will be elicited. First, relational bonds between helpers and recipients are posited to be important, an idea which is consistent with a recent evolutionary theory of social bonds and altruism (S. L. Brown & Brown, 2006). Indeed, there is experimental evidence that relationship variables themselves (e.g., closeness) can activate caregiving-system hormones such as progesterone (S. L. Brown, Fredrickson, et al., 2009). Thus, the stress-regulating effects of giving to others should be especially strong when givers are close, interdependent, or familiar with recipients. Studies described previously have provided evidence for this possibility (McClellan et al., 1993; Poulin et al., 2010), but the caregiving literature, which focuses predominantly on spouse caregiving, has suggested that other factors may also be at play. Thus, future studies should focus on relationship type and quality to examine when giving predicts better health outcomes.

Individual Differences

There are a number of individual differences that are hypothesized to affect whether giving will be beneficial or costly to givers' health. We hypothesize that gender plays a role in such outcomes and, in particular, that women whose caregiving systems have been primed with pregnancy and childbirth should be more likely to benefit from giving. Some research, described previously, found that women were more likely to benefit from giving (Schwartz et al., 2009); however, these effects were not consistent (Pinquart & Sörensen, 2006; Vitaliano et al., 2003). Many of the studies controlled for gender, but we recommend also testing for its moderating role in future research.

Traits that help people to form bonds more easily with others should facilitate the activation of the caregiving system. Thus, individual differences that are associated with bonding capacity such as attachment style (secure vs. insecure) and dispositional empathy should also moderate the relationship between helping and stress regulation. As reviewed earlier, having an empathic or compassionate personality is associated with a number of health benefits, and it is possible that this is because of a chronic activation of the caregiving system.

Resources

The availability of time, attention, money, and energy should predict better health outcomes associated with giving because these resources can keep the motivational focus on the recipient of care rather than on the giver's own worries. This is consistent with the energy-resource model of empathic responding (Konrath & Fuhrel-Forbis, 2011a), which posits that each act of empathizing or caring for another is costly in terms of energy units, and some people find these acts costlier than others. Resources likely interact with relationship variables and individual differences to predict optimal health outcomes from giving to others. For example, a high empathy person may find a small act of giving to be less depleting than a low empathy person would, because the more frequent flexing of empathic capacities in higher empathy people likely renders them more automatic (Konrath & Fuhrel-Forbis, 2011a).

This example highlights the contextual nature of resources, and we caution future researchers to avoid being overly literal in defining them. The subjective report of participants (e.g., "I barely have time to think") likely matters just as much as any objective indicators (e.g., only having a part-time job). That being said, one clear finding in the caregiving literature is that caregivers who objectively have more resources are less likely to suffer from negative health consequences (Pinquart & Sörensen, 2007).

Possible Alternative Routes

It is possible that positive emotions also explain why the altruism and health relationship exists. Helping behavior increases positive emotions in helpers (Yinon & Landau, 1987), and positive emotions themselves can accelerate recovery from stressors (Fredrickson, 2000). Positive emotions also predict increased longevity (Danner, Snowdon, & Friesen, 2001). Similarly, giving to others may also buffer stress and improve health outcomes because it increases a sense of purpose or meaning in volunteers' lives (Greenfield & Marks, 2004; Musick et al., 1999), which has independently been linked to greater longevity (Boyle, Barnes, Buchman, & Bennett, 2009). In other words, perhaps helping behavior, however it is activated (i.e., through the caregiving system or not), triggers positive emotions or an increased sense of purpose, which then enhance stress regulation, with implications for long-term health. Future research should also examine these other potential explanations for the health benefits of giving to others.

FUTURE RESEARCH DIRECTIONS

This review of the literature on the health effects of giving on givers has revealed a number of gaps that need addressing. In particular, mechanisms of the giving behavior–health relationship are not well understood, and these could be elucidated by experimental studies that examine the immediate and longer term causal effects (both positive and negative) of helping and giving behavior. In our lab, we are examining the immediate psychophysiological consequences of helping a partner within a laboratory context. In a series of experiments, we are examining whether characteristics of the helper (i.e., individual differences such as gender or empathy) affect whether there will be positive physiological consequences of helping for helpers (e.g., lower cardiovascular reactivity). We are also experimentally manipulating the degree of closeness between helpers and recipients to see how relationship variables affect physiological responses. Laboratory studies can allow researchers to systematically vary a number of other situational features to see how they influence immediate physiological outcomes. In addition, longer-term experiments (interventions) could examine how these processes work over time once they have been established in the lab.

Moreover, nearly all of the studies described in this paper have been conducted in Western cultures and on predominantly White samples, and there is a need to examine whether positive effects of giving on givers extend to people of different ethnic and cultural backgrounds. This would be an important test of the biological caregiving model, which is hypothesized to be fundamental to humans. Although there may be cultural variations in moderators of the altruism–health relationship, we hypothesize that once caregiving motivation is activated (see Figure 2.1), the stress regulatory consequences should be more universal.

Another potentially interesting area for further research is apparent after reviewing the literature. Many studies have examined processes among older adult populations; no study that we are aware of has examined whether there are immediate physiological benefits of helping among young children. This would also clarify the limits of this theoretical model. It is possible, for example, that caregiving motivation buffers people from stress only when this motivation becomes biologically critical for the survival of the species (i.e., at the age of childbearing potential). It is also possible that even young children experience physiological benefits from nurturing and caring for others, and if so, this would provide evidence for the generalizability of the caregiving system outside of parental behavior to also include a wide variety of caring and giving behaviors by a number of potential actors.

Finally, we have noted a number of important meta-analyses that have focused on three of the five literatures reviewed earlier. Notably missing are meta-analyses focusing on giving social support and health, and self-focus and health. Although these are both emerging areas of research, at this point there are enough studies available that some sort of integration would be informative.

CONCLUSION

Is it better to give than to receive? On the basis of this review, the answer is complex. Giving can have health benefits and health costs, and a number of factors influence whether the consequences will lean one way or the other. We recommend that future researchers move beyond simplistic questions of whether giving is good or bad for health and instead examine these five basic questions: Who benefits from giving to others? What types of giving are associated with better health outcomes? When is giving beneficial to health; that is, under which circumstances is it beneficial? Where is giving associated with health benefits? And the big question: Why? Answering these questions will not only theoretically integrate a number of related literatures but will also have the important practical benefit of determining the most appropriate low-cost giving-related health interventions for our aging population.

REFERENCES

Adams, A. (2010). *The relationship among illness representations, risk representations, empathy, and preventive health behaviors.* Unpublished doctoral dissertation, Marywood University, Scranton, PA.

Aknin, L. B., Barrington-Leigh, C. P., Dunn, E. W., Helliwell, J. F., Biswas-Diener, R., Kemeza, I., . . . Norton, M. I. (2010). *Prosocial spending and well-being: Cross-cultural evidence for a psychological universal* (Working Paper No. 16415). Retrieved from *National Bureau of Economic Research* website: http://www.hbs.edu/research/pdf/11-038.pdf

Au, A. M. L., Wong, A. S. K., Lai, M. K., & Chan, C. C. H. (2011). Empathy, coping, social support, and mental health in local and migrant adolescents in Beijing. *International Journal on Disability and Human Development, 10,* 173–178. doi:10.1515/ijdhd.2011.030

Bolger, N., & Amarel, D. (2007). Effects of social support visibility on adjustment to stress: Experimental evidence. *Journal of Personality and Social Psychology, 92,* 458–475. doi:10.1037/0022-3514.92.3.458

Boyle, P. A., Barnes, L. L., Buchman, A. S., & Bennett, D. A. (2009). Purpose in life is associated with mortality among community-dwelling older persons. *Psychosomatic Medicine, 71,* 574–579. doi:10.1097/PSY.0b013e3181a5a7c0

Brown, S. L., & Brown, R. M. (2006). Selective investment theory: Recasting the functional significance of close relationships. *Psychological Inquiry, 17,* 1–29. doi:10.1207/s15327965pli1701_01

Brown, S. L., Brown, R. M., House, J. S., & Smith, D. M. (2008). Coping with spousal loss: Potential buffering effects of self-reported helping behavior. *Personality and Social Psychology Bulletin, 34,* 849–861. doi:10.1177/0146167208314972

Brown, S. L., Brown, R. M., & Preston, S. (2011). A neuroscience model of caregiving motivation. In S. Brown, R. M. Brown, & L. Penner (Eds.), *Moving beyond self interest: Perspectives from evolutionary biology, neuroscience, and the social sciences* (pp. 75–88). New York, NY: Oxford University Press. doi:10.1093/acprof:oso/9780195388107.003.0026

Brown, S. L., Fredrickson, B., Wirth, M., Poulin, M., Meier, E., Heaphy, E., . . . Schultheiss, O, C. (2009). Social closeness increases salivary progesterone in humans. *Hormones and Behavior, 56,* 108–111. doi:10.1016/j.yhbeh.2009.03.022

Brown, S. L., Konrath, S., Seng, J., & Smith, D. (2011, September). *Measuring oxytocin and progesterone (compassion hormones) in a laboratory vs. ecological setting and results from recent studies.* Paper presented at The Neuroscience of Compassion Conference, Stony Brook, NY.

Brown, S. L., Nesse, R. M., Vinokur, A. D., & Smith, D. M. (2003). Providing social support may be more beneficial than receiving it: Results from a prospective study of mortality. *Psychological Science, 14,* 320–327. doi:10.1111/1467-9280.14461

Brown, S. L., & Okun, M. A., (in press). Using the caregiver system model to explain the resilience-related benefits older adults derive from volunteering. In M. Kent, M. Davis, & J. Reich (Eds.), *The resilience handbook: Approaches to stress and trauma*. New York, NY: Routledge. Retrieved from http://www.public.asu.edu/~iacmao/Handbook_of_Resilience_chapter_Brown%20_Okun.pdf

Brown, S. L., Smith, D. M., Schulz, R., Kabeto, M. U., Ubel, P. A., Poulin, M., . . . Langa, K. M. (2009). Caregiving behavior is associated with decreased mortality risk. *Psychological Science, 20*, 488–494. doi:10.1111/j.1467-9280.2009.02323.x

Brown, W. M., Consedine, N. S., & Magai, C. (2005). Altruism relates to health in an ethnically diverse sample of older adults. *The Journals of Gerontology: Series B. Psychological Sciences and Social Sciences, 60*, P143–P152. doi:10.1093/geronb/60.3.P143

Bucci, W., & Freedman, N. (1981). The language of depression. *Bulletin of the Menninger Clinic, 45*, 334–358.

Burtson, P. L., & Stichler, J. F. (2010). Nursing work environment and nurse caring: Relationship among motivational factors. *Journal of Advanced Nursing, 66*, 1819–1831. doi:10.1111/j.1365-2648.2010.05336.x

Buunk, B. P., Doosje, B. J., Jans, L. G. J. M., & Hopstaken, L. E. M. (1993). Perceived reciprocity, social support, and stress at work: The role of exchange and communal orientation. *Journal of Personality and Social Psychology, 65*, 801–811. doi:10.1037/0022-3514.65.4.801

Campbell, C., Campbell, D., Krier, D., Kuehlthau, R., Hilmes, T., & Stromberger, M. (2009). Reduction in burnout may be a benefit for short-term medical mission volunteers. *Mental Health, Religion & Culture, 12*, 627–637. doi:10.1080/13674670903124541

Campbell, W. K., Foster, C., & Finkel, E. J. (2002). Does self-love lead to love for others? A story of narcissistic game playing. *Journal of Personality and Social Psychology, 83*, 340–354. doi:10.1037/0022-3514.83.2.340

Cosley, B. J., McCoy, S. K., Saslow, L. R., & Epel, E. S. (2010). Is compassion for others stress buffering? Consequences of compassion and social support for physiological reactivity to stress. *Journal of Experimental Social Psychology, 46*, 816–823. doi:10.1016/j.jesp.2010.04.008

Crandall, R. (Ed.). (1973). *The measurement of self-esteem and related constructs*. Ann Arbor, MI: Institute for Social Research.

Danner, D. D., Snowdon, D. A., & Friesen, W. V. (2001). Positive emotions in early life and longevity: Findings from the nun study. *Journal of Personality and Social Psychology, 80*, 804–813. doi:10.1037/0022-3514.80.5.804

Davis, M. (1983). Measuring individual differences in empathy: Evidence for a multi-dimensional approach. *Journal of Personality and Social Psychology, 44*, 113–126. doi:10.1037/0022-3514.44.1.113

De Jong Giefveld, J., & Dykstra, P. (2008). Virtue is its own reward? Support-giving in the family and loneliness in middle and old age. *Ageing & Society, 28*, 271–287.

Diener, E. (1984). Subjective well-being. *Psychological Bulletin, 95*, 542–575. doi:10.1037/0033-2909.95.3.542

Dillon, M., & Wink, P. (2007). *In the course of a lifetime: Tracing religious belief, practice, and change*. Los Angeles, CA: University of California Press.

Dunn, E. W., Aknin, L. B., & Norton, M. I. (2008, March 21). Spending money on others promotes happiness. *Science, 319*, 1687–1688. doi:10.1126/science.1150952

Dyrbye, L. N., Massie, F. S., Eacker, A., Harper, W., Power, D., Durning, S. J., . . . Shanafelt, T. D. (2010, September 15). Relationship between burnout and professional conduct and attitudes among US medical students. *JAMA, 304*, 1173–1180. doi:10.1001/jama.2010.1318

Edelstein, R. S., Yim, I. S., & Quas, J. A. (2010). Narcissism predicts heightened cortisol reactivity to a psychosocial stressor in men. *Journal of Research in Personality, 44*, 565–572. doi:10.1016/j.jrp.2010.06.008

Feldman, R., Gordon, I., Schneiderman, I., Weisman, O., & Zagoory-Sharon, O. (2010). Natural variations in maternal and paternal care are associated with systematic changes in oxytocin following parent–infant contact. *Psychoneuroendocrinology, 35*, 1133–1141. doi:10.1016/j.psyneuen.2010.01.013

Field, T. M., Hernandez-Reif, M., Quintino, O., Schanberg, S., & Kuhn, C. (1998). Elder retired volunteers benefit from giving massage therapy to infants. *Journal of Applied Gerontology, 17*, 229–239. doi:10.1177/073346489801700210

Fredrickson, B. (2000). Cultivating positive emotions to optimize health and well-being. *Prevention & Treatment, 3*. Retrieved from http://www.rickhanson.net/wp-content/files/papers/CultPosEmot.pdf

Fujiwara, T. (2009). Is altruistic behavior associated with major depression onset? *PLoS ONE, 4*(2), e4557. doi:10.1371/journal.pone.0004557

Gleason, M. E. J., Iida, M., Bolger, N., & Shrout, P. E. (2003). Daily supportive equity in close relationships. *Personality and Social Psychology Bulletin, 29*, 1036–1045. doi:10.1177/0146167203253473

Greenfield, E. A., & Marks, N. F. (2004). Formal volunteering as a protective factor for older adults' psychological well-being. *The Journals of Gerontology: Series B. Psychological Sciences and Social Sciences, 59*, S258–S264. doi:10.1093/geronb/59.5.S258

Harris, A. H. S., & Thoresen, C. E. (2005). Volunteering is associated with delayed mortality in older people: Analysis of the longitudinal study of aging. *Journal of Health Psychology, 10*, 739–752. doi:10.1177/1359105305057310

Holt-Lunstad, J., Smith, T. B., & Layton, J. B. (2010). Social relationships and mortality risk: A meta-analytic review. *PLoS Medicine, 7*(7), e1000316. doi:10.1371/journal.pmed.1000316

House, J. S., Landis, K., & Umberson, D. (1988, July 29). Social relationships and health. *Science, 241*, 540–545. doi:10.1126/science.3399889

Ironson, G. (2007). Altruism and health in HIV. In S. Post (Ed.), *Altruism and health* (pp. 70–81). New York, NY: Oxford University Press. doi:10.1093/acprof:oso/9780195182910.003.0007

Ironson, G., Solomon, G., Balbin, E., O'Cleirigh, C., George, A., Kumar, M., . . . Woods, T. E. (2002). The Ironson-Woods Spirituality/Religiousness Index is associated with long survival, health behaviors, less distress, and low cortisol in people with HIV/AIDS. *Annals of Behavioral Medicine, 24*, 34–48. doi:10.1207/S15324796ABM2401_05

Kalliopuska, M. (1992). Attitudes towards health, health behaviour, and personality factors among school students very high on empathy. *Psychological Reports, 70*, 1119–1122. doi:10.2466/pr0.1992.70.3c.1119

Katz, J., Monnier, J., Libet, J., Shaw, D., & Beach, S. R. H. (2000). Individual and cross-over effects of stress on adjustment in medical student marriages. *Journal of Marital and Family Therapy, 26*, 341–351. doi:10.1111/j.1752-0606.2000.rb00303.x

Kelsey, R. M., Ornduff, S. R., McCann, C. M., & Reiff, S. (2001). Psychophysiological characteristics of narcissism during active and passive coping. *Psychophysiology, 38*, 292–303. doi:10.1111/1469-8986.3820292

Kelsey, R. M., Ornduff, S. R., Reiff, S., & Arthur, C. M. (2002). Psychophysiological correlates of narcissistic traits in women during active coping. *Psychophysiology, 39*, 322–332. doi:10.1111/1469-8986.3930322

Konrath, S., & Fuhrel-Forbis, A. (2011a). *The energy-resource model of empathic responding*. Unpublished manuscript.

Konrath, S., & Fuhrel-Forbis, A. (2011b). *Self-rated caring traits are associated with lower mortality in older adults*. Unpublished raw data.

Konrath, S., Fuhrel-Forbis, A., Lou, A., & Brown, S. L. (2012). Motives for volunteering are associated with mortality risk in older adults. *Health Psychology, 31*, 87–96. doi:10.1037/a0025226

Konrath, S. H., O'Brien, E., & Hsing, C. (2011). Changes in dispositional empathy in American college students over time: A meta-analysis. *Personality and Social Psychology Review, 15*, 180–198. doi:10.1177/1088868310377395

Krause, N., & Shaw, B. A. (2000). Giving social support to others, socioeconomic status, and changes in self-esteem in late life. *The Journals of Gerontology: Series B. Psychological Sciences and Social Sciences, 55*, S323–S333. doi:10.1093/geronb/55.6.S323

Langer, E. J., & Rodin, J. (1976). The effects of choice and enhanced personal responsibility for the aged: A field experiment in an institutional setting. *Journal of Personality and Social Psychology, 34*, 191–198. doi:10.1037/0022-3514.34.2.191

Lee, H. S., Brennan, P. F., & Daly, B. J. (2001). Relationship of empathy to appraisal, depression, life satisfaction, and physical health in informal caregivers of older adults. *Research in Nursing & Health, 24*, 44–56. doi:10.1002/1098-240X(200102)24:1<44::AID-NUR1006>3.0.CO;2-S

Liang, J., Krause, N. M., & Bennett, J. M. (2001). Social exchange and well-being: Is giving better than receiving? *Psychology and Aging, 16,* 511–523. doi:10.1037/0882-7974.16.3.511

Lindorff, M. (2000). Is it better to perceive than receive? Social support, stress and strain for managers. *Psychology, Health & Medicine, 5,* 271–286. doi:10.1080/713690199

Lorenz, M., & Cobb, S. (1952). Language behavior in manic patients. *Archives of Neurology and Psychiatry, 67,* 763–770.

Lu, L. (1997). Social support, reciprocity, and well-being. *The Journal of Social Psychology, 137,* 618–628. doi:10.1080/00224549709595483

Lu, L., & Argyle, M. (1992). Receiving and giving support: Effects on relationships and well-being. *Counselling Psychology Quarterly, 5,* 123–133. doi:10.1080/09515079208254456

Lum, T. Y., & Lightfoot, E. (2005). The effects of volunteering on the physical and mental health of older people. *Research on Aging, 27,* 31–55. doi:10.1177/0164027504271349

Luoh, M.-C., & Herzog, A. (2002). Individual consequences of volunteer and paid work in old age: health and mortality. *Journal of Health and Social Behavior, 43,* 490–509. doi:10.2307/3090239

McClellan, W. M., Stanwyck, D., & Anson, C. (1993). Social support and subsequent mortality among patients with end-stage renal disease. *Journal of the American Society of Nephrology, 4,* 1028–1034.

McClelland, D., & Krishnit, C. (1988). The effect of motivational arousal through films on salivary immunoglobulin A. *Psychology & Health, 2,* 31–52. doi:10.1080/08870448808400343

Monahan, D. J., & Hooker, K. (1995). Health of spouse caregivers of dementia patients: The role of personality and social support. *Social Work, 40,* 305–314.

Morf, C. C., & Rhodewalt, F. (2001). Unraveling the paradoxes of narcissism: A dynamic self-regulatory processing model. *Psychological Inquiry, 12,* 177–196. doi:10.1207/S15327965PLI1204_1

Morrow-Howell, N., Hinterlong, J., Rozario, P. A., & Tang, F. (2003). Effects of volunteering on the well-being of older adults. *The Journals of Gerontology: Series B. Psychological Sciences and Social Sciences, 58,* S137–S145. doi:10.1093/geronb/58.3.S137

Musick, M. A., Herzog, A. R., & House, J. S. (1999). Volunteering and mortality among older adults: Findings from a national sample. *The Journals of Gerontology: Series B. Psychological Sciences and Social Sciences, 54,* S173–S180. doi:10.1093/geronb/54B.3.S173

Musick, M. A., & Wilson, J. (2003). Volunteering and depression: The role of psychological and social resources in different age groups. *Social Science & Medicine, 56,* 259–269.

Numan, M. (2006). Hypothalamic neural circuits regulating maternal responsiveness toward infants. *Behavioral and Cognitive Neuroscience Reviews, 5*, 163–190. doi:10.1177/1534582306288790

O'Connor, L. E., Berry, J. W., Weiss, J., & Gilbert, P. (2002). Guilt, fear, submission, and empathy in depression. *Journal of Affective Disorders, 71*, 19–27. doi:10.1016/S0165-0327(01)00408-6

Oman, D., Thoresen, C. E., & Mcmahon, K. (1999). Volunteerism and mortality among the community-dwelling elderly. *Journal of Health Psychology, 4*, 301–316. doi:10.1177/135910539900400301

Piferi, R. L., & Lawler, K. A. (2006). Social support and ambulatory blood pressure: An examination of both receiving and giving. *International Journal of Psychophysiology, 62*, 328–336. doi:10.1016/j.ijpsycho.2006.06.002

Piliavin, J. A., & Siegl, E. (2007). Health benefits of volunteering in the Wisconsin Longitudinal Study. *Journal of Health and Social Behavior, 48*, 450–464. doi:10.1177/002214650704800408

Pinquart, M., & Sörensen, S. (2005). Ethnic differences in stressors, resources, and psychological outcomes of family caregiving: A meta-analysis. *The Gerontologist, 45*, 90–106. doi:10.1093/geront/45.1.90

Pinquart, M., & Sörensen, S. (2006). Gender differences in caregiver stressors, social resources, and health: An updated meta-analysis. *The Journals of Gerontology: Series B. Psychological Sciences and Social Sciences, 61*, P33–P45. doi:10.1093/geronb/61.1.P33

Pinquart, M., & Sörensen, S. (2007). Correlates of physical health of informal caregivers: A meta-analysis. *The Journals of Gerontology: Series B. Psychological Sciences and Social Sciences, 62*, P126–P137. doi:10.1093/geronb/62.2.P126

Poulin, M. J., Brown, S. L., Ubel, P. A., Smith, D. M., Jankovic, A., & Langa, K. M. (2010). Does a helping hand mean a heavy heart? Helping behavior and well-being among spouse caregivers. *Psychology and Aging, 25*, 108–117. doi:10.1037/a0018064

Reinhard, D. A., Konrath, S., Cameron, H., & Lopez, W. (2012). Expensive egos: Narcissistic males have high cortisol. *PLoS ONE, 7*(1), e30858. doi:10.1371/journal.pone.0030858

Robins, R. W., & Beer, J. S. (2001). Positive illusions about the self: Short-term benefits and long-term costs. *Journal of Personality and Social Psychology, 80*, 340–352. doi:10.1037/0022-3514.80.2.340

Rosenthal, S. A., & Hooley, J. M. (2010). Narcissism assessment in social–personality research: Does the association between narcissism and psychological health result from a confound with self-esteem? *Journal of Research in Personality, 44*, 453–465. doi:10.1016/j.jrp.2010.05.008

Rude, S., Gortner, E.-M., & Pennebaker, J. (2004). Language use of depressed and depression-vulnerable college students. *Cognition and Emotion, 18*, 1121–1133. doi:10.1080/02699930441000030

Sarid, O., Melzer, I., Kurz, I., Shahar, D. R., & Ruch, W. (2010). The effect of helping behavior and physical activity on mood states and depressive symptoms of elderly people. *Clinical Gerontologist, 33*, 270–282. doi:10.1080/07317115.2010.502105

Scherwitz, L., & Canick, J. (1988). Self-reference and coronary heart disease risk. In H. Kent & C. Snyder (Eds.), *Type A behavior pattern: Research, theory, and intervention* (pp. 146–167). Oxford, England: Wiley.

Scherwitz, L., Graham, L., & Ornish, D. (1985). Self-involvement and the risk factors for coronary heart disease. *Advances, 2*(2), 6–18.

Schwartz, C., Keyl, P., Marcum, J., & Bode, R. (2009). Helping others shows differential benefits on health and well-being for male and female teens. *Journal of Happiness Studies, 10*, 431–448. doi:10.1007/s10902-008-9098-1

Schwartz, C., Meisenhelder, J. B., Ma, Y., & Reed, G. (2003). Altruistic social interest behaviors are associated with better mental health. *Psychosomatic Medicine, 65*, 778–785. doi:10.1097/01.PSY.0000079378.39062.D4

Schwartz, C., & Sendor, R. M. (1999). Helping others helps oneself: Response shift effects in peer support. *Social Science & Medicine, 48*, 1563–1575.

Sedikides, C., Rudich, E. A., Gregg, A. P., Kumashiro, M., & Rusbult, C. (2004). Are normal narcissists psychologically healthy? Self-esteem matters. *Journal of Personality and Social Psychology, 87*, 400–416. doi:10.1037/0022-3514.87.3.400

Smith, A. M., Loving, T. J., Crockett, E. E., & Campbell, L. (2009). What's closeness got to do with it? Men's and women's cortisol responses when providing and receiving support. *Psychosomatic Medicine, 71*, 843–851. doi:10.1097/PSY.0b013e3181b492e6

Smith, C., Fernengel, K., Holcroft, C., Gerald, K., & Marien, L. (1994). Meta-analysis of the associations between social support and health outcomes. *Annals of Behavioral Medicine, 16*, 352–362.

Smith, K. D. (1992). Trait sympathy and perceived control as predictors of entering sympathy-arousing situations. *Personality and Social Psychology Bulletin, 18*, 207–216. doi:10.1177/0146167292182012

Sommer, K. L., Kirkland, K. L., Newman, S. R., Estrella, P., & Andreassi, J. L. (2009). Narcissism and cardiovascular reactivity to rejection imagery. *Journal of Applied Social Psychology, 39*, 1083–1115. doi:10.1111/j.1559-1816.2009.00473.x

Steffen, P. R., & Masters, K. (2005). Does compassion mediate the intrinsic religion-health relationship? *Annals of Behavioral Medicine, 30*, 217–224. doi:10.1207/s15324796abm3003_6

Stirman, S. W., & Pennebaker, J. W. (2001). Word use in the poetry of suicidal and nonsuicidal poets. *Psychosomatic Medicine, 63*, 517–522.

Strazdins, L., & Broom, D. H. (2007). The mental health costs and benefits of giving social support. *International Journal of Stress Management, 14*, 370–385. doi:10.1037/1072-5245.14.4.370

Tennen, H., & Herzberger, S. (1987). Depression, self-esteem, and the absence of self-protective attributional biases. *Journal of Personality and Social Psychology, 52,* 72–80. doi:10.1037/0022-3514.52.1.72

Thoits, P. A., & Hewitt, L. (2001). Volunteer work and well-being. *Journal of Health and Social Behavior, 42,* 115–131. doi:10.2307/3090173

Thorsteinsson, E., & James, J. (1999). A meta-analysis of the effects of experimental manipulations of social support during laboratory stress. *Psychology & Health, 14,* 869–886. doi:10.1080/08870449908407353

Twenge, J. M. (1997). Changes in masculine and feminine traits over time: A meta-analysis. *Sex Roles, 36,* 305–325. doi:10.1007/BF02766650

Twenge, J. M., & Campbell, W. K. (2001). Age and birth cohort differences in self-esteem: A cross-temporal meta-analysis. *Personality and Social Psychology Review, 5,* 321–344. doi:10.1207/S15327957PSPR0504_3

Twenge, J. M., & Campbell, W. K. (2008). Increases in positive self-views among high school students. *Psychological Science, 19,* 1082–1086. doi:10.1111/j.1467-9280.2008.02204.x

Twenge, J. M., Campbell, W. K., & Gentile, B. (in press). Generational increases in agentic self-evaluations among American college students, 1966–2009. *Self and Identity.* doi:10.1080/15298868.2011.576820

Twenge, J. M., Konrath, S., Foster, J., Campbell, W. K., & Bushman, B. (2008). Egos inflating over time: A cross-temporal meta-analysis of the Narcissistic Personality Inventory. *Journal of Personality, 76,* 875–901.

Uchino, B. N. (2006). Social support and health: A review of physiological processes potentially underlying links to disease outcomes. *Journal of Behavioral Medicine, 29,* 377–387. doi:10.1007/s10865-006-9056-5

Uchino, B. N., Cacioppo, J., & Kiecolt-Glaser, J. (1996). The relationship between social support and physiological processes: A review with emphasis on underlying mechanisms and implications for health. *Psychological Bulletin, 119,* 488–531. doi:10.1037/0033-2909.119.3.488

Van Willigen, M. (2000). Differential benefits of volunteering across the life course. *The Journals of Gerontology: Series B. Psychological Sciences and Social Sciences, 55,* S308–S318. doi:10.1093/geronb/55.5.S308

Vitaliano, P. P., Zhang, J., & Scanlan, J. M. (2003). Is caregiving hazardous to one's physical health? A meta-analysis. *Psychological Bulletin, 129,* 946–972. doi:10.1037/0033-2909.129.6.946

Warren, M. (1993). *The effectiveness of volunteer service: An occupational therapy intervention for post-traumatic stress disorder* (Unpublished master's thesis). San Jose State University, San Jose, CA.

Watson, P. J., & Biderman, M. (1993). Narcissistic Personality Inventory factors, splitting, and self-consciousness. *Journal of Personality Assessment, 61,* 41–57. doi:10.1207/s15327752jpa6101_4

Weintraub, W. (1981). *Verbal behavior: Adaptation and psychopathology.* New York, NY: Springer.

Windsor, T. D., Anstey, K. J., & Rodgers, B. (2008). Volunteering and psychological well-being among young–old adults: How much is too much? *The Gerontologist, 48,* 59–70. doi:10.1093/geront/48.1.59

Wink, P., & Dillon, M. (2002). Spiritual development across the adult life course: Findings from a longitudinal study. *Journal of Adult Development, 9,* 79–94. doi:10.1023/A:1013833419122

Yinon, Y., & Landau, M. O. (1987). On the reinforcing value of helping behavior in a positive mood. *Motivation and Emotion, 11,* 83–93. doi:10.1007/BF00992215

II

ROMANTIC RELATIONSHIPS

3

MARRIAGE, AFFECTIONATE TOUCH, AND HEALTH

MARY H. BURLESON, NICOLE A. ROBERTS, TARA M. VINCELETTE, AND XIN GUAN

Social relationships, especially satisfying marriages, are good for health. According to a review of 148 studies, strong social relationships reduce mortality by an average of 50% (Holt-Lunstad, Smith, & Layton, 2010). Beneficial effects of marriage on health have been documented across multiple societies (Manzoli & Villari, 2007) and even among individuals living over 100 years ago (Murray, 2000). For example, at one time, unmarried American men were 250% more likely to die than married men (Litwak et al., 1989). Social influences on health are just as powerful as diet, smoking, and exercise. Nevertheless, the behavioral and physiological pathways through which these social benefits occur are not fully understood.

Marriage appears to be an especially potent influence on health outcomes. Married people not only live longer, but evidence also suggests that they are generally healthier than those who are unmarried (Burman & Margolin,

This work is supported in part by a grant from the National Heart, Lung, and Blood Institute (B21 IIL088612-01A2; principal investigator Mary H. Burleson).

DOI: 10.1037/14036-004
Health and Social Relationships: The Good, the Bad, and the Complicated, Matthew L. Newman and Nicole A. Roberts (Editors)

1992; Kiecolt-Glaser & Newton, 2001). This is the case regardless of whether the comparison groups are never-married, separated, widowed, divorced, or (in some studies) living with a romantic partner (Carr & Springer, 2010). For this reason, many have speculated that marriage (or marital-type relationships) may cause health to improve or at the very least slow its decline. Of course, linkages between marriage and health are complicated in that relationships may both influence and be influenced by health. Further, by necessity, much research on the potential effects of relationships is correlational, preventing strong causal attributions. Nevertheless, the association between marital-type relationships and beneficial health outcomes is robust.

However, much less is known about the pathways through which these potential health effects might take place. Marriage and marital-type relationships can be seen as a special form of social connection, in which many of the different aspects of connection are found within a single relationship. One major difference between marital-type and other relationships is the opportunity that they provide for extensive close positive physical contact, including both physical affection and sexual relations, both of which have been linked to beneficial physiological changes. In this chapter, we present a brief review of studies on marriage, health, and associated physiological processes that were published after 1999, which was the publication cutoff for an earlier review by Kiecolt-Glaser and Newton (2001) on this topic. These studies link marital status (e.g., married, divorced, widowed) or characteristics of marital-type relationships (e.g., marital satisfaction) with effects on indicators of physiological functioning or with more downstream health outcomes such as disease severity. We then focus on research supporting the possibility that physical intimacy and affection may serve as important contributory mechanisms for the beneficial effects of spousal-type relationships on health.

RECENT EVIDENCE: BOTH MARITAL STATUS AND MARITAL QUALITY PREDICT HEALTH

Earlier reviews by Burman and Margolin (1992) and Kiecolt-Glaser and Newton (2001) reached the conclusion that a diverse range of health outcomes, from self-reported global health to mortality, are related to marital status and quality. By and large, studies of marital influences on health published after 1999 have confirmed this conclusion. Here we provide a brief review of these recent findings. Kiecolt-Glaser and Newton also found evidence for different pathways for these effects in husbands versus wives: Marital status had a stronger effect on men's health and mortality than on women's, whereas marital quality was more consequential for women's health and mortality. Recent results largely support this conclusion. As noted by Robles and Kiecolt-Glaser

(2003), activity in the cardiovascular, neuroendocrine, and immune systems likely mediates a significant share of the relationship between social influences and health outcomes. Therefore, with the presumption that they are predictive of longer term health conditions (Uchino, 2006), researchers continue to measure biomarkers of these systems along with actual health outcomes.

Marital Status Continues to Predict Health Outcomes and Related Biomarkers

One question is whether simply being married is sufficient to promote health or whether health outcomes are moderated by qualities of the marital relationship. We reviewed six reports that compared the effects of marital status and relationship quality in the same sample. By and large, these studies suggest that at least for cardiovascular health (and perhaps for levels of norepinephrine, a stress hormone), a poor marital-type relationship is associated with worse health outcomes than being single, and this may be especially true for women.

Four studies used multiyear follow-ups to study cardiovascular health and mortality. Eaker, Sullivan, Kelly-Hayes, D'Agostino, and Benjamin (2007) found that marital status predicted mortality for men but not women, whereas qualities of the marital relationship predicted mortality for women. In three studies, Gallo and colleagues also found relationship quality to be more predictive of health outcome for women than marital status. They compared cardiovascular risk factors (Gallo, Troxel, Matthews, & Kuller, 2003), carotid atherosclerosis (Gallo, Troxel, Kuller, et al., 2003), and metabolic syndrome (Troxel, Matthews, Gallo, & Kuller, 2005) among mid-aged women who were married or cohabiting and women who were single, divorced, or widowed. *Atherosclerosis* is the thickening and stiffening of the arterial walls due to accumulation of fat deposits and is a leading cause of heart attack and stroke. *Metabolic syndrome* is a clustering of cardiovascular risk factors, including central fat deposition, elevated blood lipids, high blood pressure, and/or blood glucose dysregulation, and is associated with cardiovascular disease and Type 2 diabetes. Women in satisfying relationships had fewer risk factors, less metabolic syndrome, less carotid atherosclerosis at baseline, and slower progression of atherosclerosis after over a decade of follow-up than women who were single, divorced, or widowed, whereas women in unhealthy relationships had the least favorable outcomes.

Two of these studies used ambulatory methods to measure blood pressure (BP) over 24-hour periods. Chronic high BP (hypertension) can damage the cardiovascular system, kidneys, and brain and is a risk factor for multiple diseases (Pencina, D'Agostino, Larson, Massaro, & Vasan, 2009), and there is evidence to suggest that high acute BP reactivity to stressors predicts later hypertension (Matthews, Woodall, & Allen, 1993). Greater drops in nighttime BP ("dipping") predict lower cardiovascular morbidity and mortality (Muxfeldt, Cardoso, & Salles, 2009). Grewen, Girdler, and Light (2005) found that urinary norepinephrine was higher in single adults, suggesting greater activation of the sympathetic nervous system, which carries health risks. Partnered adults reporting the highest relationship quality had the lowest ambulatory BP (ABP) during waking hours, and this effect was strongest in men. Holt-Lunstad, Birmingham, and Jones (2008) measured 24-hour ABP in married and unmarried individuals. Results showed that the nighttime drop in BP (dipping) was greater among the married than the unmarried, regardless of marital quality. However, both 24-hour and waking ABP were higher for those in low-quality marriages than in the unmarried. Interestingly, in this study, findings were consistent for both men and women.

Several additional studies reported linkages between marital status and diverse health indicators or outcomes without examining marital quality. Similar to findings from the Kiecolt-Glaser and Newton (2001) review, Dupre, Beck, and Meadows (2009) found mortality risk was higher for divorced and widowed adults versus currently married or never-married adults; however, women who were divorced for more than 10 years or widowed for more than 5 years had lower mortality, suggesting they may have eventually recovered from the stressful transition out of marriage. Perhaps divorced or widowed women were able to develop and/or take greater advantage of extended social networks that ultimately are more health-promoting than some marital relationships (Klinenberg, 2012). Nevertheless, simply being married (or cohabiting, in some studies) has predicted several important biomarkers of ongoing health-related processes, including slowed cellular aging (as indicated by leukocyte telomere length; Mainous et al., 2011), higher ambulatory 24-hour heart rate variability (HRV, an indicator of parasympathetic nervous system activation, which is associated with relaxation and self-regulation; Randall, Bhattacharyya, & Steptoe, 2009), and less systemic inflammation (as indicated by circulating C-reactive protein; Sbarra, 2009).

Marital Quality Continues to Predict Better Physiological Indicators and Health Outcomes

Looking further beyond marital status, variations in marital quality[1] have also been consistently associated with physiological markers, including cardiovascular and metabolic function, hypothalamic–pituitary–adrenal (HPA)

---

[1]For this chapter, when summarizing results, we follow Slatcher (2010) and use the terms *marital strength* and *marital strain* to refer respectively to positive and negative aspects of marital functioning.

axis activity, inflammation processes, and activity levels, along with health outcomes such as atherosclerosis and wound healing. We briefly review evidence for each of these next.

Indicators of Cardiovascular Function, Metabolic Syndrome, and Related Health Outcomes

Studying marital interaction offers an important window into couple functioning (Roberts, Tsai, & Coan, 2007). Physiological responses during discussions about areas of relationship conflict, and even in response to routine marital interactions such as conversations about one's day, can predict relationship functioning and outcomes, and possibly longer term outcomes (Driver & Gottman, 2004). Studies assessing BP and other cardiovascular responses to spousal interactions in the laboratory generally have found that conflict interactions are associated with greater cardiovascular activation than supportive or neutral interactions (e.g., Smith et al., 2009). Yuan, McCarthy, Holley, and Levenson (2010) also reported that in the course of a conflict interaction, positive emotion behaviors were found during periods of sympathetic nervous system down-regulation.

Some of these studies offered potential explanations for the frequently reported sex differences in marital effects on health. For example, if women are more affected by marital strain because they place a higher priority on intimate relationships, as proposed by Gottman and Carrère (1994), there could be systematic differences in speaking time or level of engagement during marital interactions, which could explain sex differences in reactivity. Nealey-Moore, Smith, Uchino, Hawkins, and Olson-Cerny (2007) found support for this hypothesis using a highly structured task to equate task engagement and speaking time. Spouses in the negative interaction condition had higher cardiovascular reactivity, but there were no sex differences. Testing another potential explanation, Newton and Sanford (2003) suggested that because wives typically desire more change in marriage than do husbands (Margolin, Talovic, & Weinstein, 1983), findings of greater reactivity in wives may result from inadvertent selection of conflict topics in which the wife desires the change. Spouses were asked to discuss two conflict topics: one in which the husband desired a change and the other in which the wife desired a change. Exchanges that were more negative were associated with higher systolic blood pressure (SBP) and diastolic blood pressure (DBP) reactivity, and as proposed, DBP reactivity was highest for the spouse requesting the change. Finally, Smith and colleagues (2011) speculated that women's health may be differentially affected in marital-type relationships due to their greater efforts at relationship maintenance. They used a series of tasks of varying hedonic tone to test the effects of self-regulation on high frequency HRV, an indicator of parasympathetic cardiac activation. As expected, women's HRV suggested that they were depleted by efforts to regulate, whereas men's HRV was not affected.

Four studies of marital quality published in the past decade have used ambulatory methods to monitor BP for at least 24 hours. Marital strength predicted greater drops in nocturnal BP for healthy husbands and wives (Holt-Lunstad, Jones, & Birmingham, 2009) and lower 24-hour DBP and left ventricular mass in mildly hypertensive men and women after a 3-year follow-up (Baker, Szalai, Paquette, & Tobe, 2003). It is notable that these effects were enhanced by greater spousal contact during the measurement period (Baker et al., 2000). However, marital strain predicted elevated mean DBP during workday hours for both men and women (Barnett, Steptoe, & Gareis, 2005) and attenuated drops in nocturnal DBP for wives (Holt-Lunstad et al., 2009). In other studies of cardiovascular health, marital strength predicted lower resting BP and better blood glucose regulation among husbands and wives (Trief et al., 2006) and among wives only (Whisman, Uebelacker, & Settles, 2010), less severe congestive heart failure for women (Coyne et al., 2001) and for both men and women (Rohrbaugh, Mehl, Shoham, Reilly, & Ewy, 2008), shorter hospital stays for women but not men after cardiac bypass surgery (Kulik & Mahler, 2006), lower all-cause mortality among patients with congestive heart failure after both 4-year (Coyne et al., 2001) and 8-year (Rohrbaugh, Shoham, & Coyne, 2006) follow-up, and higher risk of recurrent cardiac events in a female sample (Orth-Gomér et al., 2000).

Finally, in the only study reviewed that linked marital strength with a negative health outcome, Janicki, Kamarck, Shiffman, Sutton-Tyrrell, and Gwaltney (2005) found that amount of spousal interaction predicted smaller increases in carotid wall thickness (an indicator of atherosclerosis) in men with high marital adjustment but larger increases in women with high marital adjustment. This effect disappeared when women's total social interaction scores (also positively associated with increased carotid wall thickness) were included in the model, but the overall quality (conflictual vs. agreeable) of those interactions did not account for the effect. The authors suggested that *unmitigated communion* (i.e., a focus on others to the exclusion of the self; Fritz & Helgeson, 1998) might be an explanation.

Indicators of Activity in the Hypothalamic–Pituitary–Adrenal Axis

In addition to cardiovascular reactivity, which has a quick onset and offset but may contribute to longer term cardiovascular problems, HPA functioning is linked to multiple mental as well as physical illnesses (e.g., depression, diabetes). Most studies of the HPA axis measured cortisol either on awakening, at multiple times during the day, and before bed (for diary and ambulatory studies), or before and after laboratory interactions (one study measured adrenocorticotropic hormone, a pituitary hormone that triggers cortisol release from the adrenal cortex). Cortisol regulates glucose metabolism and has widespread additional effects, including potential inhibition of the immune and reproductive systems (Tsigos & Chrousos, 2002). In the absence of a stress response, circulating cortisol typically manifests a predictable daily rhythm that involves a rise before awakening, another usually sharper increase during the first 30 to 45 minutes after awakening (the cortisol awakening response, which is independent of the diurnal cycle), and a decline throughout the rest of the day to basal levels during the first half of the night. Acute stressors of sufficient strength adaptively activate the HPA axis and result in transient increases in circulating cortisol, whereas chronic stress can result in continuous higher levels and eventual resistance to cortisol effects (Miller, Cohen, & Ritchey, 2002).

Ambulatory studies have consistently found marital strain to be associated with lower morning levels and flatter cortisol slopes during the day (Adam & Gunnar, 2001, in a sample of mothers; Saxbe, Repetti, & Nishina, 2008, in only female participants; Barnett et al., 2005, in both men and women). Marital strength weakened the relation between work stress and cortisol level for wives but not husbands in two studies (Saxbe et al., 2008; Slatcher, Robles, Repetti, & Fellows, 2010), suggesting that for women, marital strength can serve as a buffer against external stressors. Both positive and negative communication behavior independently predicted slower recovery in wives' cortisol after a conflict interaction, and wife positive behavior also predicted faster recovery of her adrenocorticotropic hormone (Robles, Shaffer, Malarkey, & Kiecolt-Glaser, 2006). Evidence for an influence from one partner on the other partner's HPA activity was also found (Saxbe & Repetti, 2010; Slatcher et al., 2010). Finally, studies using marital interactions found moderating effects of demand–withdraw behavior (Heffner et al., 2006), relative marital power (Loving, Heffner, Kiecolt-Glaser, Glaser, & Malarkey, 2004), and satisfaction with spousal support (Heffner et al., 2004) on HPA responses to conflict. Again, these results offer specific physiological mechanisms through which relationship dynamics may be associated with each partner's health.

Wound Healing and Indicators of Inflammation

Four studies measured wound healing and/or inflammatory biomarkers in relation to marital quality. In short-term responses to stress, cortisol suppresses both antigen-specific and innate immune responses (of which inflammation is a major part), which can lead to higher susceptibility to infectious disease and slower healing of wounds. In addition, chronic stress produces long-term higher cortisol levels that enhance central fat deposition (Tsigos & Chrousos, 2002). This often fosters elevated systemic inflammation because adipose tissue is a source of proinflammatory cytokines such as interleukin-6 (IL-6; Coppack, 2001), which in turn further stimulate the HPA axis (Tsigos & Chrousos, 2002). Systemic inflammation is associated with a number of disease processes, ranging from atherosclerosis and coronary heart disease to rheumatoid arthritis, cancer, and Alzheimer's disease (e.g., Ershler & Keller, 2000; Kaplan & Frishman, 2001).

Three studies by Kiecolt-Glaser and colleagues (2005) reported various aspects of the effects of marital interactions, particularly conflict interactions, on wound healing and cytokine production. Standardized suction-blister wounds healed more slowly after conflict interactions than after support interactions, and more hostility during the conflicts was associated with slower healing as well as higher circulating IL-6 and tumor necrosis factor-alpha (TNF-a; IL-6 and TNF-a are proinflammatory cytokines produced by the immune system) on the morning after the interaction. Cognitive word use during conflict interactions was also associated with lower circulating IL-6 and TNF-a (Graham et al., 2009). More positive communication behaviors during the supportive interaction were associated with higher circulating oxytocin, which in turn was associated with faster wound healing (Gouin et al., 2010). Finally, marital stress predicted circulating C-reactive protein in women with large waist circumferences (Shen, Farrell, Penedo, Schneiderman, & Orth-Gomér, 2010). Therefore, a strong marriage arguably can help build immune functioning, whereas a stressful one can compromise it.

Self-Reported Health and Functional Impairment

Studies of marital interaction and health have expanded over the years to incorporate a broader demographic of couples, including older couples. Longitudinal and cross-sectional studies have revealed implications of marriage for health over time with respect to reports of physical and mental health symptoms. Two long-term multiwave surveys found that reports of marital strain were associated with accelerated age-related decline in self-reported health after 8-year follow-up for both men and women, especially in older participants (Umberson, Williams, Powers, Liu, & Needham, 2006), and increased depression and functional impairment after 6 years for both men and women (Choi & Marks, 2008). In cross-sectional surveys, marital strain predicted a greater number of physical symptoms and chronic health problems, greater physical disability (Bookwala, 2005), and poorer global perceived health (Bookwala, 2005; Whisman & Uebelacker, 2006). However, Carrère, Mittmann, Woodin, Tabares, and Yoshimoto (2005) found no relationship between marital quality and self-reported health. Finally, Tower,

Kasl, and Darefsky (2002) found a complex relationship between marital closeness and mortality in couples over 65, consistent with marital roles prescribing a strong husband with a dependent wife. In other words, strong traditional gender roles in these older couples were associated with decreased mortality for both husbands and wives.

In sum, good physical health or disease processes may comprise many separate, fundamental physiological processes. By shaping these processes, marital relationships can influence each partner's individual health and, through couple dynamics, the health of the other (see Chapter 5, this volume).

HOW DO RESEARCHERS EXPLAIN HEALTH EFFECTS OF MARRIAGE?

In recent years, researchers have moved beyond the mere documentation of health benefits to more targeted explorations of potential mechanisms for these effects, often set within a particular theoretical framework. Many investigators believe that the provision and receipt of social support, broadly defined, is the most important way in which spousal or spousal-type relationships enhance health. As discussed elsewhere in the present volume (see Chapters 1 and 2), social support is thought to be beneficial in two major ways: through main effects and through stress buffering (Cohen & Wills, 1985). A *stress-buffering model* proposes that social support can reduce the effects of stress but has little to no effect when stress is absent. Much evidence suggests that social support dampens stress responses, thereby reducing any health-damaging effects they might have (Cohen & Wills, 1985; Uchino, Cacioppo, & Kiecolt-Glaser, 1996). However, a *main-effect model* of support suggests that social support enhances health regardless of stress level. Bolstering this perspective are studies showing that supportive relationships are associated with more positive events and positive emotional states (Cohen & Wills, 1985; Salovey, Rothman, Detweiler, & Steward, 2000), both of which can be linked with improved physiological functioning and health outcomes (Dockray & Steptoe, 2010; Pressman & Cohen, 2005; Zautra, Affleck, Tennen, Reich, & Davis, 2005).

Another important perspective addressing the physiological effects of marriage is that of *adult attachment theory* (Hazan & Shaver, 1987). This framework proposes that adult romantic relationships often lead to (or are concurrent with) the development of attachment bonds between partners. These bonds are similar in many ways to those between infants and their caregivers, except that in adult relationships, attachment and caregiving behaviors are reciprocal, and sexuality plays an important role. More recent work has suggested that attached adult partners provide both physiological and psychological coregulation for each other (Coan, 2008; Diamond, 2001; Selcuk, Zayas, & Hazan, 2010) and that the potency of coregulation reflects the strength of the attachment.

Coregulation, which is seen as distinct from stress reduction, involves an "interwoven physiology" in which each partner serves as a primary regulator of the other's ongoing physiological state (Sbarra & Hazan, 2008). This kind of mutual regulation has been likened to the influence of *zeitgebers* (Bernieri & Rosenthal, 1991; Ehlers, Frank, & Kupfer, 1988; Hofer, 1994), which are environmental stimuli (e.g., the light–dark cycle) that can reset (entrain) intrinsic biological rhythms (e.g., the sleep–wake cycle). If coregulation maintains the partners' psychological and physiological states within an optimal range for the context (Butler & Randall, in press), which remains to be confirmed, it would presumably enhance health outcomes.

Coregulation is thought to develop through classical and operant conditioning processes (Dupre et al., 2009; Zeifman & Hazan, 1997). For example, sexual and other intimate behaviors with the partner activate oxytocin- and opioid-based reward systems in the brain, which provide a physiological basis for felt security. Repeated activations of these systems reinforce preference for the partner (Young & Wang, 2004) and make him or her a conditioned stimulus for pleasure, reduced distress, and physiological homeostasis (Sbarra & Hazan, 2008). Once established, coregulation is maintained primarily through proximity and physical contact.

A related perspective is *social baseline theory* (Coan, 2008). This model suggests that for social species, proximity and interaction conserve energy through the distribution of both risk and workload. Being social, humans have evolved such that the mere presence of other (nonthreatening) individuals reduces both the actual and perceived cost of engagement with the environment. Social proximity is thereby innately regulatory, and this effect is enhanced in the presence of an attachment figure where there is a history of mutual beneficial interaction. Thus, attachment- and coregulation-based theories may help to explain some of the negative health effects of relationship loss that are not fully accounted for by stress- and support-based models (Sbarra & Hazan, 2008).

In attachment terms, provision of social support is a product of the caregiving behavior system, a response to support-seeking behaviors that arise from the attachment behavior system. Social support that buffers stress is equivalent to providing a safe haven; social support that has beneficial main effects parallels the provision of a secure base (Collins & Feeney, 2010; Mikulincer & Shaver, 2009). Further, while considering these different theoretical perspectives, it is important to note that positive affect induction, stress buffering, activation of neural reward systems, and coregulation are not mutually exclusive. These processes may work together in multiple ways to culminate in the health improvements associated with good romantic relationships.

Accordingly, in addition to marital studies, other areas of research also can inform the issue of positive influences in marital-type relationships. For example, behaviors such as physical or verbal affection, which are common in satisfying relationships, have been measured or manipulated both inside and outside the context of marital-type relationships, and associations with biomarkers have been reported. In the next section, we focus on affectionate touch, a potential mediator for the health-related effects of social support, attachment, and other processes reviewed previously.

AFFECTION, TOUCH, AND HEALTH
IN MARITAL-TYPE RELATIONSHIPS

Social touch is a critically important aspect of social relations in most primates. Multiple studies of a number of primate species over the past decade have shown beneficial physiological and behavioral effects of social touch, including both enhancement of social cohesion and reduction of stress, particularly after conflict (Dunbar, 2010). Social touch is also crucial for normal human development and attachment during infancy, and there is a large body of literature on the beneficial effects of touch with respect to infant–parent (typically mother–infant) attachment and soothing (Field, 2010). Although less studied, touch may be similarly important in the formation and maintenance of adult relationships (King & Christensen, 1983). Research has supported the notion that relationship satisfaction is positively related to level of physical affection in romantic relationships (Gulledge, Gulledge, & Stahmannn, 2003) and in marriage (Bell, Daly, & Gonzalez, 1987; Svetlik, Dooley, Weiner, Williamson, & Walters, 2005). In a study of marital-type relationships that had lasted at least 30 years, expression of physical affection was cited as an important factor in shaping the quality of the relationship (Mackey, Diemer, & O'Brien, 2000). Displays of nonphysical affectionate behaviors, such as warmth, humor, and loving expressions certainly are important in marital success (e.g., Waldinger, Schulz, Hauser, Allen, & Crowell, 2004). We suggest that physical affection plays a unique role.

Affection exchange theory (Floyd, 2006) suggests that the giving and receiving of affection (both verbal and physical) are expressions of a fundamental human need and that fulfillment of this need contributes to reproductive success primarily by enhancing pair-bonding (both romantic and platonic) but also by contributing physiological benefits. A number of studies by Floyd and colleagues support the contribution of affection to more beneficial physiological functioning. Some of these studies did not distinguish between verbal and physical affection (Floyd, Hesse, & Haynes, 2007; Floyd, Pauley, & Hesse, 2010; Floyd & Riforgiate, 2008) or assigned participants to write about their affectionate ties and did not measure physical affection (Floyd, Mikkelson, Hesse, & Pauley, 2007; Floyd, Mikkelson, Tafoya, et al., 2007a). We focus here primarily on physical affection and its direct or indirect physiological effects.

Gulledge and colleagues (2003) defined *physical affection* as "any touch intended to arouse feelings of love in the giver and/or the recipient" (p. 234). We build on this definition by adding that, ideally, the touch is appropriate to the setting, does not interfere with goal-directed behavior, and is not oriented toward immediate sexual gratification. Marital-type relationships provide plentiful opportunities for physical affection. It appears that physical affection would be an ideal mediator of marital-type positive influences on health, because it likely contributes in unique and powerful ways to positive affect and reward, coregulation, and stress buffering. Thus, marital-type relationships may enhance health at least partially through affectionate touch.

Physical Affection and Positive Emotions

Hertenstein and colleagues showed that love can be conveyed through touch alone (Hertenstein, Keltner, App, Bulleit, & Jaskolka, 2006) and that in fact touch is the preferred modality to communicate love (App, McIntosh, Reed, & Hertenstein, 2011). Because giving physical affection is an expression of positive emotion (liking and/or love), it is inherently hedonically positive. Said in a different way, *affiliative reward* is a hard-wired phenomenon that is activated by a number of unconditioned stimuli, including physical affection (Depue & Morrone-Strupinsky, 2005). Furthermore, Lamm and Wiesmann (1997) found that experiencing positive mood when thinking about or being with the target person was the most frequently cited indicator of both liking and loving someone and the second most frequently cited indicator of being "in love" with that person, making expression of liking and loving a probable stimulus for other positive emotions. Trait assessments that reveal an individual's tendency to both receive (Floyd, 2002) and give (Floyd et al., 2005) verbal and physical affection are likewise associated with reduced depression and loneliness and a number of other positive outcomes. A diary study of mid-aged women found that the occurrence of physical affection on one day predicted less negative mood on the following day and that both higher positive and lower negative mood on a given day predicted more physical affection on the following day (Burleson, Trevathan, & Todd, 2007). Thus, although this hypothesis has not been tested explicitly, the immediate effects of receiving physical affection likely include the induction of other positive emotions, and positive emotion in the context of a relationship may promote physical affection. If so, physical affection may have synergistic health effects, both because the direct benefits of touch (reviewed later) are combined with the benefits of positive mood engendered by touch and because positive mood in turn increases the occurrence of affection.

Physical Affection and Coregulation Processes

As noted earlier, physical affection, like sexual activity and many other forms of social touch (e.g., massage), is inherently rewarding. The model proposed by Depue and Morrone-Strupinsky (2005) illustrates how conditioning may further enhance the innate regulatory effects of physical affection. At the beginning of a romantic relationship, dopamine-mediated approach motivation ("wanting"; Berridge, 1999) is high (which also is inherently rewarding), and partners typically engage in high levels of physical contact and sexual activity with each other. These behaviors are consummatory and lead to relaxation (which is often mediated by parasympathetic activity) in addition to pleasure or "liking" (Berridge, 1999; mediated by opioid mechanisms). Through classical conditioning, pleasure and relaxation become associated with the stimulus contexts in which they occur. These contexts include both the presence and salient features of the partner, and the tactile sensations themselves. Therefore, in the presence of one's partner, and especially when physical contact occurs, parasympathetic activation and relaxation are elicited.

Individuals in new romantic relationships often experience a state of limerence in which they crave physical closeness with their partner. This arguably has positive effects from an evolutionary perspective in terms of mate selection and reproduction but may offer health benefits as well. Oxytocin, a hypothalamic neuropeptide with receptors across brain regions that are involved in the control of stress, anxiety, and social behavior, is likely to play a role in these processes, as central oxytocin release appears to facilitate approach behaviors (Carter, 1998) and modulate sensory processing and the formation of affiliative memories (Winslow & Insel, 2002). These effects are most notable in romantic and caregiving relationships but likely also apply to friendships and other close relationships.

Physical Affection and Physiological Functioning

If social baseline theory is correct, physical affection should reduce stress responses. One way this could occur is by serving as "proof" of the immediate physical proximity of a trusted social partner, which presumably reduces the perceived demands of the situation. Oxytocin may contribute to these effects as well, because in addition to its roles in approach and other social behaviors, it can decrease anxiety and reduce neuroendocrine responses in social stress (Heinrichs, Baumgartner, Kirschbaum, & Ehlert, 2003). For example, Ditzen and colleagues (2009) gave married or cohabiting couples nasally administered oxytocin or a placebo before they engaged in a conflict interaction. Those receiving oxytocin not only behaved more positively but also had lower cortisol responses to the conflict. Similarly, higher circulating oxytocin predicted both more positive communication behaviors during a conflict interaction and faster wound healing after (Gouin et al., 2010).

Oxytocin may also influence physiological responses outside of the acute stressor context; studies have found women's oxytocin levels were inversely related to BP, heart rate (HR), and/or norepinephrine at baseline (Light, Grewen, & Amico, 2005) and after a touch intervention in the lab (Grewen, Girdler, Amico, & Light, 2005). Multiple forms of affiliation-related tactile stimuli, such as genital and breast stimulation, copulation, physical affection, massage, and even warmth, can stimulate central oxytocin release in both animals and humans (Depue & Morrone-Strupinsky, 2005). Accordingly, during a 4-week experiment with a manipulation that increased positive physical contact in daily life, salivary oxytocin levels were higher in the treatment group both early and late in the intervention (Holt-Lunstad, Birmingham, & Light, 2008). Further, in a laboratory study, baseline oxytocin level partially mediated the inverse relationship between frequency of spousal hugging and baseline BP (Light et al., 2005). However, in an experiment in which women in one treatment group received neck and shoulder massages from their husbands, oxytocin levels did not differ between the groups (Ditzen et al., 2007).

Multiple studies have found direct health-positive relationships between an array of cardiovascular, neuroendocrine, and immune biomarkers and various forms of positive physical contact with a relationship partner, including holding hands (Coan, Schaefer, & Davidson, 2006; Master et al., 2009), neck and shoulder massage (Ditzen et al., 2007; Holt-Lunstad, Birmingham, & Light, 2008), kissing (Floyd et al., 2009; Kimata, 2003, 2006; Matsunaga et al., 2009), physical intimacy (holding hands, touching, hugging, kissing, or sexual interaction; Ditzen, Hoppmann, & Klumb, 2008), and nonverbal affection (Floyd, Mikkelson, Tafoya, et al., 2007b).

Relationship quality moderated effects of physical touch on physiological responding in the study by Coan and colleagues (2006), who monitored brain activation in married women anticipating and receiving mild electrical shocks. When participants held the experimenter's or their husband's hand during this task, activity in threat-responsive brain areas was diminished compared with the no-hand condition. Furthermore, rating of marital quality by the wives was inversely related to brain activation but only when women held their husband's hands.

Other studies have investigated associations between physiological indicators and combinations of physical affection and social interaction. Grewen, Anderson, Girdler, and Light (2003) manipulated *warm partner contact*, described as positive, relationship-focused interaction (including talking about a topic that enhanced feeling of closeness as a couple and watching a 5-minute romantic video) while maintaining physical contact (e.g., holding hands) for 10 minutes, followed by a full ventral hug lasting for 20 seconds. In a comparison of groups with and without warm contact (Grewen et al., 2003), the group with warm contact had lower SBP, DBP, and HR responses to laboratory stress tasks. Effects were similar in men and women but stronger in African American than European American couples. These results support the notion that physical affection promotes healthier cardiovascular and endocrine responses to stress; however, because the manipulation included social interaction in addition to physical affection, the effects cannot be definitively ascribed to physical affection. Ditzen et al. (2007) addressed this issue by separately manipulating verbal social support and positive physical contact. Female participants were randomly assigned to receive neck and shoulder massage or verbal support from their spouses or cohabiting partners, or to wait alone, before performing laboratory stress tasks. Women who received neck and shoulder massage displayed lower cortisol and HR responses to the stress tasks. Verbal social support alone was not associated with reduced stress responsiveness.

Sexual Aspects of Touch, Physiology, and Health

In addition to potential psychological and physiological benefits of nonphysical and physical affection, marital-type relationships provide an opportunity for sexual relationships. Sexual relations may themselves yield physiological effects that in turn result in health benefits and also may improve (or worsen) other aspects of marital intimacy and marital quality. Sexual satisfaction is a key predictor of long-term relationship satisfaction across cultures (Heiman et al., 2011), and we suspect it may enhance health by improving marital quality. Sexual relations may also improve mood; a cross-sectional study of over 15,000 randomly selected adults showed that amount of sexual activity was strongly positively related to overall happiness (Blanchflower & Oswald, 2004). Using daily diary methods in a sample of mid-aged women, Burleson and colleagues (2007) showed that partnered sexual activity was associated with improved mood on the following day, which in turn predicted partnered sexual activity on the day after, raising the possibility of a beneficial positive feedback loop.

In addition, as noted previously, the pleasure and relaxation that accompany sexual behavior can be associated with the presence of one's partner and enhance the potential for beneficial coregulation. Further, sexual arousal and orgasm have other immediate physiological effects that may influence health, especially when they occur repeatedly over time with the same partner. These effects include changes in circulating hormones, such as cortisol (Hamilton, Rellini, & Meston, 2008), oxytocin (Blaicher et al., 1999), and norepinephrine and prolactin (Krüger et al., 2003); changes in immune parameters (Haake et al., 2004); and changes in cardiovascular functioning (Chen, Zhang, & Tan, 2009). Much less is known about the effects of sexual behavior on long-term physiological changes and health. Taken together, the findings in this area suggest that, like physical affection and other forms of positive physical contact, sexual relations can influence ongoing physiological processes across many biological systems and thus may contribute to health outcomes.

WHAT REMAINS TO BE DISCOVERED ABOUT MARRIAGE AND HEALTH?

Many questions remain for researchers to pursue. Although we now have several potential explanations for sex differences in the effects of marital quality, less is known about sex differences in the effects of marital status. Why, or how, does marital status influence men's health more than women's? Will sex differences in status and quality effects change as role expectations continue to evolve? How does having children affect marital-type influences on health? Almost nothing is known about this issue. Given that children can engender both nurturance and stress, their presence is likely a potent influence. Further, although some studies have compared health effects of marriage between couples in different stages of their marriages, much remains to be learned about potential age and cohort effects on these processes. Researchers have not investigated marital-type relationships in same-sex couples. Do they confer the same benefits as in heterosexual couples? There is a similar shortage of studies comparing effects of marriage on health between members of different racial, ethnic, or cultural groups, where traditions and practices around marriage may vary drastically (e.g., arranged marriage vs. marriages of personal choice).

Theoretical explanations for marital effects on health continue to develop. Because both seeking and providing social support can be interpreted within attachment theory, it remains difficult to distinguish between these perspectives; in fact, it may be time to fully integrate them. Social support is not uniformly beneficial; depending on context, it can engender feelings of low self-esteem and vulnerability (e.g., Uchida, Kitayama, Mesquita, Reyes, & Morling, 2008). Hence, a more fine-grained analysis of support provision might further elucidate health effects of marital-type relationships. Regarding adult attachment, how powerful is physiological coregulation? Generally speaking, conditioning processes likely occur in all contexts, and it is reasonable to assume that a person's physiological responses can be conditioned to the presence of or interactions with a given other, regardless of the attachment between them. How are the effects of coregulation moderated by other characteristics of the relationship, such as satisfaction, distress, or attachment styles?

Research focused on the health effects of physical affection and other forms of positive physical contact, such as sexual activity, is at a relatively early stage. Nevertheless, findings related to physical affection have suggested that it is likely a key mediator for beneficial effects of marital-type relationships on health, both direct (e.g., by reducing sympathetic arousal) and indirect (e.g., by reducing depression). Sexual relations likely also contribute. Direct tests of these and related hypotheses remain to be conducted. For example, to what extent, and how, does the meaning of a touch influence its effect? Further, almost nothing is known about age, sex, and ethnic differences in touch attitudes and behaviors, all of which may be consequential for health.

To summarize, research in the first decade or so of the 21st century has contributed much to the understanding of marital influences on health. Researchers have moved from documenting the effects to testing specific mediators and moderators of these effects. Sex differences continue to be found, and possible explanations for them are being examined. Nevertheless, much remains to be learned.

REFERENCES

Adam, E. K., & Gunnar, M. R. (2001). Relationship functioning and home and work demands predict individual differences in diurnal cortisol patterns in women. *Psychoneuroendocrinology, 26*, 189–208. doi:10.1016/S0306-4530(00)00045-7

App, B., McIntosh, D. N., Reed, C. L., & Hertenstein, M. J. (2011). Nonverbal channel use in communication of emotion: How may depend on why. *Emotion, 11*, 603–617. doi:10.1037/a0023164

Baker, B., Paquette, M., Szalai, J. P., Driver, H., Perger, T., Helmers, K., . . . Tobe, S. (2000). The influence of marital adjustment on 3-year left ventricular mass and ambulatory blood pressure in mild hypertension. *Archives of Internal Medicine, 160*, 3453–3458. doi:10.1001/archinte.160.22.3453

Baker, B., Szalai, J. P., Paquette, M., & Tobe, S. (2003). Marital support, spousal contact and the course of mild hypertension. *Journal of Psychosomatic Research, 55*, 229–233. doi:10.1016/S0022-3999(02)00551-2

Barnett, R. C., Steptoe, A., & Gareis, K. C. (2005). Marital-role quality and stress-related psychobiological indicators. *Annals of Behavioral Medicine, 30*, 36–43. doi:10.1207/s15324796abm3001_5

Bell, R. A., Daly, J. A., & Gonzalez, M. C. (1987). Affinity-maintenance in marriage and its relationship to women's marital satisfaction. *Journal of Marriage and the Family, 49*, 445–454. doi:10.2307/352313

Bernieri, F. J., & Rosenthal, R. (1991). Interpersonal coordination: Behavior matching and interactional synchrony. In R. S. Feldman & B. B. Rime (Eds.), *Fundamentals of nonverbal behavior* (pp. 401–432). Cambridge, England: Cambridge University Press.

Berridge, K. C. (1999). Pleasure, pain, desire, and dread: Hidden core processes of emotion. In D. Kahneman, E. Diener, & N. Schwarz (Eds.), *Well-being: The foundations of hedonic psychology* (pp. 525–557). New York, NY: Russell Sage Foundation.

Blaicher, W., Gruber, D., Bieglmayer, C., Blaicher, A. M., Knogler, W., & Huber, J. C. (1999). The role of oxytocin in relation to female sexual arousal. *Gynecologic and Obstetric Investigation, 47*, 125–126. doi:10.1159/000010075

Blanchflower, D. G., & Oswald, A. J. (2004). Money, sex and happiness: An empirical study. *The Scandinavian Journal of Economics, 106*, 393–415. doi:10.1111/j.0347-0520.2004.00369.x

Bookwala, J. (2005). The role of marital quality in physical health during the mature years. *Journal of Aging and Health, 17*, 85–104. doi:10.1177/0898264304272794

Burleson, M. H., Trevathan, W. R., & Todd, M. (2007). In the mood for love, or vice versa? Understanding the relations among physical affection, sexual activity, mood, and stress in the daily lives of mid-aged women. *Archives of Sexual Behavior, 36*, 357–368. doi:10.1007/s10508-006-9071-1

Burman, B., & Margolin, G. (1992). Analysis of the association between marital relationships and health problems: An interactional perspective. *Psychological Bulletin, 112*, 39–63. doi:10.1037/0033-2909.112.1.39

Butler, E. A., & Randall, A. K. (in press). Emotional coregulation in close relationships. *Emotion Review*.

Carr, D., & Springer, K. W. (2010). Advances in families and health research in the 21st century. *Journal of Marriage and Family, 72*, 743–761. doi:10.1111/j.1741-3737.2010.00728.x

Carrère, S., Mittmann, A., Woodin, E., Tabares, A., & Yoshimoto, D. (2005). Anger dysregulation, depressive symptoms, and health in married women and men. *Nursing Research, 54*, 184–192.

Carter, C. S. (1998). Neuroendocrine perspectives on social attachment and love. *Psychoneuroendocrinology, 23*, 779–818. doi:10.1016/S0306-4530(98)00055-9

Chen, X., Zhang, Q., & Tan, X. (2009). Cardiovascular effects of sexual activity. *The Indian Journal of Medical Research, 130*, 681–688.

Choi, H., & Marks, N. F. (2008). Marital conflict, depressive symptoms, and functional impairment. *Journal of Marriage and the Family, 70*, 377–390. doi:10.1111/j.1741-3737.2008.00488.x

Coan, J. A. (2008). Toward a neuroscience of attachment. In J. Cassidy & P. R. Shaver (Eds.), *Handbook of attachment: Theory, research, and clinical applications* (2nd ed., pp. 241–265). New York, NY: Guilford Press.

Coan, J. A., Schaefer, H. S., & Davidson, R. J. (2006). Lending a hand. *Psychological Science, 17*, 1032–1039. doi:10.1111/j.1467-9280.2006.01832.x

Cohen, S., & Wills, T. A. (1985). Stress, social support, and the buffering hypothesis. *Psychological Bulletin, 98*, 310–357. doi:10.1037/0033-2909.98.2.310

Collins, N. L., & Feeney, B. C. (2010). An attachment theoretical perspective on social support dynamics in couples: Normative processes and individual differences. In K. Sullivan & J. Davila (Eds.), *Support processes in intimate relationships* (pp. 89–120). New York, NY: Oxford University Press. doi:10.1093/acprof: oso/9780195380170.003.0004

Coppack, S. W. (2001). Pro-inflammatory cytokines and adipose tissue. *The Proceedings of the Nutrition Society, 60*, 349–356. doi:10.1079/PNS2001110

Coyne, J. C., Rohrbaugh, M. J., Shoham, V., Sonnega, J. S., Nicklas, J. M., & Cranford, J. A. (2001). Prognostic importance of marital quality for survival of congestive heart failure. *The American Journal of Cardiology, 88*, 526–529. doi:10.1016/S0002-9149(01)01731-3

Depue, R. A., & Morrone-Strupinsky, J. V. (2005). A neurobehavioral model of affiliative bonding: Implications for conceptualizing a human trait of affiliation. *Behavioral and Brain Sciences, 28*, 313–350. doi:10.1017/S0140525X05000063

Diamond, L. M. (2001). Contributions of psychophysiology to research on adult attachment: Review and recommendations. *Personality and Social Psychology Review, 5*, 276–295. doi:10.1207/S15327957PSPR0504_1

Ditzen, B., Hoppmann, C., & Klumb, P. (2008). Positive couple interactions and daily cortisol: On the stress-protecting role of intimacy. *Psychosomatic Medicine, 70*, 883–889. doi:10.1097/PSY.0b013e318185c4fc

Ditzen, B., Neumann, I. D., Bodenmann, G., von Dawans, B., Turner, R. A., Ehlert, U., & Heinrichs, M. (2007). Effects of different kinds of couple interaction on cortisol and heart rate responses to stress in women. *Psychoneuroendocrinology, 32*, 565–574. doi:10.1016/j.psyneuen.2007.03.011

Ditzen, B., Schaer, M., Gabriel, B., Bodenmann, G., Ehlert, U., & Heinrichs, M. (2009). Intranasal oxytocin increases positive communication and reduces cortisol levels during couple conflict. *Biological Psychiatry, 65*, 728–731. doi:10.1016/ j.biopsych.2008.10.011

Dockray, S., & Steptoe, A. (2010). Positive affect and psychobiological processes. *Neuroscience and Biobehavioral Reviews, 35*, 69–75. doi:10.1016/j.neubiorev. 2010.01.006

Driver, J. L., & Gottman, J. M. (2004). Daily marital interactions and positive affect during marital conflict among newlywed couples. *Family Process, 43*, 301–314. doi:10.1111/j.1545-5300.2004.00024.x

Dunbar, R. I. M. (2010). The social role of touch in humans and primates: Behavioural function and neurobiological mechanisms. *Neuroscience and Biobehavioral Reviews, 34*, 260–268. doi:10.1016/j.neubiorev.2008.07.001

Dupre, M. E., Beck, A. N., & Meadows, S. O. (2009). Marital trajectories and mortality among US adults. *American Journal of Epidemiology, 170*, 546–555. doi:10.1093/aje/kwp194

Eaker, E. D., Sullivan, L. M., Kelly-Hayes, M., D'Agostino, R. B., & Benjamin, E. J. (2007). Marital status, marital strain, and risk of coronary heart disease or total mortality: the Framingham Offspring Study. *Psychosomatic Medicine, 69*, 509–513. doi:10.1097/PSY.0b013e3180f62357

Ehlers, C. L., Frank, E., & Kupfer, D. J. (1988). Social zeitgebers and biological rhythms: A unified approach to understanding the etiology of depression. *Archives of General Psychiatry, 45*, 948–952. doi:10.1001/archpsyc.1988.01800340076012

Ershler, W. B., & Keller, E. T. (2000). Age-associated increased interleukin-6 gene expression, late-life diseases, and frailty. *Annual Review of Medicine, 51*, 245–270. doi:10.1146/annurev.med.51.1.245

Field, T. (2010). Touch for socioemotional and physical well-being: A review. *Developmental Review, 30*, 367–383. doi:10.1016/j.dr.2011.01.001

Floyd, K. (2002). Human affection exchange: V. Attributes of the highly affectionate. *Communication Quarterly, 50*, 135–154. doi:10.1080/01463370209385653

Floyd, K. (2006). *Communicating affection: Interpersonal behavior and social context*. Cambridge, England: Cambridge University Press. doi:10.1017/CBO9780511606649

Floyd, K., Boren, J. P., Hannawa, A. F., Hesse, C., McEwan, B., & Veksler, A. E. (2009). Kissing in marital and cohabiting relationships: Effects on blood lipids, stress, and relationship satisfaction. *Western Journal of Communication, 73*, 113–133. doi:10.1080/10570310902856071

Floyd, K., Hess, J. A., Miczo, L. A., Halone, K. K., Mikkelson, A. C., & Tusing, K. J. (2005). Human affection exchange: VIII. Further evidence of the benefits of expressed affection. *Communication Quarterly, 53*, 285–303. doi:10.1080/01463370500101071

Floyd, K., Hesse, C., & Haynes, M. T. (2007). Human affection exchange: XV. Metabolic and cardiovascular correlates of trait expressed affection. *Communication Quarterly, 55*, 79–94. doi:10.1080/01463370600998715

Floyd, K., Mikkelson, A. C., Hesse, C., & Pauley, P. M. (2007). Affectionate writing reduces total cholesterol: Two randomized, controlled trials. *Human Communication Research, 33*, 119–142. doi:10.1111/j.1468-2958.2007.00293.x

Floyd, K., Mikkelson, A. C., Tafoya, M. A., Farinelli, L., La Valley, A. G., Judd, J., . . . Wilson, J. (2007a). Human affection exchange: XIII. Affectionate communication accelerates neuroendocrine stress recovery. *Health Communication, 22*, 123. doi:10.1080/10410230701454015

Floyd, K., Mikkelson, A. C., Tafoya, M. A., Farinelli, L., La Valley, A. G., Judd, J., . . . Wilson, J. (2007b). Human affection exchange: XIV. Relational affection predicts resting heart rate and free cortisol secretion during acute stress. *Behavioral Medicine, 32,* 151–156. doi:10.3200/BMED.32.4.151-156

Floyd, K., Pauley, P. M., & Hesse, C. (2010). State and trait affectionate communication buffer adults' stress reactions. *Communication Monographs, 77,* 618–636. doi:10.1080/03637751.2010.498792

Floyd, K., & Riforgiate, S. (2008). Affectionate communication received from spouses predicts stress hormone levels in healthy adults. *Communication Monographs, 75,* 351–368. doi:10.1080/03637750802512371

Fritz, H. L., & Helgeson, V. S. (1998). Distinctions of unmitigated communion from communion: Self-neglect and overinvolvement with others. *Journal of Personality and Social Psychology, 75,* 121–140. doi:10.1037/0022-3514.75.1.121

Gallo, L. C., Troxel, W. M., Kuller, L. H., Sutton-Tyrrell, K., Edmundowicz, D., & Matthews, K. A. (2003). Marital status, marital quality, and atherosclerotic burden in postmenopausal women. *Psychosomatic Medicine, 65,* 952. doi:10.1097/01.PSY.0000097350.95305.FE

Gallo, L. C., Troxel, W. M., Matthews, K. A., & Kuller, L. H. (2003). Marital status and quality in middle-aged women: Associations with levels and trajectories of cardiovascular risk factors. *Health Psychology, 22,* 453–463. doi:10.1037/0278-6133.22.5.453

Gottman, J. M., & Carrère, S. (1994). Why can't men and women get along? Developmental roots and marital inequities. In D. J. Canary & L. Stafford (Eds.), *Communication and relational maintenance,* (pp. 203–229). San Diego, CA: Academic Press.

Gouin, J. P., Carter, C. S., Pournajafi-Nazarloo, H., Glaser, R., Malarkey, W. B., Loving, T. J., . . . Kiecolt-Glaser, J. K. (2010). Marital behavior, oxytocin, vasopressin, and wound healing. *Psychoneuroendocrinology, 35,* 1082–1090. doi:10.1016/j.psyneuen.2010.01.009

Graham, J. E., Glaser, R., Loving, T. J., Malarkey, W. B., Stowell, J. R., & Kiecolt-Glaser, J. K. (2009). Cognitive word use during marital conflict and increases in proinflammatory cytokines. *Health Psychology, 28,* 621–630. doi:10.1037/a0015208

Grewen, K. M., Anderson, B. J., Girdler, S. S., & Light, K. C. (2003). Warm partner contact is related to lower cardiovascular reactivity. *Behavioral Medicine, 29,* 123–130. doi:10.1080/08964280309596065

Grewen, K. M., Girdler, S. S., Amico, J., & Light, K. C. (2005). Effects of partner support on resting oxytocin, cortisol, norepinephrine, and blood pressure before and after warm partner contact. *Psychosomatic Medicine, 67,* 531–538. doi:10.1097/01.psy.0000170341.88395.47

Grewen, K. M., Girdler, S. S., & Light, K. C. (2005). Relationship quality: Effects on ambulatory blood pressure and negative affect in a biracial sample of men and women. *Blood Pressure Monitoring, 10,* 117–124. doi:10.1097/00126097-200506000-00002

Gulledge, A. K., Gulledge, M. H., & Stahmannn, R. F. (2003). Romantic physical affection types and relationship satisfaction. *The American Journal of Family Therapy, 31,* 233–242. doi:10.1080/01926180390201936

Haake, P., Krueger, T. H., Goebel, M. U., Heberling, K. M., Hartmann, U., & Schedlowski, M. (2004). Effects of sexual arousal on lymphocyte subset circulation and cytokine production in man. *Neuroimmunomodulation, 11,* 293–298. doi:10.1159/000079409

Hamilton, L. D., Rellini, A. H., & Meston, C. M. (2008). Cortisol, sexual arousal, and affect in response to sexual stimuli. *Journal of Sexual Medicine, 5,* 2111–2118.

Hazan, C., & Shaver, P. (1987). Romantic love conceptualized as an attachment process. *Journal of Personality and Social Psychology, 52,* 511–524. doi:10.1037/0022-3514.52.3.511

Heffner, K. L., Kiecolt-Glaser, J. K., Loving, T. J., Glaser, R., & Malarkey, W. B. (2004). Spousal support satisfaction as a modifier of physiological responses to marital conflict in younger and older couples. *Journal of Behavioral Medicine, 27,* 233–254. doi:10.1023/B:JOBM.0000028497.79129.ad

Heffner, K. L., Loving, T. J., Kiecolt-Glaser, J. K., Himawan, L. K., Glaser, R., & Malarkey, W. B. (2006). Older spouses' cortisol responses to marital conflict: Associations with demand/withdraw communication patterns. *Journal of Behavioral Medicine, 29,* 317–325. doi:10.1007/s10865-006-9058-3

Heiman, J. R., Long, J. S., Smith, S. N., Fisher, W. A., Sand, M. S., & Rosen, R. C. (2011). Intimacy and marital satisfaction in spouses. *Journal of Sex & Marital Therapy, 27,* 247–257.

Heinrichs, M., Baumgartner, T., Kirschbaum, C., & Ehlert, U. (2003). Social support and oxytocin interact to suppress cortisol and subjective responses to psychosocial stress. *Biological Psychiatry, 54,* 1389–1398. doi:10.1016/S0006-3223(03)00465-7

Hertenstein, M. J., Keltner, D., App, B., Bulleit, B. A., & Jaskolka, A. R. (2006). Touch communicates distinct emotions. *Emotion, 6,* 528–533. doi:10.1037/1528-3542.6.3.528

Hofer, M. A. (1994). Hidden regulators in attachment, separation, and loss. *Monographs of the Society for Research in Child Development, 59,* 192–207. doi:10.2307/1166146

Holt-Lunstad, J., Birmingham, W., & Jones, B. Q. (2008). Is there something unique about marriage? The relative impact of marital status, relationship quality, and network social support on ambulatory blood pressure and mental health. *Annals of Behavioral Medicine, 35,* 239–244. doi:10.1007/s12160-008-9018-y

Holt-Lunstad, J., Birmingham, W., & Light, K. C. (2008). Influence of a "warm touch" support enhancement intervention among married couples on ambulatory blood pressure, oxytocin, alpha amylase, and cortisol. *Psychosomatic Medicine, 70,* 976–985. doi:10.1097/PSY.0b013e318187aef7

Holt-Lunstad, J., Jones, B. Q., & Birmingham, W. (2009). The influence of close relationships on nocturnal blood pressure dipping. *International Journal of Psychophysiology, 71,* 211–217. doi:10.1016/j.ijpsycho.2008.09.008

Holt-Lunstad, J., Smith, T. B., & Layton, J. B. (2010). Social relationships and mortality risk: A meta-analytic review. *PLoS Medicine, 7*(7). doi:10.1371/journal.pmed.1000316

Janicki, D. L., Kamarck, T. W., Shiffman, S., Sutton-Tyrrell, K., & Gwaltney, C. J. (2005). Frequency of spousal interaction and 3-year progression of carotid artery intima medial thickness: The Pittsburgh Healthy Heart Project. *Psychosomatic Medicine, 67*, 889–896. doi:10.1097/01.psy.0000188476.87869.88

Kaplan, R. C., & Frishman, W. H. (2001). Systemic inflammation as a cardiovascular disease risk factor and as a potential target for drug therapy. *Heart Disease, 3*, 326–332. doi:10.1097/00132580-200109000-00009

Kiecolt-Glaser, J. K., Loving, T. J., Stowell, J. R., Malarkey, W. B., Lemeshow, S., Dickinson, S. L., & Glaser, R. (2005). Hostile marital interactions, proinflammatory cytokine production, and wound healing. *Archives of General Psychiatry, 62*, 1377–1384. doi:10.1001/archpsyc.62.12.1377

Kiecolt-Glaser, J. K., & Newton, T. L. (2001). Marriage and health: His and hers. *Psychological Bulletin, 127*, 472–503. doi:10.1037/0033-2909.127.4.472

Kimata, H. (2003). Kissing reduces allergic skin wheal responses and plasma neurotrophin levels. *Physiology & Behavior, 80*, 395–398. doi:10.1016/j.physbeh.2003.09.004

Kimata, H. (2006). Kissing selectively decreases allergen-specific IgE production in atopic patients. *Journal of Psychosomatic Research, 60*, 545–547. doi:10.1016/j.jpsychores.2005.09.007

King, C. E., & Christensen, A. (1983). The relationship events scale: A Guttman scaling of progress in courtship. *Journal of Marriage and the Family, 45*, 671–678. doi:10.2307/351672

Klinenberg, E. (2012). *Going solo: the extraordinary rise and surprising appeal of living alone.* New York, NY: Penguin Press.

Krüger, T. H., Haake, P., Chereath, D., Knapp, W., Janssen, O. E., Exton, M. S., . . . Hartmann, U. (2003). Specificity of the neuroendocrine response to orgasm during sexual arousal in men. *The Journal of Endocrinology, 177*, 57–64. doi:10.1677/joe.0.1770057

Kulik, J. A., & Mahler, H. I. M. (2006). Marital quality predicts hospital stay following coronary artery bypass surgery for women but not men. *Social Science & Medicine, 63*, 2031–2040. doi:10.1016/j.socscimed.2006.05.022

Lamm, H., & Wiesmann, U. (1997). Subjective attributes of attraction: How people characterize their liking, their love, and their being in love. *Personal Relationships, 4*, 271–284. doi:10.1111/j.1475-6811.1997.tb00145.x

Light, K. C., Grewen, K. M., & Amico, J. A. (2005). More frequent partner hugs and higher oxytocin levels are linked to lower blood pressure and heart rate in premenopausal women. *Biological Psychology, 69*, 5–21. doi:10.1016/j.biopsycho.2004.11.002

Litwak, E., Messeri, P., Wolfe, S., Gorman, S., Silverstein, M., & Guilarte, M. (1989). Organizational theory, social supports, and mortality rates: A

theoretical convergence. *American Sociological Review, 54*, 49–66. doi:10.2307/
2095661

Loving, T. J., Heffner, K. L., Kiecolt-Glaser, J. K., Glaser, R., & Malarkey, W. B.
(2004). Stress hormone changes and marital conflict: Spouses' relative power
makes a difference. *Journal of Marriage and Family, 66*, 595–612. doi:10.1111/
j.0022-2445.2004.00040.x

Mackey, R. A., Diemer, M. A., & O'Brien, B. A. (2000). Psychological intimacy in
the lasting relationships of heterosexual and same-gender couples. *Sex Roles, 43*,
201–227. doi:10.1023/A:1007028930658

Mainous, A. G., Everett, C. J., Diaz, V. A., Baker, R., Mangino, M., Codd, V., &
Samani, N. J. (2011). Leukocyte telomere length and marital status among
middle-aged adults. *Age and Ageing, 40*, 73–78. doi:10.1093/ageing/afq118

Manzoli, L., & Villari, P. (2007). Marital status and mortality in the elderly: A
systematic review and meta-analysis. *Social Science & Medicine, 64*, 77–94.
doi:10.1016/j.socscimed.2006.08.031

Margolin, G., Talovic, S., & Weinstein, C. D. (1983). Areas of Change Questionnaire: A practical approach to marital assessment. *Journal of Consulting and
Clinical Psychology, 51*, 920. doi:10.1037/0022-006X.51.6.920

Master, S. L., Eisenberger, N. I., Taylor, S. E., Naliboff, B. D., Shirinyan, D., &
Lieberman, M. D. (2009). A picture's worth: Partner photographs reduce experimentally induced pain. *Psychological Science, 20*, 1316–1318. doi:10.1111/
j.1467-9280.2009.02444.x

Matsunaga, M., Sato, S., Isowa, T., Tsuboi, H., Konagaya, T., Kaneko, H., & Ohira,
H. (2009). Profile of serum proteins influenced by warm partner contact in
healthy couples. *Neuroendocrinology Letters, 30*, 227–236.

Matthews, K. A., Woodall, K. L., & Allen, M. T. (1993). Cardiovascular reactivity
to stress predicts future blood pressure status. *Hypertension, 22*, 479–485.

Mikulincer, M., & Shaver, P. R. (2009). An attachment and behavioral systems perspective on social support. *Journal of Social and Personal Relationships, 26*, 7–19.
doi:10.1177/0265407509105518

Miller, G. E., Cohen, S., & Ritchey, K. A. (2002). Chronic psychological stress
and the regulation of pro-inflammatory cytokines: A glucocorticoid-resistance
model. *Health Psychology, 21*, 531–541. doi:10.1037/0278-6133.21.6.531

Murray, J. E. (2000). Marital protection and marital selection: Evidence from a
historical–prospective sample of American men. *Demography, 37*, 511–521.
doi:10.1353/dem.2000.0010

Muxfeldt, E. S., Cardoso, C. R., & Salles, G. F. (2009). Prognostic value of nocturnal
blood pressure reduction in resistant hypertension. *Archives of Internal Medicine,
169*, 874–880. doi:10.1001/archinternmed.2009.68

Nealey-Moore, J. B., Smith, T. W., Uchino, B. N., Hawkins, M. W., & Olson-Cerny, C.
(2007). Cardiovascular reactivity during positive and negative marital interactions. *Journal of Behavioral Medicine, 30*, 505–519. doi:10.1007/s10865-007-9124-5

Newton, T. L., & Sanford, J. M. (2003). Conflict structure moderates associations between cardiovascular reactivity and negative marital interaction. *Health Psychology, 22*, 270–278. doi:10.1037/0278-6133.22.3.270

Orth-Gomér, K., Wamala, S. P., Horsten, M., Schenck-Gustafsson, K., Schneiderman, N., & Mittleman, M. A. (2000, December 20). Marital stress worsens prognosis in women with coronary heart disease. *JAMA, 284*(23), 3008–3014. doi:10.1001/jama.284.23.3008

Pencina, M. J., D'Agostino, R. B., Larson, M. G., Massaro, J. M., & Vasan, R. S. (2009). Predicting the 30-year risk of cardiovascular disease The Framingham Heart Study. *Circulation, 119*, 3078–3084. doi:10.1161/CIRCULATIONAHA.108.816694

Pressman, S. D., & Cohen, S. (2005). Does positive affect influence health? *Psychological Bulletin, 131*, 925–971. doi:10.1037/0033-2909.131.6.925

Randall, G., Bhattacharyya, M. R., & Steptoe, A. (2009). Marital status and heart rate variability in patients with suspected coronary artery disease. *Annals of Behavioral Medicine, 38*, 115–123. doi:10.1007/s12160-009-9137-0

Roberts, N. A., Tsai, J. L., & Coan, J. A. (2007). Emotion elicitation using dyadic interaction tasks. In J. A. Coan & J. Allen (Eds.), *The handbook of emotion elicitation and assessment* (pp. 106–123). New York, NY: Oxford University Press.

Robles, T. F., & Kiecolt-Glaser, J. K. (2003). The physiology of marriage: Pathways to health. *Physiology & Behavior, 79*, 409–416. doi:10.1016/S0031-9384(03)00160-4

Robles, T. F., Shaffer, V. A., Malarkey, W. B., & Kiecolt-Glaser, J. K. (2006). Positive behaviors during marital conflict: Influences on stress hormones. *Journal of Social and Personal Relationships, 23*, 305. doi:10.1177/0265407506062482

Rohrbaugh, M. J., Mehl, M. R., Shoham, V., Reilly, E. S., & Ewy, G. A. (2008). Prognostic significance of spouse we talk in couples coping with heart failure. *Journal of Consulting and Clinical Psychology, 76*, 781. doi:10.1037/a0013238

Rohrbaugh, M. J., Shoham, V., & Coyne, J. C. (2006). Effect of marital quality on eight-year survival of patients with heart failure. *The American Journal of Cardiology, 98*, 1069–1072. doi:10.1016/j.amjcard.2006.05.034

Salovey, P., Rothman, A. J., Detweiler, J. B., & Steward, W. T. (2000). Emotional states and physical health. *American Psychologist, 55*, 110–121. doi:10.1037/0003-066X.55.1.110

Saxbe, D., & Repetti, R. L. (2010). For better or worse? Coregulation of couples' cortisol levels and mood states. *Journal of Personality and Social Psychology, 98*, 92–103. doi:10.1037/a0016959

Saxbe, D. E., Repetti, R. L., & Nishina, A. (2008). Marital satisfaction, recovery from work, and diurnal cortisol among men and women. *Health Psychology, 27*, 15–25. doi:10.1037/0278-6133.27.1.15

Sbarra, D. A. (2009). Marriage protects men from clinically meaningful elevations in C-reactive protein: Results from the National Social Life, Health, and Aging Project (NSHAP). *Psychosomatic Medicine, 71*, 828–835. doi:10.1097/PSY.0b013e3181b4c4f2

Sbarra, D. A., & Hazan, C. (2008). Coregulation, dysregulation, self-regulation: An integrative analysis and empirical agenda for understanding adult attachment, separation, loss, and recovery. *Personality and Social Psychology Review, 12,* 141. doi:10.1177/1088868308315702

Selcuk, E., Zayas, V., & Hazan, C. (2010). Beyond satisfaction: The role of attachment in marital functioning. *Journal of Family Theory & Review, 2,* 258–279. doi:10.1111/j.1756-2589.2010.00061.x

Shen, B. J., Farrell, K. A., Penedo, F. J., Schneiderman, N., & Orth-Gomér, K. (2010). Waist circumference moderates the association between marital stress and C-reactive protein in middle-aged healthy women. *Annals of Behavioral Medicine, 40,* 258–264. doi:10.1007/s12160-010-9211-7

Slatcher, R. B. (2010). Marital functioning and physical health: Implications for social and personality psychology. *Social and Personality Psychology Compass, 4,* 455–469. doi:10.1111/j.1751-9004.2010.00273.x

Slatcher, R. B., Robles, R. F., Repetti, R. L., & Fellows, M. D. (2010). Momentary work worries, marital disclosure, and salivary cortisol among parents of young children. *Psychosomatic Medicine, 72,* 887–896. doi:10.1097/PSY.0b013e3181f60fcc

Smith, T. W., Cribbet, M. R., Nealey-Moore, J. B., Uchino, B. N., Williams, P. G., MacKenzie, J., & Thayer, J. F. (2011). Matters of the variable heart: Respiratory sinus arrhythmic response to marital interaction and associations with marital quality. *Journal of Personality and Social Psychology, 100,* 103–119. doi:10.1037/a0021136

Smith, T. W., Uchino, B. N., Berg, C. A., Florsheim, P., Pearce, G., Hawkins, M., . . . Olsen-Cerny, C. (2009). Conflict and collaboration in middle-aged and older couples: II. Cardiovascular reactivity during marital interaction. *Psychology and Aging, 24,* 274–286. doi:10.1037/a0016067

Svetlik, R. N. D., Dooley, W., Weiner, M. F., Williamson, G. M., & Walters, A. S. (2005). Declines in satisfaction with physical intimacy predict caregiver perceptions of overall relationship loss: A study of elderly caregiving spousal dyads. *Sexuality and Disability, 23,* 65–79. doi:10.1007/s11195-005-4670-7

Tower, R. B., Kasl, S. V., & Darefsky, A. S. (2002). Types of marital closeness and mortality risk in older couples. *Psychosomatic Medicine, 64,* 644.

Trief, P. M., Morin, P. C., Izquierdo, R., Teresi, J., Starren, J., Shea, S., & Weinstock, R. S. (2006). Marital quality and diabetes outcomes: The IDEATel Project. *Families, Systems, & Health, 24,* 318–331. doi:10.1037/1091-7527.24.3.318

Troxel, W. M., Matthews, K. A., Gallo, L. C., & Kuller, L. H. (2005). Marital quality and occurrence of the metabolic syndrome in women. *Archives of Internal Medicine, 165,* 1022–1027. doi:10.1001/archinte.165.9.1022

Tsigos, C., & Chrousos, G. P. (2002). Hypothalamic–pituitary–adrenal axis, neuroendocrine factors and stress. *Journal of Psychosomatic Research, 53,* 865–871. doi:10.1016/S0022-3999(02)00429-4

Uchida, Y., Kitayama, S., Mesquita, B., Reyes, J. A. S., & Morling, B. (2008). Is perceived emotional support beneficial? Well-being and health in independent and interdependent cultures. *Personality and Social Psychology Bulletin, 34*, 741–754. doi:10.1177/0146167208315157

Uchino, B. N. (2006). Social support and health: a review of physiological processes potentially underlying links to disease outcomes. *Journal of Behavioral Medicine, 29*, 377–387. doi:10.1007/s10865-006-9056-5

Uchino, B. N., Cacioppo, J. T., & Kiecolt-Glaser, J. K. (1996). The relationship between social support and physiological processes: A review with emphasis on underlying mechanisms and implications for health. *Psychological Bulletin, 119*, 488–531. doi:10.1037/0033-2909.119.3.488

Umberson, D., Williams, K., Powers, D. A., Liu, H., & Needham, B. (2006). You make me sick: Marital quality and health over the life course. *Journal of Health and Social Behavior, 47*, 1–16. doi:10.1177/002214650604700101

Waldinger, R. J., Schulz, M. S., Hauser, S. T., Allen, J. P., & Crowell, J. A. (2004). Reading others' emotions: The role of intuitive judgments in predicting marital satisfaction, quality, and stability. *Journal of Family Psychology, 18*, 58–71. doi:10.1037/0893-3200.18.1.58

Whisman, M. A., & Uebelacker, L. A. (2006). Impairment and distress associated with relationship discord in a national sample of married or cohabiting adults. *Journal of Family Psychology, 20*, 369–377. doi:10.1037/0893-3200.20.3.369

Whisman, M. A., Uebelacker, L. A., & Settles, T. D. (2010). Marital distress and the metabolic syndrome: Linking social functioning with physical health. *Journal of Family Psychology, 24*, 367–370. doi:10.1037/a0019547

Winslow, J. T., & Insel, T. R. (2002). The social deficits of the oxytocin knockout mouse. *Neuropeptides, 36*, 221–229. doi:10.1054/npep.2002.0909

Young, L. J., & Wang, Z. (2004). The neurobiology of pair bonding. *Nature Neuroscience, 7*, 1048–1054. doi:10.1038/nn1327

Yuan, J. W., McCarthy, M., Holley, S. R., & Levenson, R. W. (2010). Physiological down-regulation and positive emotion in marital interaction. *Emotion, 10*, 467–474. doi:10.1037/a0018699

Zautra, A. J., Affleck, G. G., Tennen, H., Reich, J. W., & Davis, M. C. (2005). Dynamic approaches to emotions and stress in everyday life: Bolger and Zuckerman reloaded with positive as well as negative affects. *Journal of Personality, 73*, 1511–1538. doi:10.1111/j.0022-3506.2005.00357.x

Zeifman, D., & Hazan, C. (1997). A process model of adult attachment formation. In S. Duck (Ed.), *Handbook of personal relationships: Theory, research and interventions* (2nd ed.), (pp. 179–195). Hoboken, NJ: Wiley.

4

ROMANTIC SEPARATION, LOSS, AND HEALTH: A REVIEW OF MODERATORS

ASHLEY E. MASON AND DAVID A. SBARRA

The loss of a spouse or romantic partner due to separation, divorce, or death can be a difficult if not devastating experience (Booth & Amato, 1991; M. S. Stroebe, Schut, & Stroebe, 2007). Our routines are disrupted, we miss work, our bank accounts often shrink, we hire lawyers, we reschedule our children's lives, and we often move our residence—in addition to a number of other chores. There are few other emotional and psychological experiences in life as potentially devastating as ending our committed romantic relationships. Those who initiate romantic separations often experience guilt, uncertainty, and fear, whereas those who are left by their partners may feel acute rejection, loneliness, and shame. For those who miss former partners, longing can evolve into clinical depression, prolonged grief, and/or substance abuse. In short, romantic separations open the door for a variety of difficult life experiences.

Loss due to divorce or death of a romantic partner is associated with increased risk of poor psychological and physical health, sadness, and distress

DOI: 10.1037/14036-005
Health and Social Relationships: The Good, the Bad, and the Complicated, Matthew L. Newman and Nicole A. Roberts (Editors)

(Amato, 2000; Kiecolt-Glaser et al., 1987; Pinquart, 2003; M. S. Stroebe, Hansson, Stroebe, & Schut, 2001; W. Stroebe & Schut, 2001; W. Stroebe & Stroebe, 1987). Studies have suggested that the experience of romantic loss—not simply the lack of a romantic partner—may be responsible for these poorer health outcomes (e.g., Hemström, 1996). For example, Pienta, Hayward, and Jenkins (2000) found that the end of a marriage, through divorce or widowhood, is associated with poorer health consequences than never having been married at all.

A number of researchers have devoted attention to the mechanisms (i.e., mediators) that explain these poor outcomes (Sbarra, 2012). For instance, *social selection*, or the idea that some people possess characteristics that increase risk of separation or divorce and poor health, may implicate third variables as potential causal explanations (e.g., Amato, 2000; Goldman, 1993; Osler, McGue, Lund, & Christensen, 2008; Wade & Pevalin, 2004). Other data have implicated macrolevel processes, such as poorer socioeconomic status (SES), decreases in finances (especially for women), and decreases in social network sizes (see Sbarra, Law, & Portley, 2011, for a review).

Relatively less attention has been paid to the variables that increase or decrease risk of poor outcomes in the wake of a social loss (i.e., the *moderators*). It is critical to investigate moderators of health outcomes following social loss to better identify those at risk of these outcomes, to investigate effective interventions, and to develop policies and programs targeting these individuals.

Research reviews of individual differences that confer risk following divorce and bereavement are accumulating with respect to psychological health outcomes (e.g., Amato, 2010; Booth & Amato, 1991; Kitson & Morgan, 1990; Parkes & Prigerson, 2010; M. S. Stroebe et al., 2007; W. Stroebe & Schut, 2001; Wang & Amato, 2000). Perhaps not surprisingly, such reviews have revealed that divorced individuals (compared with married individuals) report more symptoms of depression and anxiety, more substance use, more social isolation, more negative life events, poorer self-concepts, and lower levels of happiness (see Amato, 2000, for a review). Similarly, data have suggested that bereaved individuals (compared with matched controls) report more physical complaints (including headaches, indigestion, chest pain, and dizziness), greater rates of general illness and disability, more medication use, more frequent hospitalization, and increases in depressive symptoms (see M. S. Stroebe et al., 2007, for a review).

The present chapter examines multiple types of loss—including separation, divorce, and widowhood—and focuses on the individual differences that may increase or decrease risk of poor physical health outcomes among those who experience such a loss. For some of these moderators, as reviewed later, data on actual physical health are lacking; in these cases, we draw on the literature on psychological outcomes in an attempt to understand the potential physical outcomes. This chapter adopts an interdisciplinary framework, discussing health correlates of social loss based on sociological, epidemiological, and psychological research.

MORBIDITY AND MORTALITY FOLLOWING ROMANTIC LOSS

Many negative health consequences follow from romantic loss. Compared with matched controls, bereaved adults report more headaches, dizziness, indigestion, and chest pain, as well as higher rates of disability and physical illness (see M. S. Stroebe, 2010). However, these health consequences do not seem to lead to a corresponding increase in doctor visits among bereaved individuals (e.g., Prigerson et al., 2001; Thompson, Breckenridge, Gallagher, & Peterson, 1984), indicating that this population may not receive the care they need. Similar to bereavement, being or becoming divorced (or separated) is associated with increased risks for a variety of poor physical health outcomes, including decreased immune function (Gerra et al., 2003; Kiecolt-Glaser et al., 1987), cardiovascular disease (Ebrahim, Wannamethee, McCallum, Walker, & Shaper, 1995; Pienta et al., 2000), respiratory disease (Ikeda et al., 2007; Lorenz, Wickrama, Conger, & Elder, 2006), and liver disease (Johnson, Backlund, Sorlie, & Loveless, 2000), among others.

Research has suggested that the notion that one can "die of a broken heart" may be true. The loss of a romantic partner is associated with heightened mortality, even after accounting for a number of lifestyle and socioeconomic factors (e.g., Kposowa, 2000; Parkes, Benjamin, & Fitzgerald, 1969; M.S. Stroebe et al., 2007). Mortality risk is greater during the first 6 months following the death of a spouse, with a spike in mortality in the weeks immediately following the loss, although data have also suggested that increased risk can persist beyond this time frame (e.g., Buckley, McKinley, Tofler, & Bartrop, 2010; Jones, Bartrop, Forcier, & Penny, 2010). This pattern of increased mortality risk is labeled the *widowhood effect* (Elwert & Christakis, 2008). Although explanations for the widowhood effect are debated in the literature (see M. S. Stroebe et al., 2007), considerable evidence supports its existence. One problem associated with documenting the widowhood effect is the low base rate of deaths among bereaved individuals. Only approximately 5% of widowers aged 55 and older die in the 6 months following their loss, versus 3% of married adults in this same period (M. S. Stroebe, Strobe, & Schut, 2001).

Mortality risk for those who divorce is greater than that of their married counterparts. In an analysis of 14 total effects from five separate studies, Manzoli, Villari, Pirone, and Boccia (2007) reported an average risk hazard of 1.16 for death among divorced adults relative to the married. This finding indicates that, on average, men and women who were at least 65 years old and divorced (at the start of a given study) experienced a 16% increase in mortality risk at each follow-up period relative to their married counterparts.

MODERATORS OF MORBIDITY AND MORTALITY FOLLOWING ROMANTIC LOSS

In the remainder of this chapter, we focus on the variables that moderate the probability of better or worse health outcomes following a romantic loss. We focus on individual demographic variables that heighten or decrease risk, as well as other interpersonal or social–cognitive processes (e.g., real or imagined contact with a former partner) that may interact with romantic loss to predict health. We present moderators of bereavement and divorce separately, because research suggests that although they both have a common ingredient (romantic loss), the mode by which one loses a romantic partner can affect health outcomes. A number of studies have suggested that there may be differences in the prevalence and severity of health outcomes such as cardiovascular disease and cancer (e.g., Ebrahim et al., 1995) following the different events. For a review of mechanisms of action (e.g., changes in health behaviors, psychological stress), we direct the reader to other papers (e.g., Fine & Harvey, 2006; Hall & Irwin, 2001; Sbarra, 2012).

Preloss Psychological Functioning

Disentangling the moderating and main effects of prior psychological function on divorce and bereavement health outcomes remains a challenge for researchers for several reasons. First, people with poor psychological functioning in general are more likely to experience a variety of poor physical health outcomes (Taylor, 2007). Second, poor psychological functioning predicts increased risk of divorce (e.g., Whisman, Tolejko, & Chatav, 2007). It is likely that at least some of the association between preloss psychological functioning and the alleged consequences of social loss can be explained by third variables (e.g., hostility) and genetic selection (Lichtenstein, Gatz, & Berg, 1998; Osler et al., 2008; Saudino, Pedersen, Lichtenstein, McClearn, & Plomin, 1997). Not surprisingly, people with preloss histories of mental illness and insecure attachment patterns are more vulnerable to poorer psychological health outcomes following romantic loss (e.g., Parkes & Prigerson, 2010; Wade & Pevalin, 2004). However, limited research has carefully separated the main and moderating effects of preloss psychological functioning on physical health following romantic loss. Hence, as previously, we discuss what literature exists that addresses both physical health outcomes and findings that are highly correlated and concerned with physical health.

Bereavement

Although some people coping with bereavement experience chronic grief, most people adapt well over the course of bereavement and evidence little distress (Bonanno, 2004). A growing body of literature implicates a number of both transient psychological and stable personality factors that moderate this trajectory. For example, people who experience depression, anxiety, or other psychological disorders prior to the death of a romantic partner are more likely to experience difficulty adjusting to widowhood or widowerhood (Boerner, Wortman, & Bonanno, 2005; Raphael, Minkov, & Dobson, 1993). People with secure attachment styles evidence better adjustment during bereavement than those with insecure attachment styles (e.g. W. Stroebe, Schut, & Stroebe, 2005; van der Houwen et al., 2010). In addition, people who maintain external control beliefs (as opposed to internal control beliefs) report more somatic complaints following an unexpected loss of a partner (W. Stroebe, Stroebe, & Domittner, 1988). Bonanno et al. (2002) found that among bereaved people, chronic grief following spousal loss was associated with both overall interpersonal dependency and dependency on the spouse, as measured preloss. Future research should aim to separate main effects of individual differences (e.g., personality, attachment style) on social loss from moderating effects, because people with secure attachment styles, less neuroticism, and less psychopathology experience better health in general (e.g., Friedman, 2007; Musselman, Evans, & Nemeroff, 1998).

Divorce

Compared with those who remain married, people who divorce report both poorer psychological well-being (Waite, Luo, & Lewin, 2009) and poorer physical health (Kiecolt-Glaser et al., 1987). However, few study designs have targeted the impact of prior psychological health on subsequent physical health outcomes. Given robust correlations among psychological and physical health (see Taylor, 2007, for a review), teasing apart direct and moderating effects of prior psychological functioning on physical health outcomes following divorce presents a sizeable challenge. As an example, assume that Joan is married to Bob, who experiences recurrent episodes of major depression. When Bob experiences a depressive episode, Joan cooks all of Bob's meals, makes his doctor appointments, and picks up Bob's prescriptions from the pharmacy. If Joan leaves Bob, and Bob subsequently eats poorly, skips doctor appointments, and forgets to pick up his prescriptions at the pharmacy, his risks for poorer physical and psychological health increase. Are Bob's increased risks for poorer health outcomes due to a main effect of his depression, or due to an interactive effect of Bob's depression and Joan's leaving him?

Data that have captured psychological functioning both before and after divorce have lent support to the ideas that psychological dysfunction may both contribute to and follow from divorce. Using data from nine annual waves of the British Household Panel Survey, Wade and Pevalin (2004) found that people who divorce experience poor psychological health both prior to and following the separation. What about unhappy, conflict-ridden marriages? Might those who exit these sorts of relationships fare better following divorce? Data have been mixed. Some studies have suggested that people who do not leave these troubled marriages report similar levels of emotional well-being when compared with people who do leave (Kalmijn & Monden, 2006; Waite et al., 2009). Applied to the earlier example, if Bob and Joan are unhappily married and obtain a divorce, results from Waite and colleagues' (2009) study would suggest that they will not experience the precipitous decrease in well-being that a happy couple would on obtaining a divorce, and therefore they may have less to lose. Other data, however, have shown that adults who leave troubled marriages may have some reduction in risk of poor outcomes (Amato & Hohmann-Marriott, 2007; Overbeek et al., 2006). Overbeek and colleagues (2006) found that divorce was prospectively associated with increased alcohol abuse, dysthymia, and social phobias. However, divorced adults were not more likely to develop a psychological disorder if they reported lower levels of marital quality prior to their divorce. The authors concluded that marital discord prior to the actual divorce might be responsible for the subsequent development of psychological disorders.

Social Support

Social support is associated with a range of psychological and physical health outcomes across the life span (Allen, Blieszner, & Roberto, 2000; Taylor, 2007; Uchino 2004, 2006). A recent meta-analysis found that people who report stronger social relationships are 50% more likely to survive than those who report poor or insufficient social relationships (Holt-Lunstad, Smith, & Layton, 2010). People who are not married tend to report lower levels of social integration than their married counterparts (House, Landis, & Umberson, 1988).

Bereavement

Understandably, social support is commonly assumed to moderate bereavement outcomes (e.g., M. S. Stroebe, Folkman, Hansson, & Schut,

2006; W. Stroebe & Stroebe, 1987); however, limited data directly link social support and physical health following bereavement. Some data, however, reveal links between social support and psychological health indices that are often correlated with physical health (these data are reviewed elsewhere in this book). For example, social support reduces psychological distress due to depression, negative mood states, and anxiety (Taylor, 2007). These sorts of psychological distress increase the risk of heart disease for healthy individuals as well as poorer outcomes for people who already have heart disease (Appels, Golombeck, Gorgels, de Vreede, & van Breukelen, 2000; Barefoot, Brummett, Helms, Mark, Siegler, & Williams, 2000; Rugulies, 2002). In general, however, much more data is needed to understand whether changes in social support (or the presence or absence of support) increases or decreases risk of poor health outcomes specifically following bereavement.

Divorce

Divorced individuals report greater social isolation than their married counterparts (e.g., Amato, 2000) and also experience decreases in their social network size and social support following divorce (e.g., Duffy, 1993; Duran-Aydintug, 1998; Nelson, 1995). In a meta-analysis examining the effects of social relationships on post-divorce health outcomes, Kramrei, Coit, Martin, Fogo, and Mahoney (2007) reported a main effect such that divorced people who reported a greater number of social relationships following their divorces also reported less maladjustment. The authors further found that the type of social relationship moderated the association between divorce and maladjustment. Specifically, they found that having one-on-one relationships was associated with less maladjustment, whereas being a member of a social network group (e.g., church group) was not. If Joan maintains three close friends, yet Bob belongs to three bowling league groups, these data would suggest that, upon a romantic separation, Joan would experience a greater protective benefit than would Bob. Unfortunately, the authors did not report on physical health outcomes separately, which makes it difficult to discern whether the effect of social support moderated each index of maladjustment individually.

Continuing Ties to a Loved One

The end of a romantic relationship does not indicate that a former partner will no longer involve an ex-partner in his or her life. People may cross paths, physically or psychologically, with their ex-partners amidst gatherings of family and/or friends, and this continued contact can hold important consequences for subsequent well-being (Adams & Pasley, 2006; Bonanno, 2009; Masheter, 1991; Masuda, 2006; Parkes & Prigerson, 2010; Sprecher, Felmlee, Schmeeckle, & Shu, 2006). The roles of ex-partner contact are slowly emerging in the literature, and here we review what exists with respect to varied health outcomes.

Bereavement

Although one cannot interact with a deceased spouse, it is not uncommon to hear of people who speak with their deceased spouses, and to date, no literature has documented that this practice is especially harmful (Bonanno, 2009). Although data do not yet paint a clear picture, the concept of maintaining a relationship with a deceased partner is well accepted outside of Western society and may be associated with a host of benefits, such as feelings of comfort, support, and solace (Bonanno & Kaltman, 1999; Klass & Walter, 1993). Shuchter and Zisook (1993) found that some 39% of widows and widowers in the 2 months following their loss reported talking with their deceased spouses regularly. Datson and Marwit (1997) found that 86% of widows and widowers considered sensing the presence of their deceased spouse to be comforting; however, those who reported sensing their deceased loved ones also scored higher in neuroticism than those who did not. Field and colleagues (2003) found that continued attachment behaviors (e.g., maintaining the possessions of the deceased) were associated with more grief 5 years following spousal loss but were not associated with other measures of psychological well-being. Bonanno, Mihalecz, and LeJeune (1999) evaluated core emotion themes from bereaved individuals' verbal accounts of their previous relationships 6 months after their loss and found that some 80% reported a continued bond with their ex-partners. These themes were associated with fewer somatic complaints in the following months. Thus, emerging evidence suggests that the ways in which we conceptualize our relationships with deceased partners may moderate our subsequent physical health. Future research should uncover the circumstances under which continued relationships with the deceased lead to better or worse health outcomes.

Divorce

Divorced individuals often must maintain some sort of relationship with an ex-partner, be it to coordinate their children's lives or maintain social relationships with friends. Approximately 50% of divorced individuals report continued contact with their former spouses 2 and then 10 years after separating (Fischer, de Graaf, & Kalmijn, 2005; Masheter, 1991). Little research has documented the psychological effects of contact with an ex-partner (e.g., Masheter, 1991; Sbarra & Emery, 2005), and even less research has documented physical health correlates of contact with an ex-partner. In a longitudinal investigation of recovery following divorce, recently separated individuals reported thinking about their former partners an average of 15.5 minutes per hour (Sbarra, Law, Lee, & Mason, 2009). The amount of time individuals reported thinking about their ex-partners at study intake (interpreted as preoccupation with an ex-spouse) predicted changes in their self-reported health over the following 3 months. Those who reported more time spent thinking about their ex-partners also reported poorer health 3 months later. Data on actual contact with an ex-partner is sorely lacking in the study of divorce. The absence of this work is conspicuous because interpersonal conflict, for example, can have a direct effect on physiological stress responses that if maintained over time, have clear health relevance.

Gender

Men and women may differ in how they initiate, experience, and move past their dissolved relationships (Duck & Wood, 2006). Consequently, a sizeable body of research addresses gender differences with respect to health outcomes following bereavement and divorce, and we briefly summarize the conclusions from this body of work.

Bereavement

Because men tend to die earlier than women, it follows that women are significantly more likely to become widows than men are to become widowers (B. R. Williams, Baker, Allman, & Roseman, 2007). M. S. Stroebe et al. (2007) stated that although both men and women who lose their marital partners are at a significantly higher risk of mortality and morbidity than their married peers, widowers are generally at a greater risk of mortality than are widows during the weeks immediately following loss. Other data have supported this notion, indicating that widowers report poorer physical health outcomes than widows (e.g., Parkes & Prigerson, 2010; Pienta et al., 2000; M. S. Stroebe, Hansson, et al., 2001; M. S. Stroebe, Stroebe, et al., 2001; K. Williams & Umberson, 2004). There are several potential explanations as to why women often fare better following spousal loss than men. The tendency for women to assume responsibility for the health of their family members (Depner & Ingersoll-Dayton, 1985), to discourage negative health behaviors such as drinking and driving (Umberson 1987, 1992), and to complete household responsibilities (Lennon & Rosenfield, 1994) indicates that lifestyle changes following spousal loss may differ in ways that affect men's day-to-day lives. These practical differences may contribute to gender differences in bereavement outcomes.

Divorce

A diverse body of research on gender differences in divorce outcomes has suggested that men fare more poorly in terms of emotional health than women (Braver, Shapiro, & Goodman, 2006), but researchers have yet to isolate differences in physical health that follow from divorce. Hu and Goldman (1990) found that divorced men, compared with women as well as married, widowed, and single men, evidenced significantly elevated mortality rates. In more than half of the countries sampled, however, divorced women experienced greater mortality than widowed or single women. In a Swedish study, Hemström (1996) found that compared with their married counterparts, divorced men's excess mortality was 143% (divorced women's excess mortality was 63% compared with their married counterparts).

In contrast to these data, however, some findings have not revealed gender effects across divorce outcomes. Tucker, Friedman, Wingard, and Schwartz (1996) found no evidence that the detrimental aspects of divorce or romantic separation on health differ by gender; married men and married women were both at a significantly reduced mortality risk compared with those who had experienced a divorce or romantic separation. Zhang and Hayward (2006) found that the risk of cardiovascular disease among divorced (and widowed) men is not different from that of their married counterparts. Divorced women, however, were significantly more likely to experience cardiovascular disease than their married counterparts, but this association became nonsignificant after accounting for SES and self-reported mental distress. Hemström (1996) also found a large reduction in excess mortality risk for men after accounting for SES, employment status, and number of children in the household, concluding, "gender differences are smaller than is usually believed" (p. 376). Hence, psychosocial situational variables may underlie observed gender differences.

Additional data have implicated gender differences as potential statistical artifacts. In a 40-year prospective study, Sbarra and Nietert (2009) examined the possibility that gender moderates an association between divorce and death. The authors found no evidence for a gender effect, despite a main effect of men's tendency to die earlier than women. Other data have suggested a similar conclusion: One meta-analysis of 53 studies included extensive follow-up data ranging from 1.3 to 20.0 years, with an average of 8.7 years. Forty-six of these studies included follow-up data from 5 or more years and seven studies included follow-up data from 1 to 5 years. In this data set, Manzoli et al. (2007) found that the prospective association between divorce and death was roughly equivalent for men and women. Because almost all epidemiological studies have reported their effects separately for men and women, what may appear to be a Divorce × Gender interaction on health outcomes following divorce may in fact be a main effect gender difference that is frequently misinterpreted in the literature.

Ethnocultural Factors

There are several documented racial and ethnic differences in family structure, including relationships with extended kin (e.g., Hays & Mindel, 1973), household division of labor (e.g., Orbuch & Eyster, 1997), and attitudes toward women working outside of the home (e.g., Blee & Tickamyer, 1995). It follows that sizeable changes to family structure, such as the loss of a romantic partner, might differentially affect members of various races and ethnicities. Given evidence that SES in the United States is significantly associated with race (D. R. Williams, 1999) and that lower SES status is associated with poorer health (House, 2002), teasing apart the differential impacts of race and SES on health outcomes in general, let alone following social loss, poses substantial difficulty (Kaufman, Cooper, & McGee, 1997; Orbuch & Fine, 2003).

Bereavement

Little research has focused on racial and SES differences in the context of the widowhood effect (see Elwert & Christakis, 2006, for a notable exception). The data that have emerged concerning race have painted an unclear picture (Johnson et al., 2000; Schaefer, Quesenberry, & Wi, 1995). A large-scale study of elderly couples in the United States by Elwert and Christakis (2006) reported a greater risk of bereavement-related mortality in Whites who were married to Whites, after accounting for demographic, SES, health, and other contextual factors. However, the authors did not detect a widowhood effect operating among African Americans married to African Americans. For interracial couples, the authors noted that men whose deceased wives were White, but not those whose wives were African American, experienced increased mortality risk. Data on the differential effects of SES on bereavement outcomes have not yielded meaningful differences; researchers have suggested that ties between race and SES may have made detecting independent contributions of SES to bereavement outcomes more difficult (M. S. Stroebe, Hansson, et al., 2001; W. Stroebe & Stroebe, 1987). Future research should tease apart cultural from SES-based practices.

Elwert and Christakis attribute their findings concerning the lack of widowerhood effect among African American men to three racial differences among African Americans and Whites. First, more unmarried elderly African Americans live with kin than do their White counterparts (see Coward, Lee, Netzer, Cutler, & Danigelis, 1996; Taylor & Chatters, 1991), and therefore they may receive those health benefits conferred by having a spouse. Second, greater religiosity in the African American community may afford spiritual comfort and additional social connections that are beneficial in the aftermath of losing a spouse. Third, the less-gendered division of household chores and child rearing in African American households may render African Americans more self-sufficient and prepared to deal with the practical demands of widower life. Other data indicate that African Americans experience a lower lifetime prevalence of major depressive disorder than Whites, and this differential susceptibility may interact with spousal loss to influence postloss outcomes (D. R. Williams et al., 2007). These are tractable hypotheses that can be translated into future psychological research questions, and the literature in this area will benefit by understanding the psychological processes linking race and health outcomes following spousal loss.

Divorce

Although divorce rates vary widely by race, most research on the associations between race and divorce has focused on structural factors that account for racial differences in frequency and not on interactional factors that may predict outcomes following divorce (Orbuch & Brown, 2006). Some reports have presented health differences among divorced people by race. Kobrin and Hendershot (1977) stated that mortality due to diabetes mellitus and arteriosclerotic heart disease is higher among divorced non-White men. Data from the National Center for Health Statistics (1970) revealed that among White women and both White and non-White men, the suicide rate was higher for those who divorced than for any other marital status. More recently, Schaefer and colleagues (1995) and Johnson and colleagues (2000) found no differences in suicide among divorced or separated African Americans and Whites. Lillard and Waite (1995) also found no significant differences across African American and White divorcees with respect to mortality risk, when measures of household income were included; however, when household income was removed from the analysis, race emerged a significant predictor of mortality such that African Americans experienced a higher mortality risk than Whites. Similarly, in a study conducted with retired people aged 51 to 61, Pienta and colleagues (2000) found that compared with Whites, African Americans and Hispanics experienced significantly poorer health outcomes following divorce; however, this study did not take into account measures of SES. Thus far there is limited evidence that SES moderates divorce outcomes, but this may be due to (a) complex interactive factors of race and SES and/or (b) race and SES accounting for overlapping variance in outcomes and therefore being difficult to statistically tease apart (see M. S. Stroebe, Hansson, et al., 2001; W. Stroebe & Stroebe, 1987).

Orbuch and Brown (2006) summarized that most research on associations between race and divorce has focused on structural predictors of divorce, echoing a call to focus instead on how interactions among various predictors (e.g. race, SES) forecast divorce outcomes. For example, Varner and Mandara

(2009) found that among divorced African American women, those with fewer financial resources experienced greater symptoms of depression. The authors noted that this effect has previously not been observed among White women, suggesting a possible interaction of race and SES on psychological well-being. Thus, evidence indicates that differences in sociodemographic variables between married and divorced adults may partially account for differences in all-cause mortality (e.g., Dupre, Beck, & Meadows, 2009). To date, no data have implicated changes in finances as a unique factor in the association between divorce and poorer health outcomes; however, differences in SES between married and divorced adults do account for substantial differences in all-cause mortality (Lillard & Waite, 1995).

Age

Despite a general negative association between age and health outcomes, younger people tend to suffer more than older people following romantic loss (Sbarra et al., 2011; W. Stroebe & Schut, 2001). For example, in the meta-analysis conducted by Sbarra et al. (2011), adults who were younger at the time of their divorce evidenced greater risk of early death than those who were older at the time of their divorce. Although causal conclusions cannot be generated from these correlational data, the findings suggest that those who seem to suffer the most are those who stand to lose the most life-years in an established partnership.

Bereavement

Contrary to popular notions (e.g., Gove, 1973), younger bereaved people experience greater mortality risk than older bereaved people (Hu & Goldman, 1990; Johnson et al., 2000). In a large-scale study of spousal pairs, Schaefer and colleagues (1995) found that the relative risks of mortality for bereaved men and women in the youngest age category (ages 40–49) were 3 to 4 times that of their same-sex, married peers. Similarly, in an investigation of mortality following bereavement in a Finnish cohort, Martikainen and Valkonen (1996) found that younger bereaved adults (ages 35–64) experienced significantly increased mortality, and this excess was significantly higher for men (70%) than for women (25%). Older widowed adults (ages 65–74) evidenced lower rates of excess mortality (20% for men, 10% for women), and among those in the oldest group (ages 75+), there was no excess mortality risk for women; however, there remained some risk for men (10%). Similarly, Hu and Goldman (1990) found that widowed individuals in their 20s and 30s had as much as a tenfold increase in mortality risk compared with their same-sex married peers.

One potential explanation for this effect is that younger people are more likely to lose a spouse to an unanticipated, traumatic event, whereas older people more often lose their partners to chronic diseases, such as cancer and cardiovascular disease (W. Stroebe & Schut, 2001). Some data have suggested that unexpected deaths, especially for those who hold external control beliefs, are associated with greater depression and more somatic complaints (W. Stroebe et al., 1988). In addition, Smith and Zick (1986) found that widowers experience increased mortality risk when their wives' deaths are sudden, rather than after prolonged illness. Although younger folks may therefore suffer more in the immediate aftermath of a loss, this increased risk may disappear over time because of the greater rate of recovery of younger widows and widowers (Sanders, 1981).

M. S. Stroebe and colleagues (2007) cautioned that we must consider age effects in bereavement carefully. For example, people who reside in juvenile detention centers, nursing and retirement homes, prisons, and mental hospitals, are often excluded from analysis, and mortality risk is greater for frail individuals regardless of marital status. Thus, simply looking at age difference comparisons "detract[s] from understanding the unique natures and different contexts of bereavement in younger versus older life" (p. 2447). For example, Smith and Zick (1986) found that the younger bereaved people's increased mortality risk is primarily due to greater unexpected partner deaths among younger people. Thus, the higher rate of unexpected deaths among younger individuals may be driving an observed age effect.

Divorce

There are substantially fewer studies addressing the role of age in mortality risk following divorce, and those that do exist are often reported in tandem with data on bereavement and in the context of other moderators (e.g., Hu & Goldman, 1990; Johnson et al., 2000). In addition to their findings concerning the roles of gender and age on mortality risk following bereavement, Hu and Goldman (1990) found that divorced people in their 20s and 30s experienced greater mortality risk compared with their married peers (also see Sbarra et al., 2011). Similarly, Gove (1973) found that for men between ages 35 and 44, being single or divorced was associated with increased mortality risk. In contrast, K. Williams and Umberson (2004) found that although 30 year-old men transitioning into divorce experienced a 34% increase in the probability of reporting excellent or very good health, this advantage decreased with age such that men beyond age 54 who transition into divorce are 32% less likely to report excellent or very good health.

One explanation for these observations is that, compared with younger people, older adults may have fewer options to form new romantic relationships. In addition, some data have shown that older divorcees are less likely to remarry. Another idea is that for younger men, divorce may reduce the negative health consequences of being in an unhappy marriage and in so doing lead to improved health. Younger people may be better able to form a new social network following divorce, whereas older people, who may have long-standing relationships within a social network with their ex-spouses, may struggle more. Thus, more careful research into the aftermath of divorce among people at different stages of life may shed light on the impact of age on health following divorce. In some cases, this may simply mean returning to existing data and separately analyzing data from divorced and bereaved people.

Remarriage

Studying remarriage is important for understanding associations between loss and health; if a separation or loss experience is stressful and confers risk of increased morbidity or mortality, then these effects should be mitigated once people remarry. Remarriage may reduce mortality following bereavement and divorce (Hughes & Waite, 2009; Noda et al., 2009). In an examination of data from the Charleston Heart Study, Sbarra and Nietert (2009) found that those who divorced experienced a significantly shorter time to death than those who were married, never married, or widowed. In addition, they found that remaining separated or divorced is significantly associated with early mortality, whereas remarrying eliminated this risk. The authors concluded that "it is not the experience of separation or divorce per se that confers risk, but rather some combination of intrapersonal and situational determinants associated with not remarrying after a separation experience" (p. 111). Two obvious possibilities in this regard are depression and hostility, both of which predict the likelihood of divorce among the married. Depressed or highly hostile people may have trouble reestablishing new relationships. Over time, it is not the divorce that ultimately predicts their morbidity or mortality but rather the depression or hostility that decreases the likelihood of getting into a new relationship.

Some data, however, have suggested that remarriage following divorce does not affect health or alter baseline mortality risk (Brockmann & Klein, 2004; Zhang & Hayward, 2006). Zhang and Hayward (2006) found that, compared with their married counterparts, divorced women are at an increased risk of cardiovascular disease in late midlife regardless of remarriage, whereas remarried (previously divorced) men evidenced less risk of cardiovascular disease. Brockmann and Klein (2004) found that over time, the negative effects of divorce and bereavement attenuated for remarried women but not remarried men. Hughes and Waite (2009) found that those with multiple marital interruptions fared no more poorly than those with a single marital interruption, which suggests that the stress surrounding the end of a marriage may not be cumulative. The observation that most acute effects of romantic loss occur in the time immediately following the loss (i.e., not when a person is remarried) may also explain the lack of effects of remarriage; that is, whatever negative aspects a separation experience exerts may take place prior to remarriage and occur regardless of subsequent remarriage. Future investigations should take care to measure and better account for the changing aspects of the relationship-dissolution process when examining the role of remarriage in subsequent health, because some benefits of marriage may be more important for some people than for others. For example, perhaps those with chronic health conditions may experience greater benefits from remarriage than those without such difficulties. If Bob relies on Joan for his blood pressure medication, and on obtaining a divorce from Joan, he remarries a woman who will remind him to take his blood pressure medication, remarriage may attenuate the negative impact that Bob's high blood pressure has on his health by ensuring that he takes his blood pressure medication (see Chapter 5, this volume, for further discussion of health behaviors).

CONCLUSION

In this chapter, we reviewed a diverse body of data collected across several disciplines to provide an overview of the literature on moderators of outcomes following divorce and bereavement. A key issue for future research is that most moderators with empirical support are sociodemographic (and, therefore, fairly static) rather than psychological. That we can differentiate people along these variables suggests that methods to screen and identify those most at risk may be useful, but research is needed into the processes that mediate the moderator effects. That is, the moderators discussed in this chapter do not exert their health effects in isolation. Consider the association between gender and health outcomes following both bereavement and divorce. Why do men fare worse? Do they have worse health behaviors? Are they more stressed? Do men miss the benefits of social support, which may be easier for women to garner? If public health benefits emerge by studying these moderators, then revealing these benefits rest on identifying differential pathways between loss and health among high- and low-risk groups.

One way to begin this endeavor is to focus the research in this area more squarely on psychological variables. Few studies have examined how attachment styles, personality, or psychological well-being interact with health-relevant biological processes to increase or decrease risk of poor health outcomes following romantic loss. In doing so, we can begin to ask questions about differential pathways. Why are younger people more likely to die early after a social loss experience? What types of contact with an ex-partner are associated with chronic activation of the physiological stress response? If remarriage attenuates risk, what social and behavioral changes might explain the protection afforded by a new relationship? These questions and others like them will form the basis of the next generation of research on social loss and health.

REFERENCES

Adams, K., & Pasley, K. (2006). Coparenting following divorce and relationship dissolution. In M. A. Fine & G. H. Harvey (Eds.), *Handbook of divorce and relationship dissolution* (pp. 241–261). Mahwah, NJ: Erlbaum.

Allen, K. R., Blieszner, R., & Roberto, K. A. (2000). Families in the middle and later years: A review and critique of research in the 1990s. *Journal of Marriage and Family, 62*, 911–926. doi:10.1111/j.1741-3737.2000.00911.x

Amato, P. R. (2000). The consequences of divorce for adults and children. *Journal of Marriage and Family, 62*, 1269–1287. doi:10.1111/j.1741-3737.2000.01269.x

Amato, P. R. (2010). Research on divorce: Continuing trends and new developments. *Journal of Marriage and Family, 72*, 650–666. doi:10.1111/j.1741-3737.2010.00723.x

Amato, P. R., & Hohmann-Marriott, B. (2007). A comparison of high- and low-distress marriages that end in divorce. *Journal of Marriage and Family, 69*, 621–638. doi:10.1111/j.1741-3737.2007.00396.x

Appels, A., Golombeck, B., Gorgels, A., de Vreede, J., & van Breukelen, G. (2000). Behavioral risk factors of sudden cardiac arrest. *Journal of Psychosomatic Research, 48*, 463–469. doi:10.1016/S0022-3999(99)00087-2

Barefoot, J. C., Brummett, B. H., Helms, M. J., Mark, D. B., Siegler, I. C., & Williams, R. B. (2000). Depressive symptoms and survival of patients with coronary artery disease. *Psychosomatic Medicine, 62*, 790–795.

Blee, K., & Tickamyer, A. (1995). Racial differences in men's attitudes about women's gender roles. *Journal of Marriage and Family, 57*, 21–30. doi:10.2307/353813

Boerner, K., Wortman, C. B., & Bonanno, G. A. (2005). Resilient or at risk? A 4-year study of older adults who initially showed high or low distress following conjugal loss. *The Journals of Gerontology: Series B. Psychological Sciences and Social Sciences, 60*, P67–P73. doi:10.1093/geronb/60.2.P67

Bonanno, G. A. (2004). Loss, trauma, and human resilience: Have we underestimated the human capacity to thrive after extremely adverse events? *American Psychologist, 59*, 20–28. doi:10.1037/0003-066X.59.1.20

Bonanno, G. A. (2009). *The other side of sadness*. New York, NY: Basic Books.

Bonanno, G. A., & Kaltman, S. (1999). Toward an integrative perspective on bereavement. *Psychological Bulletin, 125*, 760–776. doi:10.1037/0033-2909.125.6.760

Bonanno, G. A., Mihalecz, M. C., & LeJeune, J. T. (1999). The core emotion themes of conjugal loss. *Motivation and Emotion, 23,* 175–201. doi:10.1023/A:1021398730909

Bonanno, G. A., Wortman, C. B., Lehman, D. R., Tweed, R. G., Haring, M., Sonnega, J., . . . Nesse, R. M. (2002). Resilience to loss and chronic grief: A prospective study from preloss to 18-months postloss. *Journal of Personality and Social Psychology, 83,* 1150–1164. doi:10.1037/0022-3514.83.5.1150

Booth, A., & Amato, P. (1991). Divorce and psychological stress. *Journal of Health and Social Behavior, 32,* 396–407. doi:10.2307/2137106

Braver, S. L., Shapiro, J. R., & Goodman, M. R. (2006). Consequences of divorce for parents. In M. A. Fine & G. H. Harvey (Eds.), *Handbook of divorce and relationship dissolution* (pp. 313–337). Mahwah, NJ: Erlbaum.

Brockmann, H., & Klein, T. (2004). Love and death in Germany: The marital biography and its effect on mortality. *Journal of Marriage and Family, 66,* 567–581. doi:10.1111/j.0022-2445.2004.00038.x

Buckley, T., McKinley, S., Tofler, G., & Bartrop, R. (2010). Cardiovascular risk in early bereavement: A literature review and proposed mechanisms. *International Journal of Nursing Studies, 47,* 229–238. doi:10.1016/j.ijnurstu.2009.06.010

Coward, R. T., Lee, G. R., Netzer, J. K., Cutler, S. J., & Danigelis, N. L. (1996). Racial differences in the household composition of elders by age, gender, and area of residence. *International Journal of Aging & Human Development, 42,* 205–227. doi:10.2190/WD8G-450Q-HC77-2K2G

Datson, S. L., & Marwit, S. J. (1997). Personality constructs and perceived presence of deceased loved ones. *Death Studies, 21,* 131–146. doi:10.1080/074811897202047

Depner, C. E., & Ingersoll-Dayton, B. (1985). Conjugal social support: Patterns in later life. *Journal of Gerontology, 40,* 761–766.

Duck, S., & Wood, J. T. (2006). What goes up may come down: Sex and gendered patterns in relationship dissolution. In M. A. Fine & G. H. Harvey (Eds.), *Handbook of divorce and relationship dissolution* (pp. 169–187). Mahwah, NJ: Erlbaum.

Duffy, M. E. (1993). Social networks and social support of recently divorced women. *Public Health Nursing, 10,* 19–24. doi:10.1111/j.1525-1446.1993.tb00015.x

Dupre, M. E., Beck, A. N., & Meadows, S. O. (2009). Marital trajectories and mortality among US adults. *American Journal of Epidemiology, 170,* 546–555. doi:10.1093/aje/kwp194

Duran-Aydintug, C. (1998). Emotional support during separation. *Journal of Divorce & Remarriage, 29,* 121–141. doi:10.1300/J087v29n03_08

Ebrahim, S., Wannamethee, G., McCallum, A., Walker, M., & Shaper, A. G. (1995). Marital status, change in marital status, and mortality in middle-aged British men. *American Journal of Epidemiology, 142,* 834–842.

Elwert, F., & Christakis, N. (2006). Widowhood and race. *American Sociological Review, 71,* 16–41. doi:10.1177/000312240607100102

Elwert, F., & Christakis, N. (2008). Wives and ex-wives: A new test for homogamy bias in the widowhood effect. *Demography, 45,* 851–873. doi:10.1353/dem.0.0029

Field, N. P., Gal-Oz, E., & Bonanno, G. A. (2003). Continuing bonds and adjustment at 5 years after the death of a spouse. *Journal of Consulting and Clinical Psychology, 71,* 110–117. doi:10.1037/0022-006X.71.1.110

Fine, M. A., & Harvey, J. H. (Eds.). (2006). *Handbook of divorce and relationship dissolution.* Mahwah, NJ: Erlbaum.

Fischer, T. F. C., de Graaf, P. M., & Kalmijn, M. (2005). Friendly and antagonistic contact between former spouses after divorce: Patterns and determinants. *Journal of Family Issues, 26,* 1131–1163. doi:10.1177/0192513X05275435

Friedman, H. S. (2007). Personality, disease, and self-healing. In H. S. Friedman & R. C. Silver (Eds.), *Foundations of health psychology* (pp. 172–199). New York, NY: Oxford University Press.

Gerra, G., Monti, D., Panerai, A. E., Sacerdote, P., Anderlini, R., Avanzini, P., . . . Franceschi, C. (2003). Long-term immune-endocrine effects of bereavement: Relationships with anxiety levels and mood. *Psychiatry Research, 121,* 145–158. doi:10.1016/S0165-1781(03)00255-5

Goldman, N. (1993). Marriage selection and mortality patterns: Inferences and fallacies. *Demography, 30,* 189–208. doi:10.2307/2061837

Gove, W. R. (1973). Sex, marital status, and mortality. *American Journal of Sociology, 79,* 45–67. doi:10.1086/225505

Hall, M., & Irwin, M. (2001). Physiological indices of functioning in bereavement. In M. S. Stroebe, R. O. Hansson, W. Stroebe, & H. Schut (Eds.), *Handbook of bereavement research: Consequences, coping, and care* (pp. 473–492). Washington, DC: American Psychological Association. doi:10.1037/10436-020

Hays, W. C., & Mindel, C. H. (1973). Extended kinship relations in Black and White families. *Journal of Marriage and Family, 35,* 51–57. doi:10.2307/351096

Hemström, Ö. (1996). Is marriage dissolution linked to differences in mortality risks for men and women? *Journal of Marriage and Family, 58,* 366–378. doi:10.2307/353502

Hetherington, E. M., & Kelly, J. (2002). *For better or for worse: Divorce reconsidered.* New York, NY: Norton.

Holt-Lunstad, J., Smith, T.B., & Layton, J.B. (2010). Social relationships and mortality risk: A meta-analytic review. *PLoS Medicine, 7,* e1000316. DOI: 10.1371/journal.pmed.1000316.

House, J. S. (2002). Understanding social factors and inequalities in health: 20th century progress and 21st century prospects. *Journal of Health and Social Behavior, 43,* 125–142. doi:10.2307/3090192

House, J. S., Landis, K. R., & Umberson, D. (1988, July 29). Social relationships and health. *Science, 241*(4865), 540–545. doi:10.1126/science.3399889

Hu, Y. R., & Goldman, N. (1990). Mortality differentials by marital status: An international comparison. *Demography, 27,* 233–250. doi:10.2307/2061451

Hughes, M. E., & Waite, L. J. (2009). Marital biography and health at mid-life. *Journal of Health and Social Behavior, 50,* 344–358. doi:10.1177/002214650905000307

Ikeda, A., Iso, H., Toyoshima, H., Fujino, Y., Mizoue, T., Yoshimura, T., . . . Tamakoshi, A. (2007). Marital status and mortality among Japanese men and women: The Japan Collaborative Cohort Study. *BMC Public Health, 7,* 73–80. doi:10.1186/1471-2458-7-73

Johnson, N. J., Backlund, E., Sorlie, P. D., & Loveless, C. A. (2000). Marital status and mortality: The National Longitudinal Mortality Study. *Annals of Epidemiology, 10,* 224–238. doi:10.1016/S1047-2797(99)00052-6

Jones, M. P., Bartrop, R. W., Forcier, L., & Penny, R. (2010). The long-term impact of bereavement upon spouse health: A 10-year follow-up. *Acta Neuropsychiatrica, 22,* 212–217. doi:10.1111/j.1601-5215.2010.00482.x

Kalmijn, M., & Monden, C. W. S. (2006). Are the negative effects of divorce on well-being dependent on marital quality? *Journal of Marriage and Family, 68,* 1197–1213. doi:10.1111/j.1741-3737.2006.00323.x

Kaufman, J. S., Cooper, R. S., & McGee, D. L. (1997). Socioeconomic status and health in Blacks and Whites: The problem of residual confounding and the resiliency of race. *Epidemiology, 8,* 621–628.

Kiecolt-Glaser, J. K., Fisher, L. D., Ogrocki, P., Stout, J. C., Speicher, C. E., & Glaser, R. (1987). Marital quality, marital disruption, and immune function. *Psychosomatic Medicine, 49,* 13–34.

Kitson, G. C., & Morgan, L. A. (1990). The multiple consequences of divorce: A decade review. *Journal of Marriage and Family, 52,* 913–924. doi:10.2307/353310

Klass, D., & Walter, J. (1993). Processes of grieving: How bonds are continued. In M. S. Stroebe, W. Stroebe, & R. O. Hansson (Eds.), *Handbook of bereavement: Theory, research, and intervention* (pp. 431–448). Cambridge, England: Cambridge University Press.

Kobrin, F. E., & Hendershot, G. E. (1977). Do family ties reduce mortality? Evidence from the United States, 1966–1968. *Journal of Marriage and Family, 39,* 737–745. doi:10.2307/350478

Kposowa, A. J. (2000). Marital status and suicide in the national longitudinal mortality study. *Journal of Epidemiology and Community Health, 54,* 254–261. doi:10.1136/jech.54.4.254

Kramrei, E., Coit, C., Martin, S., Fogo, W., & Mahoney, A. (2007). Post-divorce adjustment and social relationships: A meta-analytic review. *Journal of Divorce & Remarriage, 46,* 145–166. doi:10.1300/J087v46n03_09

Lennon, M. C., & Rosenfield, S. (1994). Relative fairness and the division of housework: The importance of options. *American Journal of Sociology, 100,* 506–531.

Lichtenstein, P., Gatz, M., & Berg, S. (1998). A twin study of mortality after spousal bereavement. *Psychological Medicine, 28,* 635–643. doi:10.1017/S0033291798006692

Lillard, L. A., & Waite, L. J. (1995). 'Til death do us part: Marital disruption and mortality. *American Journal of Sociology, 100*, 1131–1156. doi:10.1086/230634

Lorenz, F. O., Wickrama, K. A. S., Conger, R. D., & Elder, G. H. (2006). The short-term and decade-long effects of divorce on women's midlife health. *Journal of Health and Social Behavior, 47*, 111–125. doi:10.1177/002214650604700202

Manzoli, L., Villari, P., Pirone, G. M., & Boccia, A. (2007). Marital status and mortality in the elderly: A systematic review and meta-analysis. *Social Science & Medicine, 64*, 77–94. doi:10.1016/j.socscimed.2006.08.031

Martikainen, P., & Valkonen, T. (1996). Mortality after the death of a spouse: Rates and causes of death in a large Finnish cohort. *American Journal of Public Health, 86*, 1087–1093. doi:10.2105/AJPH.86.8_Pt_1.1087

Masheter, C. (1991). Postdivorce relationships between ex-spouses: The roles of attachment and interpersonal conflict. *Journal of Marriage and Family, 53*, 103–110. doi:10.2307/353136

Masuda, M. (2006). Perspectives on premarital postdissolution relationships: Account-making of friendships between former romantic partners. In M. A. Fine & G. H. Harvey (Eds.), *Handbook of divorce and relationship dissolution* (pp. 113–132). Mahwah, NJ: Erlbaum.

Musselman, D. L., Evans, D. L., & Nemeroff, C. B. (1998). The relationship of depression to cardiovascular disease. *Archives of General Psychiatry, 55*, 580–592. doi:10.1001/archpsyc.55.7.580

National Center for Health Statistics. (1970). *Mortality from selected causes by marital status* (Series 20, Nos. 8A & 8B, USDHEW). Washington, DC: U.S. Government Printing Office.

Nelson, G. (1995). Women's social networks and social support following marital separation. *Journal of Divorce & Remarriage, 23*, 149–170. doi:10.1300/J087v23n01_10

Noda, T., Ojima, T., Hayasaka, S., Hagihara, A., Takayanagi, R., & Nobutomo, K. (2009). The health impact of remarriage behavior on chronic obstructive pulmonary disease: Findings from the US longitudinal survey. *BMC Public Health, 9*(412). doi:10.1186/1471-2458-9-412

Orbuch, T. L., & Brown, E. (2006). Divorce in the context of being African American. In M. A. Fine & G. H. Harvey (Eds.), *Handbook of divorce and relationship dissolution* (pp. 481–498). Mahwah, NJ: Erlbaum.

Orbuch, T. L., & Eyster, S. L. (1997). Division of household labor among Black couples and White couples. *Social Forces, 76*, 301–332.

Orbuch, T. L., & Fine, M. A. (2003). The context of race/ethnicity in interpersonal relationships: Crossing the chasm. *Journal of Social and Personal Relationships, 20*, 147–152.

Osler, M., McGue, M., Lund, R., & Christensen, K. (2008). Marital status and twins' health and behavior: An analysis of middle-aged Danish twins. *Psychosomatic Medicine, 70*, 482–487. doi:10.1097/PSY.0b013e31816f857b

Overbeek, G., Vollebergh, W., de Graaf, R., Scholte, R., de Kemp, R., & Engels, R. (2006). Longitudinal associations of marital quality and marital dissolution with the incidence of DSM–III–R disorders. *Journal of Family Psychology, 20*, 284–291. doi:10.1037/0893-3200.20.2.284

Parkes, C. M., Benjamin, B., & Fitzgerald, R. G. (1969). Broken heart: A statistical study of increased mortality among widowers. *BMJ, 1*, 740–743. doi:10.1136/bmj.1.5646.740

Parkes, C. M., & Prigerson, H. G. (2010). *Bereavement: Studies of grief in adult life*. New York, NY: Routledge.

Pienta, A., Hayward, M. D., & Jenkins, K. R. (2000). Health consequences of marriage for the retirement years. *Journal of Family Issues, 21*, 559–586. doi:10.1177/019251300021005003

Pinquart, M. (2003). Loneliness in married, widowed, divorced, and never-married older adults. *Journal of Social and Personal Relationships, 20*, 31–53.

Prigerson, H., Silverman, G. K., Jacobs, S., Maciejewski, P., Kasl, S. V., & Rosenheck, R. (2001). Traumatic grief, disability and the underutilization of health services: A preliminary look. *Primary Psychiatry, 8*, 61–69.

Raphael, B., Minkov, C., & Dobson, M. (1993). Psychotherapeutic and pharmacological intervention for bereaved persons. In M. S. Stroebe, W. Stroebe, & R. O. Hansson (Eds.), *Handbook of bereavement: Theory, research, and intervention* (pp. 587–612). Cambridge, England: Cambridge University Press.

Rugulies, R. (2002). Depression as a predictor for coronary heart disease: A review and meta-analysis. *American Journal of Preventive Medicine, 23*, 51–61. doi:10.1016/S0749-3797(02)00439-7

Sanders, C. M. (1981). Comparison of younger and older spouses in bereavement outcome. *Omega, 11*, 217–232.

Saudino, K. J., Pedersen, N. L., Lichtenstein, P., McClearn, G. E., & Plomin, R. (1997). Can personality explain genetic influences on life events? *Journal of Personality and Social Psychology, 72*, 196–206. doi:10.1037/0022-3514.72.1.196

Sbarra, D. A. (2012). Marital dissolution and physical health outcomes: A review of mechanisms. In L. Campbell, J. La Guardia, J. Olson, & M. Zanna (Eds.), *The science of the couple: The Ontario Symposium* (Vol. 12, pp. 205–227). Florence, KY: Psychology Press.

Sbarra, D. A., & Emery, R. E. (2005). The emotional sequelae of nonmarital relationship dissolution: Analysis of change and intraindividual variability over time. *Personal Relationships, 12*, 213–232. doi:10.1111/j.1350-4126.2005.00112.x

Sbarra, D. A., Law, R. L., Lee, L. A., & Mason, A. E. (2009). Marital dissolution and blood pressure reactivity: Evidence for the specificity of emotional intrusion-hyperarousal and task-rated emotional difficulty. *Psychosomatic Medicine, 71*, 532–540. doi:10.1097/PSY.0b013e3181a23eee

Sbarra, D. A., Law, R. W., & Portley, R. M. (2011). Divorce and death: A meta-analysis and research agenda for clinical, social, and health psychology. *Perspectives on Psychological Science, 6*, 454–474. doi:10.1177/1745691611414724

Sbarra, D. A., & Nietert, P. J. (2009). Divorce and death: Forty years of the Charleston Heart Study. *Psychological Science, 20,* 107–113. doi:10.1111/j.1467-9280.2008.02252.x

Schaefer, C., Quesenberry, C. P., & Wi, S. (1995). Mortality following conjugal bereavement and the effects of a shared environment. *American Journal of Epidemiology, 141,* 1142–1152.

Shuchter, S. R., & Zisook, S. (1993). The course of normal grief. In M. S. Stroebe, W. Stroebe, & R. O. Hansson (Eds.), *Handbook of bereavement: Theory, research, and intervention* (pp. 23 43). Cambridge, England: Cambridge University Press. doi:10.1017/CBO9780511664076.003

Smith, K. R., & Zick, C. D. (1986). Risk of mortality following widowhood: Age and sex differences by mode of death. *Biodemography and Social Biology, 43,* 59–71. doi:10.1080/19485565.1996.9988913

Sprecher, S., Felmlee, D., Schmeeckle, M., & Shu, X. (2006). No breakup occurs on an island: Social networks and relationship dissolution. In M. A. Fine & G. H. Harvey (Eds.), *Handbook of divorce and relationship dissolution* (pp. 457–478). Mahwah, NJ: Erlbaum.

Stroebe, M. S. (2010). Coping with bereavement. In S. Folkman (Ed.), *The Oxford handbook of stress, health, and coping* (pp. 148–172). New York, NY: Oxford University Press.

Stroebe, M. S., Folkman, S., Hansson, R. O., & Schut, H. (2006). The prediction of bereavement outcome: Development of an integrative risk factor framework. *Social Science & Medicine, 63,* 2440–2451. doi:10.1016/j.socscimed.2006.06.012

Stroebe, M. S., Hansson, R. O., Stroebe, W., & Schut, H. (Eds.). (2001). *Handbook of bereavement research: Consequences, coping, and care.* Washington, DC: American Psychological Association. doi:10.1037/10436-000

Stroebe, M. S., Schut, H., & Stroebe, W. (2007). Health outcomes of bereavement. *The Lancet, 370,* 1960–1973. doi:10.1016/S0140-6736(07)61816-9

Stroebe, M. S., Stroebe, W., & Schut, H. (2001). Gender differences in adjustment to bereavement: An empirical and theoretical review. *Review of General Psychology, 5,* 62–83. doi:10.1037/1089-2680.5.1.62

Stroebe, W., & Schut, H. (2001). Risk factors in bereavement outcome: A methodological and empirical review. In M. S. Stroebe, R. O. Hansson, W. Stroebe, & H. Schut (Eds.), *Handbook of bereavement research: Consequences, coping, and care* (pp. 349–371). Washington, DC: American Psychological Association. doi:10.1037/10436-015

Stroebe, W., Schut, H., & Stroebe, M. (2005). Grief work, disclosure and counseling: Do they help the bereaved? *Clinical Psychology Review, 25,* 395–414. doi:10.1016/j.cpr.2005.01.004

Stroebe, W., & Stroebe, M. S. (1987). *Bereavement and health: The psychological and physical consequences of partner loss.* New York, NY: Cambridge University Press. doi:10.1017/CBO9780511720376

Stroebe, W., Stroebe, M. S., & Domittner, G. (1988). Individual and situational differences in recovery from bereavement: A risk group identified. *Journal of Social Issues, 44*, 143–158. doi:10.1111/j.1540-4560.1988.tb02082.x

Taylor, R. J., & Chatters, L. M. (1991). Extended family networks of older Black adults. *The Journals of Gerontology: Series B. Social Sciences, 46*, S210–S217.

Taylor, S. (2007). Social support. In H. S. Friedman & R. C. Silver (Eds.), *Foundations of health psychology* (pp. 145–171). New York, NY: Oxford University Press.

Thompson, L. W., Breckenridge, J. N., Gallagher, D., & Peterson, J. A. (1984). Effects of bereavement on self-perceptions of physical health in elderly widows and widowers. *Journal of Gerontology, 39*, 309–314.

Tucker, J. S., Friedman, H. S., Wingard, D. L., & Schwartz, J. E. (1996). Marital history at midlife as a predictor of longevity: Alternative explanations to the protective effects of marriage. *Health Psychology, 15*, 94–101. doi:10.1037/0278-6133.15.2.94

Uchino, B. N. (2004). *Social support and physical health: Understanding the health consequences of relationships.* New Haven, CT: Yale University Press.

Uchino, B. N. (2006). Social support and health: A review of physiological processes potentially underlying links to disease outcomes. *Journal of Behavioral Medicine, 29*, 377–387. doi:10.1007/s10865-006-9056-5

Umberson, D. (1987). Family status and health behaviors: Social control as a dimension of social integration. *Journal of Health and Social Behavior, 28*, 306–319. doi:10.2307/2136848

Umberson, D. (1992). Gender, marital status and the social control of health behavior. *Social Science & Medicine, 34*, 907–917. doi:10.1016/0277-9536(92)90259-S

van der Houwen, K., Stroebe, M. S., Stroebe, W., Schut, H., van den Bout, J., & Wijngaards-de Meig, L. (2010). Risk factors for bereavement outcome: A multivariate approach. *Death Studies, 34*, 195–220. doi:10.1080/07481180903559196

Varner, F., & Mandara, J. (2009). Marital transitions and changes in African American mothers' depressive symptoms: The buffering role of financial resources. *Journal of Family Psychology, 23*, 839–847. doi:10.1037/a0017007

Wade, T. J., & Pevalin, D. J. (2004). Marital transitions and mental health. *Journal of Health and Social Behavior, 45*, 155–170. doi:10.1177/002214650404500203

Waite, L. J., Luo, Y., & Lewin, A. C. (2009). Marital happiness and marital stability: Consequences for psychological well-being. *Social Science Research, 38*, 201–212. doi:10.1016/j.ssresearch.2008.07.001

Wang, H., & Amato, P. R. (2000). Predictors of divorce adjustment: Stressors, resources, and definitions. *Journal of Marriage and Family, 62*, 655–668. doi:10.1111/j.1741-3737.2000.00655.x

Whisman, M. A., Tolejko, N., & Chatav, Y. (2007). Social consequences of personality disorders: Probability and timing of marriage and probability of marital disruption. *Journal of Personality Disorders, 21*, 690–695. doi:10.1521/pedi.2007.21.6.690

Williams, B. R., Baker, P. S., Allman, R. M., & Roseman, J. M. (2007). Bereavement among African American and White older adults. *Journal of Aging and Health, 19,* 313–333. doi:10.1177/0898264307299301

Williams, D. R. (1999). Race, socioeconomic status, and health: The added effects of racism and discrimination. *Annals of the New York Academy of Sciences, 896,* 173–188. doi:10.1111/j.1749-6632.1999.tb08114.x

Williams, D. R., Gonzalez, H. M., Neighbors, H., Nesse, R., Abelson, J. M., Sweetman, J., & Jackson, J. S. (2007). Prevalence and distribution of major depressive disorder in African Americans, Caribbean Blacks, and non-Hispanic Whites. *Archives of General Psychiatry, 64,* 305–315. doi:10.1001/archpsyc.64.3.305

Williams, K., & Umberson, D. (2004). Marital status, marital transitions, and health: A gendered life course perspective. *Journal of Health and Social Behavior, 45,* 81–98. doi:10.1177/002214650404500106

Zhang, Z., & Hayward, M. D. (2006). Gender, the marital life course, and cardiovascular disease in late midlife. *Journal of Marriage and Family, 68,* 639–657. doi:10.1111/j.1741-3737.2006.00280.x

5

HEALTH BEHAVIOR AND EMOTION REGULATION IN COUPLES

JANE A. SKOYEN, ANYA V. KOGAN, SARAH A. NOVAK,
AND EMILY A. BUTLER

Health behaviors can act as a form of emotion regulation—people drink to forget their troubles, smoke to relax or be more alert, exercise to feel better, or eat to cope with distress (e.g., Berking et al., 2011; Butler, Young, & Randall, 2010; Davey, Fitzpatrick, Garland, & Kilgour, 2009; Ikard, Green, & Horn, 1969; S. H. Stewart, Morris, Mellings, & Komar, 2006). This connection between emotion regulation and health behaviors becomes particularly pronounced in the context of committed romantic relationships, where it has an added layer of complexity. In addition to regulating their own emotions and health behaviors, partners in relationships become involved in each other's health-related and emotion regulation processes. Depending on the quality of the relationship and individual partner characteristics, their bond may have positive and negative effects on emotion and health (for reviews, see Kiecolt-Glaser & Newton, 2001; and Walker & Luszcz, 2009).

DOI: 10.1037/14036-006
Health and Social Relationships: The Good, the Bad, and the Complicated, Matthew L. Newman and Nicole A. Roberts (Editors)

To fully understand the complex mechanisms linking partners' health behaviors to their emotional well-being and relationship functioning, we need to consider a wide range of individual and dyadic factors. Individual factors include both partners' health conditions, their health habits and beliefs, and their capacity for emotion regulation (e.g., Aimé, Sabourin, & Ratté, 2006; Berking et al., 2011; Brennan & Shaver, 1995; Davies, Bekker, & Roosen, 2011; Davis, Shaver, & Vernon, 2003; Jáuregui Lobera, Estébanez, Santiago Fernández, Álvarez Bautista, & Garrido, 2009; S. H. Stewart et al., 2006). Dyadic factors may include relationship quality (Markey, Markey, & Birch, 2001; Ren, 1997; Rohrbaugh, Shoham, & Coyne, 2006; Schafer, Keith, & Schafer, 2000; Schafer, Schafer, & Keith, 1997), match or mismatch between the partners' health beliefs (Skoyen, Blank, Corkery, & Butler, 2012), and couples' deliberate attempts to regulate each other's emotions and behaviors. In this chapter, we suggest that the key to understanding these mechanisms is to take into account the interwoven nature of interpersonal relationships and health maintenance practices, as well as to consider the potential moderators of these effects. Although situational and personality factors undoubtedly play a role in these mechanisms as well, here we outline the models that are internal to the ongoing relationship because they allow for a better focus on the dynamic connections between emotions, relationships, and health.

Health behaviors and relationship functioning are interrelated: Health helps maintain couples' well-being, and relationship factors contribute to overall health and specific health behaviors. To better understand these associations, it is important to first differentiate between health-enhancing and health-compromising behaviors and their potential role in dyadic emotion regulation. *Health-enhancing* behaviors, such as exercise, healthy diet, and adequate sleep, along with strategies used to effectively cope with chronic illness, may improve partners' physical health and increase physical endurance (for a review, see Baum & Posluszny, 1999). These behaviors are also associated with higher health-related quality of life (Schmitz, Kruse, & Kugler, 2004; Villaverde-Gutiérrez et al., 2006). In turn, better health is linked to higher relationship quality (e.g., McPheters & Sandberg, 2010; Uchino, Cacciopo, & Kiecolt-Glaser, 1996; Wickrama, Lorenz, & Conger, 1997); therefore, health-enhancing behaviors may be associated with better relationships as well.

In contrast, *health-compromising* behaviors, such as smoking, poor dietary practices, excessive alcohol use, and lack of exercise, may undermine overall health; poorer health is in turn associated with lower relationship functioning (e.g., Dethier, Counerotte, & Blairy, 2011; Rotunda, Scherer, & Imm, 1995). However, these health-compromising behaviors may ironically contribute to couples' well-being and cohesion in the short term by temporarily improving mood by providing a distraction or an outlet for relationship conflict (Rohrbaugh, Shoham, Butler, Hasler, & Berman, 2009; Shoham, Butler, Rohrbaugh, & Trost, 2007).

Both health-enhancing and health-compromising behaviors may play a role in couples' emotion regulation, for example, when smoking, drinking, engaging in sports, dieting, or overeating become routinized ways by which partners relate to each other or self-soothe to cope with relationship stressors. Even benign health behaviors such as having an occasional drink or an over-indulgent meal may become incorporated into relationship and emotion regulation processes in a way that reinforces and exacerbates these behaviors, in which case they may contribute to more pathological forms of alcoholism or eating disorders. Although both health-enhancing and health-compromising behaviors may play a role in dyadic processes, the majority of the investigations reviewed in this chapter focused on health-compromising behaviors. Such behaviors are notoriously hard to change, and knowing what function these health habits serve for a given couple may be the key to altering them.

In this chapter, we outline several pathways through which dyadic emotion regulation and health behaviors may be linked. In the first section, we review the links between emotion, self-regulation, and health behaviors within individuals. We then discuss the connection between relationship quality and health and consider health behaviors as one of the potential mechanisms underlying this connection. In the third section, we address the role of emotion regulation strategies and focus on the reciprocal influence of partners' health habits and associated emotions. Finally, we discuss the links between partners' emotion regulation strategies and health behaviors in a dyadic context. We review several mechanisms in this final section: partners reacting to each other's health behaviors, partners making emotionally charged attempts to influence each other's health actions, and partners engaging in health behaviors to cope with relationship conflict. We address these mechanisms from a systemic viewpoint—that is, assuming that actions of one partner are interwoven with actions of the other and that patterns of dyadic health behaviors and emotion regulation (e.g., match or mismatch of health habits and emotion regulation strategies) also play a role in dyadic functioning.

WITHIN-INDIVIDUAL PROCESSES LINKING EMOTION REGULATION AND HEALTH BEHAVIORS

Within individuals, affective or cognitive states may be connected to health behaviors and attempts to self-regulate emotionally. Affective and cognitive states may be negative or positive. *Positive states* refer to emotions such as joy and happiness, as well as positive self-image and high self-efficacy;

negative states refer to fear or sadness, as well as catastrophic thinking and poor self-image. Health behavior may be used to cope with negative states directly or with the failure of another self-regulation strategy.

People experiencing negative states may attempt to cope with them through health behaviors (e.g., Aimé et al., 2006; Brennan & Shaver, 1995; Davis et al., 2003; Jáuregui Lobera et al., 2009; S. H. Stewart et al., 2006). For instance, they may consume alcohol to cope with negative emotions (e.g., Berking et al., 2011; S. H. Stewart et al., 2006) or to enhance positive emotions (Cooper, Frone, Russell, & Mudar, 1995). Changes in the relationship status may also engender both negative emotions and poor health behaviors. For example, people who are distressed due to relationship dissolution are more likely to use coping strategies that include drug or alcohol use (Davis et al., 2003).

Although some people may directly engage in a particular health behavior to alter mood, others may first attempt a different coping strategy, such as thinking positively, seeking out social support, or suppressing thoughts and emotions. Should these attempts fail, people may then engage in health behaviors to escape the aversive states that follow unsuccessful coping. For example, individuals with eating pathology tend to use maladaptive coping strategies (e.g., emotion-oriented and passive coping styles, cognitive catastrophizing), which perpetuate problematic eating habits (Aimé et al., 2006; Davies et al., 2011; Jáuregui Lobera et al., 2009).

Although the extant literature highlights examples of individuals using health-compromising behaviors to alter mood states, it is conceivable that health-enhancing behaviors are also used in this way. For example, people might exercise or engage in restorative behaviors to relieve stress or distance themselves from a conflict (e.g., Hsiao & Thayer, 1998).

RELATIONSHIP QUALITY AND HEALTH BEHAVIORS

In addition to within-individual processes linking emotion regulation and health behaviors, the quality of one's romantic relationship may play a role in these processes. A growing body of literature has provided evidence that relationship quality is positively associated with health (e.g., Burman & Margolin, 1992; Ren, 1997; Rohrbaugh et al., 2006). Higher quality of marital relationships can be linked to health-enhancing behaviors, and over time, this contributes to overall health status. The notion that relationship quality may lead to differential health behavior has received some empirical support (e.g., Markey et al., 2001; Troxel, Robles, Hall, & Buysse, 2007). Of course, the converse association is also likely and being healthy may contribute to higher quality relationships (Burman & Margolin, 1992). Health limitations or crises add stress to daily life and may detract from pleasurable shared activities. Good health, in contrast, enables partners to have more time and resources available to cope with external stressors and relationship conflict, as well as being able to engage in a wider range of pleasurable activities together.

Relationship quality, affective or cognitive states, emotion self-regulation, and health behaviors may be bidirectionally related to any or all other components. For instance, relationship quality may (a) have direct effects on one's state, self-regulatory attempts, and health behaviors or (b) moderate the relationship between any of these factors. Relationship factors may directly contribute to negative states in partners and subsequently (and indirectly) result in health behaviors in an attempt to alter those states. Relationships may also be associated with positive states and, in theory, could subsequently lead to health-enhancing behaviors. To date, the link between relationship quality and health-enhancing behaviors has not been thoroughly investigated.

Many examples of relationships contributing to negative states and subsequent health-compromising behaviors come from studies of eating habits. Schafer and colleagues examined the effects of marital discord on dietary self-efficacy (Schafer, Keith, & Schafer, 1994) as well as on dietary behaviors (Schafer et al., 1997, 2000) in married couples at different life stages. The studies used cross-sectional (Schafer et al., 1994, 1997) as well as longitudinal (Schafer et al., 2000) designs using interviews administered in the homes separately to husbands and wives. Among both husbands and wives, negative marital interactions triggered higher consumption of fat (Schafer et al., 1997), a direct association between relationship dissatisfaction and diet. Moreover, negative marital interactions predicted lower adherence to recommended dietary changes in both genders at a 10-year follow-up (Schafer et al., 2000), indicating that the effect of negative marital interactions on dietary behaviors may persist over time. Moreover, psychological distress was predictive of the extent to which husbands and wives followed recommended dietary changes (Schafer et al., 2000), providing evidence for the link between negative affective states and health-compromising behaviors.

In addition, Schafer and colleagues (1994, 1997, 2000) illustrated that for husbands and wives different factors may play a role in linking the marital relationship with health behaviors. For wives, cognitive factors such as self-esteem (Schafer et al., 1994), self-efficacy (Schafer et al., 1997), and perceived barriers to change (Schafer et al., 2000) mediated the relationship between negative marital interactions and poor dietary behaviors, whereas for husbands, negative appraisal by their spouses mediated the relationship between marital relationship and fat consumption (Schafer et al., 1997). Together, these studies suggest a pathway from negative marital interactions, through negative cognitive–affective states, to negative health behaviors.

Moreover, health behaviors may serve as tools for partners' interpersonal emotion regulation, such as when a health behavior is used to cope with a relationship issue that is hard to resolve. A daily diary study showed that on days when overweight women reported greater levels of emotional suppression, their partners reported feeling less negatively about them; however, the women also reported eating more on these days (Butler et al., 2010). Overweight women may maintain their relationships through the ineffective regulatory strategy of emotional suppression, potentially compromising their own health. In a qualitative study, Kenyon (2007) similarly demonstrated that partner emotional accessibility influenced the course and maintenance of eating disorders. Women who had an eating disorder identified their own inability to express emotion, and their husbands' emotional expression related to their disorder, as both a cause and a consequence of their eating dysregulation. The results suggest that unhealthy eating can serve a soothing function in relationships in which partners lack emotional accessibility and that partner emotion regulation is in turn affected by eating behaviors.

A recent study that focused on sleep highlights the bidirectional nature of the associations between partners' health behaviors and relationship quality (Hasler & Troxel, 2010). Theorizing that poor sleep could undermine relationship functioning and that negative partner interactions could undermine sleep, the researchers used longitudinal data collected from 29 cosleeping young adult couples over 7 days. Interestingly, for men, worse sleep predicted reports of partner interactions that were more negative, whereas for women, interpersonal interactions significantly affected their sleep. As with previous reports (Schafer et al., 1994, 1997, 2000), this study suggested gender differences in the processes by which dyadic interactions and health behaviors are linked. In this study, women's perceptions of partner interactions were predictive not just of their own sleep efficiency but also of their partners' sleep. However, men's perceptions of partner interactions were not predictive of their own or their partners' sleep patterns. This suggests that women are more "tuned-in" to the quality of partner interactions and their reports may be more predictive of the effects of relational patterns on health behaviors.

PARTNER INFLUENCES ON EMOTION REGULATION AND HEALTH BEHAVIOR

Another important contributor to our understanding of the link between relationship quality and health behavior is the role that partners play in influencing each other's emotional well-being and health habits. Evidence is presented for the following three processes: (a) partners' indirect mutual influence on health behaviors, (b) partners' deliberate attempts to control

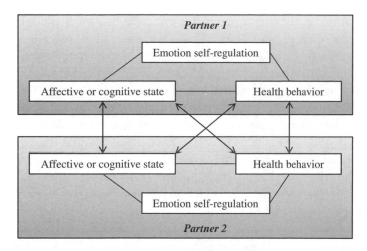

Figure 5.1. Partner influence on emotion regulation and health behaviors. Within-individual links are depicted as lines and between-partner links as bidirectional arrows.

each other's health behaviors, and (c) partners' emotional reactions to each other's health-related behaviors.

Figure 5.1 represents these three forms of influence within the dyadic framework. Partner mutual influence is reflected in the link connecting Partner 1 and Partner 2's health behaviors; emotional reactions to each other's health behaviors are reflected by the cross-over arrows starting with health behaviors and leading to affective and cognitive states; the same cross-over arrows in the opposite direction, from affective states to partners' health behaviors, represent direct partner control attempts triggered by an emotional state or a health-related belief. Evidence supporting these connections is described next.

Partners' Indirect Mutual Influence of Health Behaviors

A broad literature suggests that partners indirectly influence each other's health behavior over time. For instance, Homish and Leonard (2008) demonstrated that one partner's health behavior prior to marriage was associated with the other partner's behavior over time and that partners transmitted both positive and negative habits. Specifically, individuals whose spouses engaged in healthier eating prior to marriage were more likely to be healthy eaters later, whereas those who married unhealthy eaters were more likely to eat unhealthy foods over the first 4 years of marriage. Other studies showed that decreases in one partner's fat consumption were positively associated with dietary fat reduction in the other partner, even when these effects were not explicitly intended (e.g., Gorin et al., 2008; Shattuck, White, & Kristal, 1992).

Additional research suggests that changes in one partner's daily routine can affect the other partner's health behavior, even when partners are not in the same location (Diamond, Hicks, & Otter-Henderson, 2008). A study of 42 married or cohabiting heterosexual couples demonstrated that a short-term separation caused by work-related travel of one of the partners was associated with disturbances in sleep for both partners. Interestingly, the researchers found that a key relationship factor, attachment anxiety, moderated the effect of separation on sleep for both partners. Specifically, among the homebound partners, anxiously attached individuals exhibited greater sleep disturbances. Furthermore, the traveling partners of anxiously attached individuals also experienced greater sleep disturbances, suggesting that anxiety of the homebound partner influenced the health-enhancing behavior of both members of the dyad. Thus, attachment anxiety experienced by one of the partners may exacerbate the negative effects of physical separation on health behaviors in both partners, which supports the theoretical premise that each of the partner's affective states have mutual influence on partners' health behaviors.

Partners' Deliberate Influence Over Each Other's Health Behaviors

Research on social control highlights partner involvement in health behaviors. This literature has suggested that people attempt to influence each other's health-related behaviors through efforts to encourage, support, praise, shame, or threaten their partners to engage in or abstain from particular behaviors. These attempts are especially prevalent in married and romantically involved couples (Rook, Thuras, & Lewis, 1990; Savoca & Miller, 2001), with 73% of married individuals reporting their spouse as the primary source of social control (Lewis & Rook, 1999). Research has further suggested that social control from a partner is associated with more health-enhancing and fewer health-compromising behaviors (Lewis & Butterfield, 2007; Lewis & Rook, 1999) and predicts better health practices for people who remain consistently married over the course of 2 years (Umberson, 1992).

The results regarding social control and health behavior are somewhat mixed, however, suggesting that other dyadic and health factors, as well as the specific social control strategies used, may be important moderators. For example, Novak and Webster (2011) demonstrated that the association between social control strategies, weight-related health behavior, and well-being among married couples was moderated by the type of regulatory strategies used as well as by the target partners' weight status. Similarly, Lewis and Rook (1999) found that positive social control tactics were related to an increase in health-enhancing behaviors, whereas negative social control was unrelated to health behavior change but was associated with more distress. Furthermore, a separate study showed how affective responses could mediate behavioral reactions, as more positive influence elicited positive affect, and more frequent negative strategies contributed to negative affect (Tucker & Anders, 2001; Tucker, Orlando, Elliott, & Klein, 2006).

Partners' Emotional Reactions to Health Behaviors

Another pathway linking health and relationships is that one partner's health behavior may affect the emotional well-being of the other partner. In one study, researchers examined the reciprocal influence of marital interactions, emotional experiences, and health-promoting behaviors (Doumas, Margolin, & John, 2003). Husbands and wives reported a greater number of positive partner interactions on the days when they worked fewer hours, consumed regular meals, felt energetic, and spent time relaxing.

Clinical literature has provided copious examples of more extreme health behaviors affecting the partner. For example, a qualitative study of couples in which the female partners were diagnosed with bulimia nervosa showed that the male partners' negative emotional experiences were triggered by the women's episodes of bulimia (Huke & Slade, 2006). Furthermore, the nature of the male partner's emotional involvement and consequent influence attempts depended on his interpretation of the illness as well as his sense of both self-efficacy and partner efficacy in coping with it. Similarly, Markey (2008) showed that men and women who attempted to regulate their partners' eating behaviors tended to have relatively heavy partners and tended to be dissatisfied with their partners' bodies, suggesting that cognitions including dissatisfaction or disappointment with the partners' shape might be one of the factors driving attempts to change partners' behavior.

Studies of alcohol abuse have likewise suggested that both alcoholics and their partners experience a greater level of negative affectivity. Alcoholic families show higher levels of conflict and poorer communication, poorer problem-solving skills, and poorer emotion regulation strategies compared with those without alcohol abuse (see Rotunda et al., 1995, for a review). It also appears that alcohol use by one partner decreases a couple's capacity for emotional coordination. Dethier and colleagues (2011) showed that both partners in couples coping with alcoholism reported lower marital satisfaction, lower self-esteem, and were less congruent with each other in evaluations of each other's emotional states than partners in couples unaffected by alcoholism.

In addition, alcohol intoxication increases negative emotion because of conflict and negative perceptions of one's partner's feelings; those with low self-esteem experience more insecurity in their partners' affections and increased likelihood of blaming their partners for conflict (MacDonald, Zanna, & Holmes, 2000). Partners of alcoholics have a greater chance of exposure to cursing, yelling, ridicule, and humiliation and may experience consequences such as degraded self-esteem, feelings of uselessness, worthlessness, and self-blame (Campbell, 1995). It seems logical that people experiencing these negative consequences from their partner's health behavior would attempt to influence their partner to decrease the frequency of substance use.

DYADIC REGULATION PROCESSES AND HEALTH BEHAVIOR

The evidence outlined previously suggests that partners are affected by and respond to each other's health behaviors. An initial change can instigate a cyclical sequence, including changes in both partners' affective and cognitive states, which may alter subsequent health behaviors. These complex associations can be conceptualized better by going beyond the unidirectional causal links proposed by individual studies and shifting the focus to the continuous, reciprocal influence of health behaviors and interpersonal regulation processes. Unidirectional studies help to clarify the links between relationship factors and health behavior; however, they largely miss the dynamic process through which health behaviors are maintained, becoming integrated within dyadic emotional processes. This broader perspective becomes especially important if we consider that to have an impact on physical health, a particular health behavior must be repeated (e.g., regular exercise, not just an occasional day of activity). Therefore, the mechanisms that maintain health behaviors may be more important than the individual causal factors.

Systems theory is one framework that allows for a concise conceptualization of the dynamic interpersonal mechanisms that maintain health behaviors. From this perspective, couples are viewed as systems in a state of homeostatic balance. When a new health behavior is introduced into this dyadic system, it is much more likely to be maintained if the dyadic relationship somehow improves as a result of the behavior. Note that what constitutes "improvement" is determined by enhanced functioning for a specific couple. For a given couple, this may mean spending more time together or apart, self-soothing, or doing something that makes the couple feel more connected. Health behaviors can trigger such changes in dyadic interactions, in which case they may play an important role in maintaining relationship quality.

These dynamic processes of mutual influence are described in the systemic literature as feedback loops, which can be positive or negative. *Positive feedback loops* amplify changes that occur in the system, thereby increasing and perpetuating the behaviors and reactions involved. *Negative feedback loops* counteract changes introduced to the system and restore the system back to balance. Going beyond this simple distinction, we focus on four different dynamic processes that have empirical support: negative feedback loops, demand–withdraw cycles, protective buffering, and symptom–system fit. All of these processes are

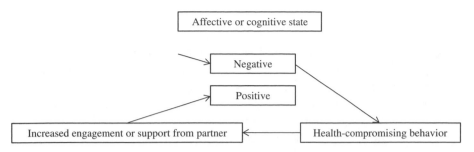

Figure 5.2. Negative feedback loop. One partner uses health-compromising behavior to reduce negative affect, and this elicits a positive response from the other partner, thus engendering positive mood in the first partner and rebalancing the system.

cyclical. Although change can be introduced at any point in the cycle (i.e., with a change in emotion, behavior, or partner involvement), for the sake of conciseness we start with the affective states, continue to health-related behaviors, then to partner involvement, and end with the affective outcome.

Negative Feedback Loops

Figure 5.2 depicts a negative feedback loop in which one partner experiences negative affect and attempts to correct it by engaging in a health behavior, which in turn elicits a positive response from the other partner, thus engendering positive mood in the first partner and rebalancing the system.

To illustrate this concept with a clinical example, if a depressed veteran is beginning to drink too much alcohol, his wife might spend more time with him to help him regain interest in life. Assuming the support she provides is sufficient to decrease his negative emotion, the undesirable health behavior might also decrease, and the dyadic system is restored to balance. In this case, the health-compromising drinking serves as a marker of distress but is reduced once dyadic balance is achieved. Thus, the husband's alcohol abuse triggers a series of supportive actions from the wife, which, in turn, restores and protects their relationship. Although this example may include clinical manifestations of health behaviors and emotional disarray, similar patterns may be observed in more day-to-day situations and among couples free of diagnosable pathology.

A number of clinical studies validate the existence of this sort of negative feedback process. Kelly, Halford, and Young (2000) showed that women experiencing problems with both alcohol abuse and relationship functioning who participated in individual therapy showed an increase in relational efficacy and marital satisfaction and a decreased need for alcohol use and depressive symptoms. The authors discussed bidirectional influences of marital problems and alcohol consumption and suggested that therapy should target whichever problem arose first. More recently, the same authors demonstrated that women with both alcohol and relationship problems had positive expectations for enhanced intimacy and increased emotional expression following alcohol consumption, whereas women with neither problem strongly rejected such expectations (Kelly, Halford, & Young, 2002). These studies support the link between emotional intimacy and alcohol and that alcohol abusers might drink to improve their relationship and emotional state. Furthermore, treatments targeting problematic health behaviors can serve to counteract this maladaptive progression.

Demand–Withdraw

Figure 5.3 illustrates one type of positive feedback loop. In this case, a negative emotion triggers a health-compromising behavior in one partner and a consequent increase in negativity from the other partner. In response, the first partner withdraws and experiences more intense negative emotion, followed by increased attempts to self-soothe through health-compromising behavior. For example, a woman may respond to a stressful workday by eating junk food, which elicits an insulting comment from her husband. Now stressed and hurt, the woman comforts herself with more junk food, engendering even more partner negativity, and perpetuating the cycle.

This pattern has often been described in the literature as a *demand-withdraw* (DW) *cycle*. DW is defined as a dyadic pattern in which one of the partners demands change by complaining, criticizing, nagging, or threatening their partner, and the recipient of this influence becomes defensive and withdraws from the interaction (e.g., Christensen & Heavey, 1990). This pattern is associated with lower relationship quality in the context of illness (e.g., Manne et al., 2006), which in turn is linked to poorer health (e.g., Coyne et al., 2001; Rohrbaugh et al., 2006).

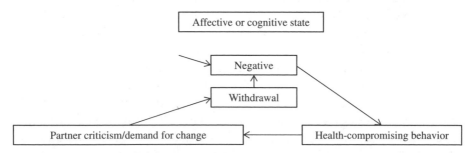

Figure 5.3. Demand–withdraw. One partner uses health-compromising behavior to reduce negative affect, and this elicits a negative reaction from the other partner. In response, the first partner withdraws and experiences even more negative emotion, followed by increased attempts to self-soothe through health-compromising behavior.

Although little research has directly identified DW dyadic interactions and their association with health behavior (see Shoham, Rohrbaugh, Stickle, & Jacob, 1998, for an exception), many studies have provided indirect evidence that this pattern is common among couples in which one partner engages in a health-compromising behavior. For example, studies of social control show how one partner's problematic health behavior can elicit frustrating, intrusive comments from the other partner, which can both increase distress and exacerbate the problematic behavior (e.g., Helgeson, Novak, Lepore, & Eton, 2004).

Other evidence for DW cycles comes from the clinical literature. For example, research has suggested that the expression of negative emotion by spouses of alcoholic patients leads to increases in drinking (e.g., Mattson, O'Farrell, Monson, Panuzio, & Taft, 2010; O'Farrell, Hooley, Fals-Stewart, & Cutter, 1998; Rotunda & O'Farrell, 1998). Positive emotionality in couples, however, might serve a protective function. For instance, a study of alcohol abusers and their spouses by Humbad, Donnellan, Iacono, and Burt (2010) showed that greater communal positive emotionality was associated with lower levels of all forms of externalizing psychopathology (including alcohol dependence) for men and with lower levels of alcohol dependence for women. In summary, these studies support the idea that DW interactions contribute to the maintenance of health-compromising behaviors through partners' negative reactions.

Protective Buffering

The literature on *protective buffering* (PB) describes another example of a positive feedback loop, depicted in Figure 5.4. PB is a relationship-focused coping strategy defined as hiding concerns, denying worries, and yielding to the partner to avoid disagreements (e.g., Coyne & Smith, 1991). Arguably,

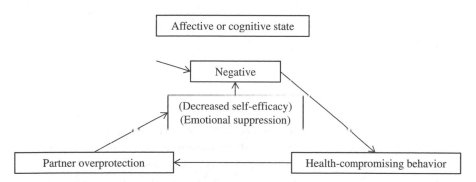

Figure 5.4. Protective buffering. One partner uses health-compromising behavior to reduce negative affect, and this elicits an overprotective reaction from the other partner. Partners avoid expressing negative affect in an attempt to protect the other partner.

this coping strategy is akin to emotional suppression because partners abstain from expressing negative affect in an attempt to protect the other partner.

To illustrate a specific case of PB, a man may experience negative affect and anxiety after losing his job and may then engage in a health-compromising behavior, such as smoking, in an attempt to cope. His wife may respond with well-intended, yet excessive support and coddling, while attempting to mask her worry and distress from her husband. This well-intentioned attempt to shield her husband is likely to backfire, however, causing him to feel less efficacious and to suppress his own negative emotions as well. This pattern may lead to a decrease in self-efficacy and ongoing experienced, but not expressed, negative affect (e.g., Dakof & Taylor, 1990; M. Stewart, Davidson, Meade, Hirth, & Makrides, 2000), thereby perpetuating the cycle.

PB has typically been studied in the context of couples coping with health challenges, in which one partner is ill and the other participates in caregiving. PB involves increased negative affect in both partners, though for different reasons. In the caregiver, the distress might be due to emotional suppression in the face of legitimate concern for the partner's well-being. The ill partner may experience PB as stressful and unhelpful, undermining self-efficacy and self-esteem (Dakof & Taylor, 1990; M. Stewart et al., 2000). Protective behavior by caregiving partners is positively associated with the ill partners' distress cross-sectionally (Hinnen, Ranchor, Baas, Sanderman, & Hagedoorn, 2009; Kuijer et al., 2000) and over time (Manne et al., 2007). This heightened distress in the ill partner might result in an increase in health-compromising behavior or a decrease in adherence to a healthy routine. No studies to our knowledge have directly tested this link between PB and health-related behaviors, but the dyadic and affectively rich nature of PB suggests that it might affect the maintenance of health behaviors. Thus, in both DW and PB dyadic patterns, the actions of one partner have an ironic effect, resulting in decreased emotional well-being of the partner who is being criticized or overprotected and an increased motivation for unhealthy behaviors.

Symptom–System Fit

The studies reviewed above suggest that health-compromising behaviors are likely to be associated with negative affectivity, poorer relationship functioning, and poorer interpersonal emotion regulation. However, a small body of work has revealed that the link between relationship quality and health behavior might be more complex and that health-compromising behaviors can benefit the couple in some circumstances. According to these studies, health behaviors may sometimes play an important—albeit ironic—role in the maintenance of couples' well-being.

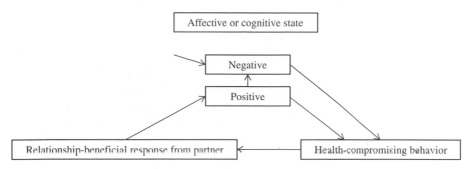

Figure 5.5. Symptom–system fit. Negative emotions are experienced by one or both partners, who self-soothe by engaging in health-compromising behavior. The behavior enhances the relationship in some way, contributing to positive emotions for both partners, which reinforces the health-compromising behavior.

Figure 5.5 shows an example of a dyadic feedback loop in which negative emotion is experienced by one or both partners, who then attempt to self-soothe by engaging in a health behavior, such as eating an indulgent, unhealthy meal. This action may improve the person's mood; if the meal is shared, it may improve the mood of both partners or provide a desired distraction, and neither partner is criticized. Even if only one partner engages in the unhealthy behavior, the other may enjoy the benefits of the first partner's improved mood and may therefore respond positively. Unlike the negative feedback loop depicted in Figure 5.4, in this case the positive response from the partner reinforces rather than counteracts the health behavior. As with a negative feedback loop, the health behavior and positive partner response return the system to balance, but in this case, the system now incorporates the health behavior so that dyadic balance becomes contingent on continuing the behavior. In the example, the couple may continue having unhealthy meals together to improve mood or distract from conflict; alternatively, one partner may benefit from the other partner self-soothing by overeating. From a systemic perspective, dyadic balance is maintained as long as one or both keep engaging in the health-related behavior and continue to somehow benefit from it as a couple.

This process has often been described in the literature as *symptom–system fit* (Rohrbaugh, Shoham, & Racioppo, 2002). Another illustration of this concept might be a couple struggling with intimacy, in which one of the partners drinks every night, thus making intimacy less desirable for the other partner. Although the other partner might condemn the drinking, it prevents the couple from directly addressing their intimacy problems, thus potentially making their couplehood more secure. The symptom in this scenario—the drinking—serves a regulatory purpose (or "fits") the dyadic system. Pearson and Anderson (1985) identified three such regulatory purposes that alcohol use may serve in a dyadic system: (a) signaling stress within the family; (b) stabilizing a chaotic system, potentially by distracting the couple from addressing problems that are harder to resolve; and (c) regulating emotional intimacy by altering the partners' ability to appropriately express affection and aggression toward each other.

Evidence for this complex interrelation of emotion, health, and dyadic processes has illustrated symptom–system fit among couples who smoke together. Although both partners might be conscious of the health risks and may want to quit smoking, sharing this health-compromising habit might provide them with an opportunity to be alone together, facilitate communication, and fulfill their emotional needs as a couple. Several studies have provided support for this concept. Shoham et al. (2007) found that when the couples were asked to smoke in the laboratory, dual-smoker couples demonstrated an increase in positive emotion, whereas single-smoker couples showed a decrease. In a follow-up study, Rohrbaugh et al. (2009) showed that affective synchrony increased in dual-smoker couples when both partners smoked and decreased in single-smoker couples when only one partner smoked. If higher emotional synchrony is indicative of better relationship quality and more successful interpersonal emotion regulation, these studies provide evidence that dual-smoker couples benefit from smoking together through an increase in emotional synchrony and positivity, though this habit undermines physical health.

CONCLUSION

Bidirectional influences between close relationships, emotion regulation, and health behaviors help to explain how health and relationships are linked. Health behaviors can serve an emotion regulatory function, both at an individual level and in dyadic relationships. These behaviors may be attempted as a way to escape or cope with a negative state directly or after a different self-regulation strategy fails. Health behaviors and health per se are also affected by relationship quality, with partners in more satisfying relationships usually experiencing better health and practicing fewer health-compromising behaviors. In addition, partners influence each other in multiple ways, ranging from adopting each other's health habits, to responding with emotionally charged reactions to them, to acting on these reactions and attempting to directly influence and control partners' behaviors.

Given that health behaviors do not go unnoticed by partners and that partners attempt to influence each other's health behaviors, it becomes inevitable that partners' affective processes and health behaviors are linked. Namely, a change in emotion or health behavior may trigger changes in the dyadic relationship. Conversely, changes in dyadic interaction may lead to changes in health behaviors. In either case, the health behavior itself may become one of the strategies used by the partners to regulate their own emotions and their dyadic well-being, thus creating a tightly connected system involving both partners' emotions, health behaviors, and relationship quality. The combined evidence reviewed here supports the interwoven nature of dyadic regulatory processes and health behaviors. However, more research is needed to further our understanding of the connections between partner interactions and health behaviors. Such research would ideally include assessment of both partners over different domains of functioning over time. Future studies could benefit from addressing factors external to the ongoing relationship and examining the interactions between individual and dyadic contributors to health. Given that health-related habits are notoriously hard to change, a better understanding of the relationship factors that may contribute to the maintenance of health behavior will provide an opportunity to sharpen health-promoting interventions.

REFERENCES

Aimé, A., Sabourin, S., & Ratté, C. (2006). The eating disturbed spectrum in relation with coping and interpersonal functioning. *Eating and Weight Disorders*, *11*, 66–72.

Baum, A., & Posluszny, D. (1999). Health psychology: Mapping biobehavioral contributions to health and illness. *Annual Review of Psychology*, *50*, 137–163. doi:10.1146/annurev.psych.50.1.137

Berking, M., Margraf, M., Ebert, D., Wupperman, P., Hofmann, S. G., & Junghanns, K. (2011). Deficits in emotion-regulation skills predict alcohol use during and after cognitive–behavioral therapy for alcohol dependence. *Journal of Consulting and Clinical Psychology*, *79*, 307–318. doi: 10.1037/a0023421

Brennan, K. A., & Shaver, P. R. (1995). Dimensions of adult attachment, affect regulation, and romantic relationship functioning. *Personality and Social Psychology Bulletin*, *21*, 267–283. doi:10.1177/0146167295213008

Burman, B., & Margolin, G. (1992). Analysis of the association between marital relationships and health problems: An interactional perspective. *Psychological Bulletin*, *112*, 39–63. doi:10.1037/0033-2909.112.1.39

Butler, E. A., Young, V. J., & Randall, A. K. (2010). Suppressing to please, eating to cope: The effect of overweight women's emotion suppression on romantic relationships and eating. *Journal of Social and Clinical Psychology*, *29*, 599–623. doi:10.1521/jscp.2010.29.6.599

Campbell, J. C. (1995). *Assessing dangerousness: Violence by sexual offenders, batterers, and child abusers*. Newbury Park, CA: Sage.

Christensen, A., & Heavey, C. L. (1990). Gender and social structure in the demand/withdraw pattern of marital conflict. *Journal of Personality and Social Psychology*, *59*, 73–81. doi:10.1037/0022-3514.59.1.73

Cooper, M. L., Frone, M. R., Russell, M., & Mudar, P. (1995). Drinking to regulate positive and negative emotions: A motivational model of alcohol use. *Journal of Personality and Social Psychology, 69,* 990–1005. doi:10.1037/0022-3514.69.5.990

Coyne, J. C., Rohrbaugh, M. J., Shoham, V., Sonnega, J. S., Nicklas, J. M., & Cranford, J. A. (2001). Prognostic importance of marital quality for survival of congestive heart failure. *The American Journal of Cardiology, 88,* 526–529. doi:10.1016/S0002-9149(01)01731-3

Coyne, J. C., & Smith, D. A. (1991). Couples coping with a myocardial infarction: A contextual perspective on wives' distress. *Journal of Personality and Social Psychology, 61,* 404–412. doi:10.1037/0022-3514.61.3.404

Dakof, G. A., & Taylor, S. E. (1990). Victims' perceptions of social support: What is helpful from whom? *Journal of Personality and Social Psychology, 58,* 80–89. doi:10.1037/0022-3514.58.1.80

Davey, J., Fitzpatrick, M., Garland, R., & Kilgour, M. (2009). Adult participation motives: Empirical evidence from a workplace exercise programme. *European Sport Management Quarterly, 9,* 141–162. doi:10.1080/16184740802571427

Davies, M. M., Bekker, M. J., & Roosen, M. A. (2011). The role of coping and general psychopathology in the prediction of treatment outcome in eating disorders. *Eating Disorders, 19,* 246–258. doi:10.1080/10640266.2011.566147

Davis, D., Shaver, P., & Vernon, M. (2003). Physical, emotional, and behavioral reactions to breaking up: The roles of gender, age, emotional involvement, and attachment style. *Personality and Social Psychology Bulletin, 29,* 871–884. doi:10.1177/0146167203029007006

Dethier, M., Counerotte, C., & Blairy, S. (2011). Marital satisfaction in couples with an alcoholic husband. *Journal of Family Violence, 26,* 151–162. doi:10.1007/s10896-010-9355-z

Diamond, L. M., Hicks, A. M., & Otter-Henderson, K. D. (2008). Every time you go away: Changes in affect, behavior, and physiology associated with travel-related separations from romantic partners. *Journal of Personality and Social Psychology, 95,* 385–403. doi:10.1037/0022-3514.95.2.385

Doumas, D. M., Margolin, G, & John, R. S. (2003). The relationship between daily marital interaction, work, and health-promoting behaviors in dual-earner couples: An extension of the work-family spillover model. *Journal of Family Issues, 24,* 3–20. doi:10.1177/0192513X02238518

Gorin, A. A., Wing, R., Fava, J., Jakicic, J., Jeffery, R., West, D., . . . DiLillo, V. (2008). Weight loss treatment influences untreated spouses and the home environment: Evidence of a ripple effect. *International Journal of Obesity, 32,* 1678–1684. doi:10.1038/ijo.2008.150

Hasler, B. P., & Troxel, W. M. (2010). Couples' nighttime sleep efficiency and concordance: Evidence for bidirectional associations with daytime relationship functioning. *Psychosomatic Medicine, 72,* 794–801. doi:10.1097/PSY.0b013e3181ecd08a

Helgeson, V. S., Novak, S. A., Lepore, S. J., & Eton, D. T. (2004). Spouse social control efforts: Relations to health behavior and well-being among men with prostate cancer. *Journal of Social and Personal Relationships, 21*, 53–68. doi:10.1177/0265407504039840

Hinnen, C., Ranchor, A., Baas, P., Sanderman, R., & Hagedoorn, M. (2009). Partner support and distress in women with breast cancer: The role of patients' awareness of support and level of mastery. *Psychology & Health, 24*, 439–455. doi:10.1080/08870440801919513

Homish, G. G., & Leonard, K. E. (2008). Spousal influence on general health behaviors in a community sample. *American Journal of Health Behavior, 32*, 754–763. doi:10.5993/AJHB.32.6.19

Hsiao, E. T., & Thayer, R. E. (1998). Exercising for mood regulation: The importance of experience. *Personality and Individual Differences, 24*, 829–836. doi:10.1016/S0191-8869(98)00013-0

Huke, K., & Slade, P. (2006). An exploratory investigation of the experiences of partners living with people who have bulimia nervosa. *European Eating Disorders Review, 14*, 436–447. doi:10.1002/erv.744

Humbad, M. N., Donnellan, M., Iacono, W. G., & Burt, S. (2010). Externalizing psychopathology and marital adjustment in long-term marriages: Results from a large combined sample of married couples. *Journal of Abnormal Psychology, 119*, 151–162. doi:10.1037/a0017981

Ikard, F. F., Green, D. E., & Horn, D. (1969). A scale to differentiate between types of smoking as related to the management of affect. *The International Journal of the Addictions, 4*, 649–659.

Jáuregui Lobera, I., Estébanez, S., Santiago Fernández, M. J., Álvarez Bautista, E., & Garrido, O. (2009). Coping strategies in eating disorders. *European Eating Disorders Review, 17*, 220–226. doi:10.1002/erv.920

Kelly, A. B., Halford, W. K., & Young, R. M. (2000). Maritally distressed women with alcohol problems: The impact of a short-term alcohol-focused intervention on drinking behavior and marital satisfaction. *Addiction, 95*, 1537–1549. doi:10.1046/j.1360-0443.2000.951015378.x

Kelly, A. B., Halford, W. K., & Young, R. M. (2002). Expectations of the effects of drinking on couple relationship functioning: An assessment of women in distressed relationships who consume alcohol at harmful levels. *Addictive Behaviors, 27*, 451–464. doi:10.1016/S0306-4603(01)00185-X

Kenyon, R. J. (2007). A grounded theory of the relationship between eating disorders and marital relationships: The role of emotional accessibility. *Dissertation Abstracts International: Section B. Sciences and Engineering, 67*(9), 5409.

Kiecolt-Glaser, J. K., & Newton, T. L. (2001). Marriage and health: His and hers. *Psychological Bulletin, 127*, 472–503. doi:10.1037/0033-2909.127.4.472

Kuijer, R., Ybema, J., Buunk, B., De Jong, G., Thijs-Boer, F., & Sanderman, R. (2000). Active engagement, protective buffering, and overprotection: Three ways of giving support by intimate partners of patients with cancer. *Journal of Social and Clinical Psychology, 19,* 256–275. doi:10.1521/jscp.2000.19.2.256

Lewis, M. A., & Butterfield, R. (2007). Social control in marital relationships: Effect of one's partner on health behaviors. *Journal of Applied Social Psychology, 37,* 298–319. doi:10.1111/j.0021-9029.2007.00161.x

Lewis, M. A., & Rook, K. S. (1999). Social control in personal relationships: Impact on health behaviors and psychological distress. *Health Psychology, 18,* 63–71. doi:10.1037/0278-6133.18.1.63

MacDonald, G., Zanna, M. P., & Holmes, J. G. (2000). An experimental test of the role of alcohol in relationship conflict. *Journal of Experimental Social Psychology, 36,* 182–193. doi:10.1006/jesp.1999.1412

Manne, S. L., Norton, T. R., Ostroff, J. S., Winkel, G., Fox, K., & Grana, G. (2007). Protective buffering and psychological distress among couples coping with breast cancer: The moderating role of relationship satisfaction. *Journal of Family Psychology, 21,* 380–388. doi:10.1037/0893-3200.21.3.380

Manne, S. L., Ostroff, J. S., Norton, T. R., Fox, K., Goldstein, L., & Grana, G. (2006). Cancer- related relationship communication in couples coping with early stage breast cancer. *Psycho-Oncology, 15,* 234–247. doi:10.1002/pon.941

Markey, C. N. (2008). Romantic relationships and eating regulation: An investigation of partners' attempts to control each others' eating behaviors. *Journal of Health Psychology, 13,* 422–432. doi:10.1177/1359105307088145

Markey, C. N., Markey, P. M., & Birch, L. L. (2001). Interpersonal predictors of dieting practices among married couples. *Journal of Family Psychology, 15,* 464–475. doi:10.1037/0893-3200.15.3.464

Mattson, R., O'Farrell, T., Monson, C., Panuzio, J., & Taft, C. (2010). Female perpetrated dyadic psychological aggression predicts relapse in a treatment sample of men with substance use disorders. *Journal of Family Violence, 25,* 33–42. doi:10.1007/s10896-009-9267-y

McPheters, J. K., & Sandberg, J. G. (2010). The relationship among couple relationship quality, physical functioning, and depression in multiple sclerosis patients and partners. *Families, Systems, & Health, 28,* 48–68. doi:10.1037/a0018818

Novak, S. A., & Webster, G. D. (2011). Spousal social control during a weight loss attempt: A daily diary study. *Personal Relationships, 18,* 224–241. doi:10.1111/j.1475-6811.2011.01358.x

O'Farrell, T. J., Hooley, J., Fals-Stewart, W., & Cutter, H. G. (1998). Expressed emotion and relapse in alcoholic patients. *Journal of Consulting and Clinical Psychology, 66,* 744–752. doi:10.1037/0022-006X.66.5.744

Pearson, D., & Anderson, S. A. (1985). Treating alcoholic family systems: Intervening in the marital subsystem. *Family Therapy, 12,* 211–220.

Ren, X. S. (1997). Marital status and quality of relationships: The impact on health perception. *Social Science & Medicine, 44,* 241–249. doi:10.1016/S0277-9536(96)00158-X

Rohrbaugh, M. J., Shoham, V., Butler, E. A., Hasler, B. P., & Berman, J. S. (2009). Affective synchrony in dual- and single-smoker couples: Further evidence of "symptom-system fit"? *Family Process, 48,* 55–67. doi:10.1111/j.1545-5300.2009.01267.x

Rohrbaugh, M. J., Shoham, V., & Coyne, J. C. (2006). Effect of marital quality on eight-year survival of patients with heart failure. *The American Journal of Cardiology, 98,* 1069–1072. doi:10.1016/j.amjcard.2006.05.034

Rohrbaugh, M. J., Shoham, V., & Racioppo, M. W. (2002). Toward family-level attribute × treatment interaction research. In H. A. Liddle, D. A. Santisteban, R. F. Levant, & J. H. Bray (Eds.), *Family psychology: Science-based intervention* (pp. 215–237). Washington, DC: American Psychological Association. doi:10.1037/10438-011

Rook, K. S., Thuras, P. D., & Lewis, M. A. (1990). Social control, health risk taking, and psychological distress among the elderly. *Psychology and Aging, 5,* 327–334. doi:10.1037/0882-7974.5.3.327

Rotunda, R. J., & O'Farrell, T. J. (1998). Understanding and managing expressed emotion in the couples treatment of alcoholism. *In Session: Psychotherapy in Practice, 4*(3), 55–71. doi:10.1002/(SICI)1520-6572(199823)4:3<55::AID-SESS5>3.0.CO;2-7

Rotunda, R., Scherer, D., & Imm, P. (1995). Family systems and alcohol misuse: Research on the effects of alcoholism on family functioning and effective family interventions. *Professional Psychology: Research and Practice, 26,* 95–104. doi:10.1037/0735-7028.26.1.95

Savoca, M., & Miller, C. (2001). Food selection and eating patterns: Themes found among people with type 2 diabetes mellitus. *Journal of Nutrition Education, 33,* 224–233. doi:10.1016/S1499-4046(06)60035-3

Schafer, R. B., Keith, P. M., & Schafer, E. (1994). The effects of marital interaction, depression and self-esteem on dietary self-efficacy among married couples. *Journal of Applied Social Psychology, 24,* 2209–2222. doi:10.1111/j.1559-1816.1994.tb02380.x

Schafer, R. B., Keith, P. M., & Schafer, E. (2000). Marital stress, psychological distress, and healthful dietary behavior: A longitudinal analysis. *Journal of Applied Social Psychology, 30,* 1639–1656. doi:10.1111/j.1559-1816.2000.tb02459.x

Schafer, R. B., Schafer, E., & Keith, P. M. (1997). Stress in marital interaction and diet behavior. *Stress Medicine, 13,* 145–150. doi:10.1002/(SICI)1099-1700(199707)13:3<145::AID-SMI731>3.0.CO;2-R

Schmitz, N., Kruse, J., & Kugler, J. (2004). The association between physical exercises and health-related quality of life in subjects with mental disorders: Results from a cross-sectional survey. *Preventive Medicine, 39,* 1200–1207. doi:10.1016/j.ypmed.2004.04.034

Shattuck, A. L., White, E., & Kristal, A. R. (1992). How women's adopted low-fat diets affect their husbands. *American Journal of Public Health, 82,* 1244–1250. doi:10.2105/AJPH.82.9.1244

Shoham, V., Butler, E. A., Rohrbaugh, M. J., & Trost, S. E. (2007). Symptom-system fit in couples: Emotion regulation when one or both partners smoke. *Journal of Abnormal Psychology, 116,* 848–853. doi:10.1037/0021-843X.116.4.848

Shoham, V., Rohrbaugh, M. J., Stickle, T. R., & Jacob, T. (1998). Demand–withdraw couple interaction moderates retention in cognitive–behavioral versus family-systems treatments for alcoholism. *Journal of Family Psychology, 12*, 557–577. doi:10.1037/0893-3200.12.4.557

Skoyen, J. A., Blank, E., Corkery, S. A., & Butler, E. A. (2012). *The interplay of partner influence and individual values predicts daily fluctuations in eating and physical activity.* Manuscript submitted for publication.

Stewart, M., Davidson, K., Meade, D., Hirth, A., & Makrides, L. (2000). Myocardial infarction: Survivors' and spouses' stress, coping, and support. *Journal of Advanced Nursing, 31*, 1351–1360. doi:10.1046/j.1365-2648.2000.01454.x

Stewart, S. H., Morris, E., Mellings, T., & Komar, J. (2006). Relations of social anxiety variables to drinking motives, drinking quantity and frequency, and alcohol-related problems in undergraduates. *Journal of Mental Health, 15*, 671–682. doi:10.1080/09638230600998904

Troxel, W. M., Robles, T. F., Hall, M., & Buysse, D. J. (2007). Marital quality and the marital bed: Examining the covariation between relationship quality and sleep. *Sleep Medicine Reviews, 11*, 389–404. doi:10.1016/j.smrv.2007.05.002

Tucker, J. S., & Anders, S. L. (2001). Social control of health behaviors in marriage. *Journal of Applied Social Psychology, 31*, 467–485. doi:10.1111/j.1559-1816.2001.tb02051.x

Tucker, J. S., Orlando, M., Elliott, M. N., & Klein, D. J. (2006). Affective and behavioral responses to health-related social control. *Health Psychology, 25*, 715–722. doi:10.1037/0278-6133.25.6.715

Uchino, B. N., Cacciopo, J. T., & Kiecolt-Glaser, J. K. (1996). The relationship between social support and physiological processes: A review with emphasis on underlying mechanisms and implications for health. *Psychological Bulletin, 119*, 488–531. doi:10.1037/0033-2909.119.3.488

Umberson, D. (1992). Gender, marital status and the social control of health behavior. *Social Science & Medicine, 34*, 907–917. doi:10.1016/0277-9536(92)90259-S

Villaverde-Gutiérrez, C., Araújo, E., Cruz, F., Roa, J., Barbosa, W., & Ruíz-Villaverde, G. (2006). Quality of life of rural menopausal women in response to a customized exercise programme. *Journal of Advanced Nursing, 54*, 11–19. doi:10.1111/j.1365-2648.2006.03784.x

Walker, R. B., & Luszcz, M. A. (2009). The health and relationship dynamics of late-life couples: A systematic review of the literature. *Ageing and Society, 29*, 455–480. doi:10.1017/S0144686X08007903

Wickrama, K. A. S., Lorenz, F. O., & Conger, R. D. (1997). Marital quality and physical illness: A latent growth curve analysis. *Journal of Marriage and Family, 59*, 143–155. doi:10.2307/353668

III

FAMILIES, PEERS, AND CULTURES

6

FAMILY RELATIONSHIPS AND PHYSICAL HEALTH: BIOLOGICAL PROCESSES AND MECHANISMS

ERIN T. TOBIN, RICHARD B. SLATCHER, AND THEODORE F. ROBLES

Family relationships, especially parent–child relationships, provide scaffolding for development across the life span. Families can range from supportive and nurturing to cold and neglectful, with potent effects on a developing child's biological functioning and physical health. Growing evidence shows that family relationships early in life can shape health outcomes into adulthood (Miller & Chen, 2010; Repetti, Taylor, & Seeman, 2002; Shonkoff, Boyce, & McEwen, 2009). Parent–child relationships that are enriched with support and nurturance provide a child with helpful coping resources and protect overall health (Meadows, 2011). In contrast, relationships between parents and children marked by frequent conflict and distress can lead to a myriad of problems ranging from emotional instability to behavioral dysregulation and even chronic illness (Davies, Sturge-Apple, Cicchetti, & Cummings, 2008; Taylor, 2010).

DOI: 10.1037/14036-007
Health and Social Relationships: The Good, the Bad, and the Complicated, Matthew L. Newman and Nicole A. Roberts (Editors)

Families with frequent conflict (e.g., repeated episodes of anger, aggression, and yelling) and cold and neglectful relationships (e.g., absence of parental emotional support, unavailability) can be especially damaging to a child's physical health (Miller & Chen, 2010; Repetti et al., 2002). The risky families model described by Repetti et al. (2002) proposes that these family characteristics can create vulnerabilities for children that have the potential to disrupt multiple biological systems and put children at risk of future chronic health problems. This model integrates influences from family characteristics and genetic predispositions, as well as environmental factors. As children in risky families grow into adolescence, risky health behaviors (e.g., smoking, poor diet, risky sexual behaviors) and deficiencies in social competence begin to develop and are then maintained through adulthood, resulting in the development of a chronic illness (Larzelere & Jones, 2008; McEwen, 2003).

Family difficulties put children at risk for a variety of health problems. For example, decreased familial support is linked to increased number of infections (Cohen, Doyle, Skoner, Rabin, & Gwaltney, 1997; Walker et al., 1999) and more frequent physical complaints (Gottman, Katz, & Hooven, 1996). A major childhood health problem exacerbated by poor family relationships is asthma, with evidence suggesting that early family environments can affect its onset and severity (Kaugars, Klinnert, & Bender, 2004). Influences of family relationships on childhood asthma include parental stress, marital conflict, and parent–child conflict (Chen, Bloomberg, Fisher, & Strunk, 2003; Northey, Griffin, & Krainz, 1998; Shalowitz, Berry, Quinn, & Wolf, 2001). In addition, children in risky families are more likely to have unfavorable lipid profiles and Type 1 diabetes, both of which increase risk for development of coronary artery disease (Dimsdale & Herd, 1982; Tiberg, Hallstrom, & Carlsson, 2010; Weidner, Hutt, Connor, & Mendell, 1992). Furthermore, exposure to family dysfunction as a child puts individuals at risk for a multitude of health problems in adulthood, including heart disease, cancer, lung disease, and liver disease (Felitti et al., 1998).

In this chapter, the potentially damaging and beneficial influences of family relationships are discussed in terms of their impact on a child's current and future health. Specifically, damaging influences such as inadequate support and high levels of conflict are considered, as well as beneficial influences such as parental support and warmth. We then focus on possible biological mediators of the effects of family relationships on child health, including the immune system, the hypothalamic–pituitary–adrenal axis (HPA), and the cardiovascular system—all key systems involved in stress response pathways that can have short- and long-term adverse effects on health. We conclude the chapter with a discussion of emerging intervention research that targets family dysfunction with an eye toward improving child health through the improvement of family relationships. Because of space limitations, there are a number of key characteristics of families with relevance for child health that we cannot review separately in this chapter, including socioeconomic status, genetic predisposition, health behaviors, and mental health issues; however, there are instances in which the influence of socioeconomic status and health behaviors is highlighted as it affects support and/or conflict in families. The biological consequences of family environments discussed in this chapter represent plausible pathways through which risky family environments can create risk of physical and mental health disorders across the life span. Investigations of the aforementioned characteristics have the potential to further clarify the moderators of the links between risky family relationships and negative health outcomes and have been covered in other more comprehensive reviews (Flinn, 2011; Francis, 2009; Kaslow, Deering, & Racusin, 1994; Reiss et al., 1995).

DAMAGING INFLUENCES OF RISKY FAMILY RELATIONSHIPS ON HEALTH

There is substantial evidence on the topic of parental involvement and its influence on social and emotional development and physical health (Belsky, Bell, Bradley, Stallard, & Stewart-Brown, 2007; Waylen, Stallard, & Stewart-Brown, 2008). Children who grow up in an unsupportive environment are prone to a variety of negative health outcomes later in life (Shonkoff et al., 2009). In this section, we first discuss what defines parenting and parental support and then review some of the research that has examined the negative impact of deficient parental support and lack of warmth across a range of health outcomes beginning in childhood and extending into adulthood.

Parenting styles are defined by the way in which parents communicate and respond to their children (Baumrind, 1991). Multiple complex factors influence how a parent acts toward his or her child, including socioeconomic status, cultural beliefs, and even genetic characteristics (Kendler, 1996). Although there are four main parenting styles—authoritarian (demanding obedience), authoritative (use of reasoning), permissive (giving in to child's demands), and uninvolved—many studies operationalize parenting as positive or negative (Jago et al., 2011). Most of the research to date has focused on the negative aspects of parenting, with the paramount features including inadequate support or communication from a parent, which together have been speculated to produce an exaggerated stress response (Meaney, 2001). Negative parenting can represent a variety of styles and actions, ranging from unlawful neglect (representing a small population subset) to unresponsive, where a child's needs for warmth and nurturance are unmet (representing a larger population subset). The bulk of the research on negative parenting characteristics discussed here has focused on the latter.

Parenting styles that are lacking support, warmth, and nurturance are linked to a number of health problems in children. For example, in a lab study of interactions between parents and children, children of parents with negative parenting styles (unstructured, cold, and unresponsive) had higher incidence of parent-reported rates of illness and higher levels of stress hormones (Gottman & Katz, 1989). Other research indicates that children from authoritarian mothers, who had high expectations for self-control and low sensitivity, were more likely to be overweight in the first grade (Rhee, Lumeng, Appugliese, Kaciroti, & Bradley, 2006). Lack of family support is also linked to management of chronic illnesses such as diabetes. In a study of children undergoing treatment for diabetes, those with less nurturing parents (less emotional support, poorer conflict resolution, and greater parental expression of anger and sadness) had less metabolic control over their diabetes as evidenced from levels of glycosylated hemoglobin (Martin, Miller-Johnson, Kitzmann, & Emery, 1998).

Evidence suggests that the negative health effects of inadequate parental support and lack of family warmth carry over into later childhood. For example, Waylen et al. (2008) investigated the long-term effects of suboptimal parenting on the number of mother-reported child health problems. They found that a child's chances of experiencing poor health in late childhood increased with exposure to maternal resentment and hostility as a toddler, with resentment playing a stronger role than hostility. These early effects of parent–child relationships are not limited to questionnaire reports of family functioning. For instance, poor interactive infant behavior at 8 to 11 months of age in videotaped mother–child interactions—defined by short face-to-face interaction and infant fretfulness—predicted chronic and/or recurrent health problems when children were 2 years of age (Mäntymaa et al., 2003). Further, a 10-year longitudinal study of Danish school-aged children indicated that lack of parental care and support predicted a greatly increased risk for obesity in young adulthood (Lissau & Sorensen, 1994). These studies suggest that parent–child difficulties can begin early in life with deleterious health effects that continue into later childhood and the early adult years. It is notable that few studies have longitudinally examined the long-term effects of family relationships on health into adulthood.

Family conflict has long been known to cause behavioral maladjustment and emotional dysregulation problems in a developing child; when family conflict is high, children exhibit greater levels of subjective and behavioral distress (Cummings, Schermerhorn, Davies, Goeke-Morey, & Cummings, 2006). A growing body of research has suggested that the negative effects of family conflict extend to physical health.

Much like deficient support, the presence of family conflict can affect a growing child as early as infancy and continue through childhood (Luecken

& Lemery, 2004). For example, in an at-home observation study of mother–infant interactions, greater conflict in the home was associated with lower infant weight attainment (Stein, Woolley, Cooper, & Fairburn, 1994). In another study of over 6,500 children, observed family conflict was associated with less height attainment at age 7 and into adulthood (Montgomery, Bartley, & Wilkinson, 1997). These studies emphasize the impact of conflict on a child's growth and development. It has also been demonstrated that high-conflict families—in which parents report open expressions of anger and aggression—are associated with higher levels of total cholesterol and high-density lipoprotein in sons between the ages of 8 and 18 (Weidner et al., 1992). This unfavorable lipid profile may leave children at increased risk for future cardiac illness. Although that study did take factors such as personality and family climate into account, it did not address influential health behaviors such as diet and physical activity. As a whole, these studies have highlighted the impact specific family characteristics have on the immediate health of growing children.

Further research suggests that family conflict has long-term effects. For example, in a retrospective study of young adults from intact and divorced families, higher levels of early family conflict in both groups were associated with increased somatic symptoms, illness reports, and health care visits in young adulthood (Luecken & Fabricius, 2003). In addition, in a study of late adolescents, early family conflict was linked to an avoidant coping style and low self-concept and had a negative impact on later health habits (including short sleeping periods and smoking; Michael, Torres, & Seemann, 2007). It is important to note that family conflict here was not directly linked to health but rather affected the development of poor health behaviors and coping strategies. In a demonstration of the prospective effects of family conflict on major health problems, men who described tumultuous relationships with either their mother or father were more likely to be diagnosed with a serious medical condition 35 years later, including asthma, arthritis, heart problems, and depression (Stewart-Brown, Fletcher, & Wadsworth, 2005). This research highlights the extensive negative impact that family conflict has on a wide range of health outcomes across human development.

BENEFICIAL INFLUENCES OF FAMILY RELATIONSHIPS ON HEALTH

Although deficient support and the presence of conflict can negatively affect health, supportive and warm parenting conversely appears to reduce stress and promote better health outcomes. Both parental warmth and sensitivity are associated with a cooperative relationship between parent and child

(Campbell, 2002), and the presence of warmth and sensitivity by a parent is correlated with a child's ability to regulate negative emotions (Denham & Kochanoff, 2002). From an extensive review of marital conflict and child adjustment, Grych and Fincham (1990) concluded that supportive parent–child relationships not only promote a child's well-being but also buffer children from the effects of marital conflict.

Multiple studies have investigated the mechanisms through which high-quality family relationships are beneficial. Family support positively influences adaptive coping styles and the effectiveness of coping responses to stressful events (Valentiner, Holahan, & Moos, 1994). Positive family relationships can also help prevent the emergence of negative health behaviors. For instance, in a national school survey of children from Grades 7 through 11, parent–child connectedness was demonstrated to be protective against cigarette and alcohol use while controlling for family structure and poverty status (Resnick, 1997). In addition, family connectedness and mealtime frequency are associated with a reduction in tobacco and alcohol consumption in adolescent girls (White & Halliwell, 2011). Further, children from families with high-quality relationships report consistently better overall health and less destructive health behaviors (including smoking, alcohol use, and illegal substance use) compared with children from families of low-quality relationships, when using family income and parental education as covariates (Hair et al., 2009). While providing insightful information about positive family influences, this study also clarified the mechanisms linking family relationships and poor health outcomes by showing that unfavorable health outcomes in families were associated with lower family income and lower parental education. Long-term benefits of positive family relationships also have been reported: A 35-year prospective study indicated that college students who rated their parents high in parental caring had a lower risk of being diagnosed with a chronic disease (including cardiovascular disease, duodenal ulcers, and alcoholism) in midlife compared with those who rated their parents low in parental care (Russek & Schwartz, 1997). In short, the research to date provides evidence that family support and warmth may have the ability to buffer the effects of stress and positively influence long-term health outcomes and health behaviors. Later, we discuss possible intervention opportunities for increasing warmth and support in families.

BIOLOGICAL MEDIATORS

With robust evidence indicating strong links between family relationships and health, researchers recently have begun to examine how family relationships "get under the skin" to affect health in childhood and beyond.

Despite ample evidence that growing up in a risky family environment is associated with more physical health problems later in life, little is known about the biological and behavioral pathways through which risky family environments exert their deleterious effects on health. For the remainder of this chapter, we discuss the growing body of research that is attempting to elucidate three biological pathways involved in the stress-response pathways with links to family relationships and health—immunity, HPA reactivity, and cardiovascular reactivity.

Immunity

The immune system is affected by challenges in the environment (i.e., stress; Segerstrom & Miller, 2004), and extensive research shows that chronic stress can suppress the immune system's protective abilities (Cohen, Miller, & Rabin, 2001; Herbert & Cohen, 1993; Kiecolt-Glaser, Glaser, Gravenstein, Malarkey, & Sheridan, 1996). In recent years, there has been increasing interest in the immune system as a key pathway through which family relationships affect child health, with particular emphasis on studies of children with chronic inflammatory diseases such as asthma that are both immune-regulated and have known links to psychological stress.

Deficient Parental Support

Studies of children with asthma indicate that lack of quality family relationships and presence of family difficulties affect both symptom expression and onset of asthma attacks (Chen, Chim, Strunk, & Miller, 2007; Sandberg et al., 2000). Research has demonstrated, for example, that children with asthma who have a strained parent–child relationships produce immune cells that are more resistant to the anti-inflammatory effects of hydrocortisone (a main ingredient in rescue inhalers) in controlling production of interleukin-5 and interferon-gamma, which are key proteins that regulate airway inflammation (Miller, Gaudin, Zysk, & Chen, 2009). Children with asthma and low levels of family support also have poorer pulmonary function and more nighttime asthma symptoms during a 2-week period (Chen et al., 2007). These findings represent emerging evidence for the direct effects of family relationships on the immune system, with poor parent–child relationships potentially exacerbating different inflammatory processes that contribute to asthma pathogenesis (Reading, 2007; Wright, 2007).

Familial Conflict

Research has suggested that family conflict is linked to immune dysregulation as well. For example, adolescent girls raised in families with moderate amounts of conflict had increased interleukin-6 production over an 18-month follow-up period (Miller & Chen, 2010) and exhibited greater glucocorticoid resistance in immune cells, which can lead to increased airway inflammation (Lee, Brattsand, & Leung, 1996). In addition, in a study comparing children with asthma and medically healthy children, children with asthma who had high levels of chronic family stress showed increased production of interleukin-4 and -5 as well as elevated interferon-gamma when they had experienced an acutely stressful event (Marin, Chen, Munch, & Miller, 2009); children with asthma who had lower levels of chronic family stress, and medically healthy children, did not exhibit these stress-related changes. Importantly, this study suggests that children who experience both acute stress and constant family stress are at increased risk for greater asthma-related immune dysfunction.

Hypothalamic–Pituitary–Adrenal Axis Reactivity

The biological system that has perhaps received the most interest as a possible mechanism of the links between family relationships and health is the HPA axis, one of the body's regulatory systems that helps individuals adapt to the demands of their environment to maintain and regulate the body's homeostasis (Kudielka & Kirschbaum, 2005). The HPA axis produces cortisol, the chief stress hormone in humans. Cortisol levels are particularly sensitive to social stressors such as those from family relationships (see Chapter 1, this volume). Although links between stress and the HPA axis are complex, chronic stress typically is associated with greater cortisol production and a high, flat diurnal cortisol profile (Miller, Chen, & Zhou, 2007), whereas acute stressors are associated with transient cortisol increases (Dickerson & Kemeny, 2004). The HPA axis appears to have key relevance for health because its dysregulation has been associated with a variety of physical and mental disorders ranging from metabolic syndrome and fibromyalgia to depression and posttraumatic stress disorder (Entringer, Kumsta, Hellhammer, Wadhwa, & Wust, 2009; Holsboer, 2000; Yehuda, 1997) and even mortality (Kumari, Shipley, Stafford, & Kivimaki, 2011; Sephton, Sapolsky, Kraemer, & Spiegel, 2000). Evidence has suggested that early environmental influences from family relationships can affect future HPA functioning. In this section, research is highlighted that has discussed deficient parental support and familial conflict in terms of its effects on the HPA axis.

Deficient Parental Support

Children with less responsive parents and less secure attachments produce higher cortisol levels when faced with acute stressors (Gunnar &

Donzella, 2002). Further, parental warmth moderates the effect of stress on cortisol output such that the less parental warmth children received in childhood, the more cortisol they secreted on days they experienced severe stress as a young adults (Hanson & Chen, 2010). Indeed, recent empirical evidence has suggested that moderate to high levels of parental warmth early in life may have the ability to buffer the biological effects of stress beyond the childhood years or perhaps that a certain threshold value of parental support can provide regulatory effects on key biological pathways (Evans, Kim, Ting, Tesher, & Shannis, 2007; Hanson & Chen, 2010). In addition to parental support, the quality of parents' marital relationships may affect children's HPA axis functioning. Evidence for this comes from a recent study showing that poor marital functioning is associated with higher average and wake-up cortisol levels in both adolescent and kindergarten-aged children (Pendry & Adam, 2007).

Additional family research has revealed a relationship between cortisol levels and family characteristics—such as child care use and moderate amounts of family expressiveness—that may potentially serve as protective factors. In one study, the use of childcare was a protective factor against the effects of deficient parental support on daily cortisol production for children with mothers who had low job role quality and frequently experienced emotional exhaustion (Chryssanthopoulou, Turner-Cobb, Lucas, & Jessop, 2005). Specifically, children in families with average amounts of expressiveness—defined by the number of opportunities and amount of encouragement to express feelings and opinions—had lower cortisol levels in both the morning and evening compared with children in highly expressive or reserved families. Further, elevated cortisol levels were found in children with mothers reporting high levels of emotional exhaustion and low job quality. This multifaceted study provided insight on the complex relationships between health and families, in that high and low levels of family expressiveness can cause stressful family environments that may put a child at risk of future physical health problems; in contrast, moderate amounts of expressiveness may allow for a more stable and less stressful family environment to help safeguard children from the development of future health problems.

Familial Conflict

A handful of studies have focused specifically on family conflict and alterations of the HPA axis. For instance, in a study of 178 families and their kindergarten children, interparental conflict was associated with lower levels of cortisol reactivity in children listening to a simulated phone argument between their parents (Davies, Sturge-Apple, Cicchetti, & Cummings, 2007); diminished cortisol reactivity to the simulated phone argument predicted child-externalizing symptoms as reported by their parents. Some of our own work has investigated everyday family conflict in preschoolers' home environments and diurnal cortisol patterns using an innovative ambulatory assessment device called an *electronically activated recorder* (EAR; Mehl, Pennebaker, Crow, Dabbs, & Price, 2001). The EAR is a digital audio recorder that allows researchers to "hear" what family members are saying to each other, providing an acoustic log of the participants' days as they unfold. We have found, for example, that EAR-assessed daily conflict in the home—beyond parents' daily reports of conflict at home—is associated with lower cortisol at wakeup and flatter cortisol slopes in young children (Slatcher & Robles, 2012) This work represents an important advance in generating an ecologically valid understanding of the links between everyday behaviors and health-related biological processes in young children. Our findings have indicated that preschoolers' everyday conflicts at home are predictive of less "healthy" diurnal cortisol rhythms, extending previous research demonstrating links between questionnaire reports of family relationship quality and child cortisol (Pendry & Adam, 2007). However, this study is the first to our knowledge to show that young children's diurnal cortisol patterns are linked to discrete social behaviors in everyday life at home, providing a more nuanced understanding of the links between family environments and stress biology.

Additional work has been conducted on the long-term effects of early family stress on HPA axis functioning in young adults. For example, one study investigated the prospective effects of early parental divorce or separation before age 10 on HPA activity in young adults (ages 20–25), finding that divorce was associated with an alteration in HPA axis activity through increased adrenocorticotropic hormone levels—an important hormone in the HPA axis, released when under stress—and decreased cortisol release in the lab (Bloch, Peleg, Koren, Aner, & Klein, 2007). This work has suggested that not only do the presence of conflict and absence of family support have negative long-term health consequences but also that parents' marital dissolution can affect biomarkers of physical health as well.

Cardiovascular Reactivity

Psychosocial factors, such as conflict and aggression, can affect the cardiovascular system by delaying its recovery from acute stressors, as evidenced by sustained cardiovascular activation above baseline levels (Chida & Steptoe, 2010; Steptoe, 2007). Cardiovascular reactivity to stress is measured in a variety of ways through changes in blood pressure and heart rate, but also through changes in respiratory sinus arrhythmia, which reflects the influence of the parasympathetic nervous system on cardiovascular activity. When these different components of the cardiovascular system are under chronic stress, wear and tear from repeated surges in blood pressure and frequent increases in heart rate on the blood vessels and vasculature can build up and eventually lead to chronic diseases such as hypertension or cardiovascular disease (Pieper & Brosschot, 2005). In this section, we describe research suggesting that negative family relationships can adversely affect the cardiovascular system.

Deficient Parental Support

There is growing evidence that deficient parental support can detrimentally affect cardiovascular physiology. Parent–child relationships with lower levels of parental support (Woodall & Matthews, 1989) and harsh parenting styles (Gump, Matthews, & Raikkonen, 1999) elicit greater systolic and diastolic blood pressure reactivity to stressors. In a 4-year prospective study, children exposed to accumulated psychosocial and physical risk factors (e.g., poor housing quality, child–family separation) had increased "wear and tear" on multiple physiological systems—including the cardiovascular system (measured by blood pressure reactivity to an acute lab stressor)—but only when mothers were low in responsiveness (Evans et al., 2007); those children at high risk also had delayed blood pressure recovery during a mental arithmetic task. In terms of longitudinal effects of parental support on the cardiovascular system, more supportive and less negative parenting before kindergarten is associated with better cardiovascular functioning in elementary school—including lower heart rate and blood pressure—especially with the presence of a positive father–son relationship (Bell & Belsky, 2008). This research demonstrated that even a small amount of support early in life is beneficial to child health.

Although blood pressure provides a wealth of knowledge about the cardiovascular system's response to stress, another important aspect of the cardiovascular system with relevance for health is respiratory sinus arrhythmia (RSA). RSA can be assessed in the resting, baseline state—which some view as an indicator of vagal tone—and in response to challenge. Higher RSA has been associated with more flexible coping responses and greater self-regulation when individuals are confronted with a stressor (Calkins, 1994; Gentzler, Santucci, Kovacs, & Fox, 2009). One study showed that children who received parental support during a challenge task displayed a greater increase in RSA, indicating a healthier response (Calkins & Keane, 2004). Another study demonstrated that children with poor quality relationships—measured through observation of mothers and children across several laboratory interactions—have less vagal tone (lower resting RSA) and less heart rate acceleration across a variety of stress-inducing tasks, suggesting a less flexible cardiovascular response (Calkins, Graziano, Berdan, Keane, & Degnan, 2008). Several studies have suggested that alterations in

RSA are associated with increased risk for cardiovascular disease and even mortality (Gorman & Sloan, 2000; Heponiemi et al., 2007). Taken together, if parental support is associated with lower RSA, this has significant implications for health and well-being. The intricacies of the relationships between parental support, self-regulatory skills, and RSA remain unclear. The contributions from these studies show that parental support may contribute to both the acquisition of self-regulatory skills and higher RSA, to each variable separately, or to a third process that affects both variables.

Familial Conflict

There are various mechanisms through which family conflict may be related to cardiovascular outcomes; here, we focus specifically on RSA. Parental conflict is known to affect children's RSA as early as infancy. Moore (2010) showed that 6-month-old infants from families with higher levels of parental conflict showed smaller change in RSA when interacting with mothers, indicating a poorer RSA response. RSA has also been shown to mitigate the negative health effects of parental conflict. In boys ages 8 to 12, both a higher resting RSA and larger change in RSA during a challenge task protected against increased respiratory and digestive health problems related to the exposure to frequent marital and verbal conflict in their family (El-Sheikh, Harger, & Whitson, 2001). These studies indicated that alterations in RSA as a function of family conflict may be part of multiple (and bidirectional) pathways through which negative family relationships can lead to greater wear and tear on the cardiovascular system and increased risk of future cardiovascular problems.

INTERVENTIONS

Considering the deleterious effects that risky family environments can have on health, researchers are now beginning to design and test family interventions tailored to improving specific aspects of family relationships. These interventions are targeted at helping parents learn behaviors that shape effective behavioral skills in children, which, ultimately, may bring about improvements in the short-term and long-term prospects of child health and continue into later development. In the literature, there has been extensive intervention work with families of children with Type 1 diabetes. Families including a child with diabetes provide a good framework for testing family interventions, because adolescents with poorly controlled diabetes are more likely to be of lower socioeconomic status, come from a single-parent family, and have low levels of parental support (Delamater et al., 1999; Liss et al., 1998; Palta et al., 1997).

Multisystemic interventions incorporate intensive home- and community-based family therapies and show particular promise for improving child health. *Multisystemic therapy* (MST) is an individualized treatment model in which families set goals for a child's treatment and collaborate with a mental health professional to design and implement an action-oriented and focused treatment plan (Henggeler, Schoenwald, Borduin, Rowland, & Cunningham, 1998). This involves conducting assessments in the home, school, and community, focusing on gathering information from the youth, parent, siblings, peers, and teachers. In MST, a mental health professional's goal is to help a family identify their problems and prioritize changes that are most likely to lead to their desired outcomes. In recent research testing the efficacy of MST for diabetes, there was improvement in adolescents' metabolic control, reduction in nonadherence to treatment plans, and decreases of inpatient admissions over a 6-month period (Ellis et al., 2005; Naar-King et al., 2009). The multisystems approach has also been effectively used to treat obesity in African American adolescents: Those receiving MST showed significantly reduced body fat and weight, whereas those in a traditional weight-loss program did not (Naar-King et al., 2009). These preliminary studies have suggested that an intensive multisystems approach may be effective in curtailing some of the vulnerabilities and deficits associated with risky family environments.

CONCLUSION

Being in a family that is deficient in parental support, lacking warmth, and marked by frequent conflict puts a child at risk of both short-term and long-term health problems. Risky families have a detrimental impact on multiple biological systems, lessening the body's ability to protect itself against common illnesses and regulate its response to stress. The research to date on the links between family relationships and health calls for an integration of biological, emotional, cognitive, and behavioral outcomes into cohesive models that can help to explain the interplay between genes, environments, and their interactive effects on health. Still needed are studies identifying the critical developmental periods (e.g., preschool, school-age, adolescence) through which children are at risk of health problems and physiological dysfunction that may last into adulthood.

The evidence reviewed here suggests that negative family relationships can have lasting effects on child health, indicating a need for increased early family intervention research. Interventions focused on reducing family conflict and anger while also increasing warmth and cohesion are likely to be particularly effective. Parents in risky families, especially those in low socioeconomic environments, could potentially benefit from learning effective behavior and self-regulatory skills to foster more positive relationships with their children; early family interventions, in turn, may lead to improvements in child health (Naar-King et al., 2009). Troubled family environments cast a long shadow on physical health. Facilitating positive, warm interactions between parents and children through psychosocial interventions has the potential to shorten that shadow.

REFERENCES

Baumrind, D. (1991). The influence of parenting style on adolescent competence and substance use. *The Journal of Early Adolescence, 11,* 56–95. doi:10.1177/0272431691111004

Bell, B. G., & Belsky, J. (2008). Parenting and children's cardiovascular functioning. *Child: Care, Health and Development, 34,* 194–203. doi:10.1111/j.1365-2214.2007.00788.x

Belsky, J., Bell, B., Bradley, R., Stallard, N., & Stewart-Brown, S. (2007). Socioeconomic risk, parenting during the preschool years and child health age 6 years. *European Journal of Public Health, 17,* 508–513. doi:10.1093/eurpub/ckl261

Bloch, M., Peleg, I., Koren, D., Aner, H., & Klein, E. (2007). Long-term effects of parental loss due to divorce on the HPA axis. *Hormones and Behavior, 51,* 516–523. doi:10.1016/j.yhbeh.2007.01.009

Calkins, S. D. (1994). Origins and outcomes of individual differences in emotion regulation. *Monographs of the Society for Research in Child Development, 59,* 53–72. doi:10.2307/1166138

Calkins, S. D., Graziano, P., Berdan, L., Keane, S., & Degnan, K. (2008). Predicting cardiac vagal regulation in early childhood from maternal-child relationship quality during toddlerhood. *Developmental Psychobiology, 50,* 751–766. doi:10.1002/dev.20344

Calkins, S. D., & Keane, S. P. (2004). Cardiac vagal regulation across the preschool period: Stability, continuity, and implications for childhood adjustment. *Developmental Psychobiology, 45,* 101–112. doi:10.1002/dev.20020

Campbell, S. (Ed.). (2002). *Behavior problems in preschool children: Clinical and developmental issues* (2nd ed.). New York, NY: Guilford Press.

Chen, E., Bloomberg, G. R., Fisher, E. B., Jr., & Strunk, R. C. (2003). Predictors of repeat hospitalization in children with asthma: The role of psychosocial and socioenvironmental factors. *Health Psychology, 22,* 12–18. doi:10.1037/0278-6133.22.1.12

Chen, E., Chim, L. S., Strunk, R. C., & Miller, G. E. (2007). The role of the social environment in children and adolescents with asthma. *American Journal of Respiratory and Critical Care Medicine, 176,* 644–649. doi:10.1164/rccm.200610-1473OC

Chida, Y., & Steptoe, A. (2010). Greater cardiovascular responses to laboratory mental stress are associated with poor subsequent cardiovascular risk status: A meta-analysis of prospective evidence. *Hypertension, 55*, 1026–1032. doi:10.1161/HYPERTENSIONAHA.109.146621

Chryssanthopoulou, C. C., Turner-Cobb, J. M., Lucas, A., & Jessop, D. (2005). Childcare as a stabilizing influence on HPA axis functioning: A reevaluation of maternal occupational patterns and familial relations. *Developmental Psychobiology, 47*, 354–368. doi:10.1002/dev.20100

Cohen, S., Doyle, W. J., Skoner, D. P., Rabin, B. S., & Gwaltney, J. M., Jr. (1997, June 25). Social ties and susceptibility to the common cold. *JAMA, 277*, 1940–1944. doi:10.1001/jama.1997.03540480040036

Cohen, S., Miller, G. E., & Rabin, B. S. (2001). Psychological stress and antibody response to immunization: A critical review of the human literature. *Psychosomatic Medicine, 63*, 7–18.

Cummings, E. M., Schermerhorn, A. C., Davies, P. T., Goeke-Morey, M. C., & Cummings, J. S. (2006). Interparental discord and child adjustment: Prospective investigations of emotional security as an explanatory mechanism. *Child Development, 77*, 132–152. doi:10.1111/j.1467-8624.2006.00861.x

Davies, P. T., Sturge-Apple, M. L., Cicchetti, D., & Cummings, E. M. (2007). The role of child adrenocortical functioning in pathways between interparental conflict and child maladjustment. *Developmental Psychology, 43*, 918–930. doi:10.1037/0012-1649.43.4.918

Davies, P. T., Sturge-Apple, M. L., Cicchetti, D., & Cummings, E. M. (2008). Adrenocortical underpinnings of children's psychological reactivity to interparental conflict. *Child Development, 79*, 1693–1706. doi:10.1111/j.1467-8624.2008.01219.x

Delamater, A., Shaw, K., Applegate, E. B., Lancelott, G., Gonzalez-Mendoza, L., & Richton, S. (1999). Risk for metabolic control problems in minority youth with diabetes. *Diabetes Care, 22*, 700–705. doi:10.2337/diacare.22.5.700

Denham, S., & Kochanoff, A. T. (2002). Parental contributions to preschoolers' understanding of emotion. *Marriage & Family Review, 34*, 311–343. doi:10.1300/J002v34n03_06

Dickerson, S. S., & Kemeny, M. E. (2004). Acute Stressors and cortisol responses: A theoretical integration and synthesis of laboratory research. *Psychological Bulletin, 130*, 355–391. doi:10.1037/0033-2909.130.3.355

Dimsdale, J. E., & Herd, J. A. (1982). Variability of plasma lipids in response to emotional arousal. *Psychosomatic Medicine, 44*, 413–430.

Ellis, D. A., Frey, M., Naar-King, S., Templin, T., Cunningham, P., & Cakan, N. (2005). Use of multisystemic therapy to improve regimen adherence among adolescents with type 1 diabetes in chronic poor metabolic control: a randomized control trial. *Diabetes Care, 28*, 1604–1610. doi:10.2337/diacare.28.7.1604

El-Sheikh, M., Harger, J., & Whitson, S. (2001). Exposure to interparental conflict and children's adjustment and physical health: The moderating role of vagal tone. *Child Development, 72,* 1617–1636. doi:10.1111/1467-8624.00369

Entringer, S., Kumsta, R., Hellhammer, D. H., Wadhwa, P. D., & Wust, S. (2009). Prenatal exposure to maternal psychosoical stress and HPA axis regulation in young adults. *Hormones and Behavior, 55,* 292–298. doi:10.1016/j.yhbeh.2008.11.006

Evans, G. W., Kim, P., Ting, A. H., Tesher, H. B., & Shannis, D. (2007). Cumulative risk, maternal responsiveness, and allostatic load among young adolescents. *Developmental Psychology, 43,* 341–351. doi:10.1037/0012-1649.43.2.341

Felitti, V. J., Anda, R. F., Nordenberg, D., Williamson, D. F., Spitz, A. M., Edwards, V., . . . Marks, J. S. (1998). Relationship of childhood abuse and household dysfunction to many of the leading causes of death in adults: The Adverse Childhood Experiences (ACE) Study. *American Journal of Preventive Medicine, 14,* 245–258. doi:10.1016/S0749-3797(98)00017-8

Flinn, M. V. (2011). Social inequalities, family relationships, and child health. In A. Booth, S. M. McHale, & N. S. Landale (Eds.), *Biosocial foundations of family processes* (pp. 205–220). New York, NY: Springer.

Francis, D. D. (2009). Conceptualizing child health disparities: A role for developmental neurogenomics. *Pediatrics, 124,* S196–S202. doi:10.1542/peds.2009-1100G

Gentzler, A. L., Santucci, A. K., Kovacs, M., & Fox, N. (2009). Respiratory sinus arrhythmia reactivity predicts emotions regulation and depressive symptoms in at-risk and control children. *Biological Psychology, 82,* 156–163. doi:10.1016/j.biopsycho.2009.07.002

Gorman, J. M., & Sloan, R. P. (2000). Heart rate variability in depressive and anxiety disorders. *American Heart Journal, 140*(4), 77–83. doi:10.1067/mhj.2000.109981

Gottman, J. M., & Katz, L. F. (1989). Effects of marital discord on young children's peer interaction and health. *Developmental Psychology, 25,* 373–381. doi:10.1037/0012-1649.25.3.373

Gottman, J. M., Katz, L. F., & Hooven, C. (1996). Parental meta-emotion philosophy and the emotional life of families: Theoretical models and preliminary data. *Journal of Family Psychology, 10,* 243–268. doi:10.1037/0893-3200.10.3.243

Grych, J. H., & Fincham, F. D. (1990). Martial conflict and children's adjustment: A cognitive-contextual framework. *Psychological Bulletin, 108,* 267–290. doi:10.1037/0033-2909.108.2.267

Gump, B. B., Matthews, K. A., & Raikkonen, K. (1999). Modeling relationships among socioeconomic status, hostility, cardiovascular reactivity, and left ventricular mass in African American and White children. *Health Psychology, 18,* 140–150. doi:10.1037/0278-6133.18.2.140

Gunnar, M. R., & Donzella, B. (2002). Social regulation of the cortisol levels in early human development. *Psychoneuroendocrinology, 27,* 199–220. doi:10.1016/S0306-4530(01)00045-2

Hair, E. C., Moore, K. A., Hadley, A. M., Kaye, K., Day, R. D., & Orthner, D. K. (2009). Parent marital quality and the parent–adolescent relationship: Effects on adolescent and young adult health outcomes. *Marriage & Family Review*, *45*, 218–248. doi:10.1080/01494920902733567

Hanson, M. D., & Chen, E. (2010). Daily stress, cortisol, and sleep: The moderating role of childhood psychosocial environments. *Health Psychology*, *29*, 394–402. doi:10.1037/a0019879

Henggeler, S. W., Schoenwald, S. K., Borduin, C. M., Rowland, M. D., & Cunningham, P. (1998). *Multisystemic treatment of antisocial behavior in children and adolescents*. New York, NY: Guilford Press.

Heponiemi, T., Elovainio, M., Pulkki, L., Puttonen, S., Raitakari, O., & Keltikangas-Jarvinen, L. (2007). Cardiac autonomic reactivity and recovery in predicting carotid atherosclerosis: The cardiovascular risk in young Finns study. *Health Psychology*, *26*, 13–21. doi:10.1037/0278-6133.26.1.13

Herbert, T. B., & Cohen, S. (1993). Stress and immunity in humans: A meta-analytic review. *Psychosomatic Medicine*, *55*, 364–379.

Holsboer, F. (2000). The corticosteroid receptor hypothesis of depression. *Neuropsychopharmacology*, *23*, 477–501. doi:10.1016/S0893-133X(00)00159-7

Jago, R., Davison, K., Brockman, R., Page, A., Thompson, J., & Fox, K. (2011). Parenting styles, parenting practices, and physical activity in 10- to 11-year olds. *Preventive Medicine*, *52*, 44–47. doi:10.1016/j.ypmed.2010.11.001

Kaslow, N. J., Deering, C. G., & Racusin, G. R. (1994). Depressed children and their families. *Clinical Psychology Review*, *14*, 39–59. doi:10.1016/0272-7358(94)90047-7

Kaugars, A. S., Klinnert, M. D., & Bender, B. G. (2004). Family influences on pediatric asthma. *Journal of Pediatric Psychology*, *29*, 475–491. doi:10.1093/jpepsy/jsh051

Kendler, K. S. (1996). Parenting: A genetic-epidemiologic perspective. *The American Journal of Psychiatry*, *153*, 11–20.

Kiecolt-Glaser, J. K., Glaser, R., Gravenstein, S., Malarkey, W. B., & Sheridan, J. (1996). Chronic stress alters the immune response to influenza virus vaccine in older adults. *Proceedings of the National Academy of Sciences of the United States of America*, *93*, 3043–3047. doi:10.1073/pnas.93.7.3043

Kudielka, B. M., & Kirschbaum, C. (2005). Sex differences in HPA axis responses to stress: A review. *Biological Psychology*, *69*, 113–132. doi:10.1016/j.biopsycho.2004.11.009

Kumari, M., Shipley, M., Stafford, M., & Kivimaki, M. (2011). Association of diurnal patterns in salivary cortisol with all-cause and cardiovascular mortality: Findings from the Whitehall II study. *The Journal of Clinical Endocrinology and Metabolism*, *96*, 1478–1485. doi:10.1210/jc.2010-2137

Larzelere, M. M., & Jones, G. N. (2008). Stress and health. *Primary Care*, *35*, 839–856. doi:10.1016/j.pop.2008.07.011

Lee, T. H., Brattsand, R., & Leung, D. Y. M. (1996). Corticosteroid action and resistance in asthma. *American Journal of Respiratory Cell and Molecular Biology*, *154*, S1–S79.

Liss, D. S., Waller, D. A., Kennard, B. D., McIntire, D., Capra, P., & Stephens, J. (1998). Psychiatric illness and family support in children and adolescents with diabetic ketoacidosis: a controlled study. *Journal of the American Academy of Child & Adolescent Psychiatry, 37*, 536–544. doi:10.1097/00004583-199805000-00016

Lissau, I., & Sorensen, T. (1994). Parental neglect during childhood and increased risk of obesity in young adulthood. *The Lancet, 343*, 324–327. doi:10.1016/S0140-6736(94)91163-0

Luecken, L. J., & Fabricius, W. V. (2003). Physical health vulnerability in adult children from divorced and intact families. *Journal of Psychosomatic Research, 55*, 221–228. doi:10.1016/S0022-3999(02)00552-4

Luecken, L. J., & Lemery, K. S. (2004). Early caregiving and physiological stress responses. *Clinical Psychology Review, 24*, 171–191. doi:10.1016/j.cpr.2004.01.003

Mäntymaa, M., Puura, K., Luoma, I., Salmelin, R., Davis, H., Tsiantis, J., . . . Tamminen, T. (2003). Infant–mother interaction as a predictor of child's chronic health problems. *Child: Care, Health and Development, 29*, 181–191. doi:10.1046/j.1365-2214.2003.00330.x

Marin, T. J., Chen, E., Munch, J. A., & Miller, G. E. (2009). Double-exposure to acute stress and chronic family stress is associated with immune changes in children with asthma. *Psychosomatic Medicine, 71*, 378–384. doi:10.1097/PSY.0b013e318199dbc3

Martin, M. T., Miller-Johnson, S., Kitzmann, K. M., & Emery, R. E. (1998). Parent–child relationships and insulin-dependent diabetes mellitus: Observational ratings of clinically relevant dimensions. *Journal of Family Psychology, 12*, 102–111. doi:10.1037/0893-3200.12.1.102

McEwen, B. S. (2003). Early life influences on life-long patterns of behavior and health. *Mental Retardation and Developmental Disabilities Research Reviews, 9*, 149–154. doi:10.1002/mrdd.10074

Meadows, S. O. (2011). The association between perceptions of social support and maternal mental health: A cumulative perspective. *Journal of Family Issues, 32*, 181–208. doi:10.1177/0192513X10375064

Meaney, M. J. (2001). Maternal care, gene expression, and the transmission of individual differences in stress reactivity across generations. *Annual Review of Neuroscience, 24*, 1161–1192. doi:10.1146/annurev.neuro.24.1.1161

Mehl, M. R., Pennebaker, J. W., Crow, M. D., Dabbs, J., & Price, J. H. (2001). The Electronically Activated Recorder (EAR): A device for sampling naturalistic daily activities and conversations. *Behavior Research Methods, 33*, 517–523. doi:10.3758/BF03195410

Michael, K. C., Torres, A., & Seemann, E. A. (2007). Adolescents health habits, coping styles and self-concept are predicted by exposure to interparental conflict. *Journal of Divorce & Remarriage, 48*, 155–174. doi:10.1300/J087v48n01_09

Miller, G. E., & Chen, E. (2010). Harsh family climate in early life presages the emergence of a proinflammatory phenotype in adolescence. *Psychological Science, 21*, 848–856. doi:10.1177/0956797610370161

Miller, G. E., Chen, E., & Zhou, E. S. (2007). If it goes up, must it come down? Chronic stress and the hypothalamic–pituitary–adrenocortical axis in humans. *Psychological Bulletin, 133,* 25–45. doi:10.1037/0033-2909.133.1.25

Miller, G. E., Gaudin, A., Zysk, E., & Chen, E. (2009). Parental support and cytokine activity in childhood asthma: The role of glucocorticoid sensitivity. *The Journal of Allergy and Clinical Immunology, 123,* 824–830. doi:10.1016/j.jaci.2008.12.019

Montgomery, S. M., Bartley, M. J., & Wilkinson, R. G. (1997). Family conflict and slow growth. *Archives of Disease in Childhood, 77,* 326–330. doi:10.1136/adc.77.4.326

Moore, G. A. (2010). Parent conflict predicts infants' vagal regulation in social interaction. *Development and Psychopathology, 22,* 23–33. doi:10.1017/S095457940999023X

Naar-King, S., Ellis, D., Kolmodin, K., Cunningham, P., Jen, K. L., Saelens, B., & Brogan, K. (2009). A randomized pilot study of multisystemic therapy targeting obesity in African-American adolescents. *Journal of Adolescent Health, 45,* 417–419. doi:10.1016/j.jadohealth.2009.03.022

Northey, S., Griffin, W. A., & Krainz, S. (1998). A partial test of the psychosomatic family model: Marital interaction patterns in asthma and nonasthma families. *Journal of Family Psychology, 12,* 220–233. doi:10.1037/0893-3200.12.2.220

Palta, M., LeCaire, T., Daniel, K., Shen, G., Allen, C., & D'Alessio, D. (1997). Risk factors for hospitalization in a cohort with Type 1 diabetes. *American Journal of Epidemiology, 146,* 627–636. doi:10.1093/oxfordjournals.aje.a009328

Pendry, P., & Adam, E. K. (2007). Associations between parents marital functioning, maternal parenting quality, maternal emotion and child cortisol levels. *International Journal of Behavioral Development, 31,* 218–231. doi:10.1177/0165025407074634

Pieper, S., & Brosschot, J. F. (2005). Prolonged stress-related cardiovascular activation: Is there any? *Annals of Behavioral Medicine, 30,* 91–103. doi:10.1207/s15324796abm3002_1

Reading, R. (2007). When home is where the stress is: Expanding the dimensions of housing that influence asthma morbidity. *Child: Care, Health and Development, 33,* 111–112. doi:10.1111/j.1365-2214.2006.00723_6.x

Reiss, D., Hetherington, M., Plomin, R., Howe, G. W., Simmens, S. J., Henderson, S. H., . . . Law, T. (1995). Genetic questions for environmental studies: Differential parenting and psychopathology in adolescence. *Archives of General Psychiatry, 52,* 925–936. doi:10.1001/archpsyc.1995.03950230039007

Repetti, R. L., Taylor, S. E., & Seeman, T. E. (2002). Risky families: Family social environments and the mental and physical health of offspring. *Psychological Bulletin, 128,* 330–366. doi:10.1037/0033-2909.128.2.330

Resnick, M. D. (1997, September 10). Protecting adolescents from harm: Findings from the National Longitudinal Study on Adolescent Health. *JAMA, 278,* 823–832. doi:10.1001/jama.1997.03550100049038

Rhee, K. E., Lumeng, J. C., Appugliese, D. P., Kaciroti, N., & Bradley, R. H. (2006). Parenting styles and overweight status in the first grade. *Pediatrics, 117,* 2047–2054. doi:10.1542/peds.2005-2259

Russek, L. G., & Schwartz, G. E. (1997). Perceptions of parental caring predict health status in midlife: A 35-year follow-up of the Harvard Mastery of Stress Study. *Psychosomatic Medicine, 59,* 144–149.

Sandberg, S., Paton, J. Y., Ahola, S., McCann, D. C., McGuinness, D., Hillary, C. R., & Oja, H. (2000). The role of acute and chronic stress in asthma attacks in children. *The Lancet, 356,* 982–987. doi:10.1016/S0140-6736(00)02715-X

Segerstrom, S. C., & Miller, G. E. (2004). Psychological stress and the human immune system: A meta-analytic study of 30 years of inquiry. *Psychological Bulletin, 130,* 601–630. doi:10.1037/0033-2909.130.4.601

Sephton, S. E., Sapolsky, R. M., Kraemer, H. C., & Spiegel, D. (2000). Diurnal cortisol rhythm as a predictor of breast cancer survival. *Journal of the National Cancer Institute, 92,* 994–1000. doi:10.1093/jnci/92.12.994

Shalowitz, M. U., Berry, C. A., Quinn, K. A., & Wolf, R. L. (2001). The relationship of life stressors and maternal depression to pediatric asthma morbidity in a subspecialty practice. *Ambulatory Pediatrics, 1,* 185–193. doi:10.1367/1539-4409(2001)001<0185:TROLSA>2.0.CO;2

Shonkoff, J. P., Boyce, W. T., & McEwen, B. S. (2009, June 3). Neuroscience, molecular biology, and the childhood roots of health disparities: Building a new framework for health promotion and disease prevention. *JAMA, 301,* 2252–2259. doi:10.1001/jama.2009.754

Slatcher, R. B., & Robles, T. F. (2012). Preschoolers' everyday conflict at home and diurnal cortisol patterns. *Health Psychology.* Advance online publication. doi:10.1037/a0026774

Stein, A., Woolley, H., Cooper, S. D., & Fairburn, C. G. (1994). An observational study of mothers with eating disorders and their infants. *Journal of Child Psychology and Psychiatry, 35,* 733–748. doi:10.1111/j.1469-7610.1994.tb01218.x

Steptoe, A. (2007). Psychophysiological contributions to behavioral medicine and psychosomatics. In J. T. Cacioppo, L. G. Tassinary, & G. G. Berntson (Eds.), *Handbook of psychophysiology* (3rd ed., pp. 2723–2751). New York, NY: Cambridge University Press.

Stewart-Brown, S. L., Fletcher, L., & Wadsworth, M. E. (2005). Parent–child relationships and health problems in adulthood in three UK national birth cohort studies. *European Journal of Public Health, 15,* 640–646. doi:10.1093/eurpub/cki049

Taylor, S. E. (2010). Mechanisms linking early life stress to adult health outcomes. *Proceedings of the National Academy of Sciences of the United States of America, 107,* 8507–8512. doi:10.1073/pnas.1003890107

Tiberg, I., Hallstrom, I., & Carlsson, A. (2010). The influence of initial management and family stress on metabolic control in children with type 1 diabetes. *International Journal of Clinical Medicine, 1,* 41–47. doi:10.4236/ijcm.2010.12008

Valentiner, D. P., Holahan, C. J., & Moos, R. H. (1994). Social support, appraisals of event controllability, and coping: An integrative model. *Journal of Personality and Social Psychology, 66,* 1094–1102. doi:10.1037/0022-3514.66.6.1094

Walker, E. A., Gelfand, A., Katon, J., Koss, M., Von Korff, M., Bernstein, D., & Russon, J. (1999). Adult health status of women with histories of childhood abuse. *The American Journal of Medicine, 107,* 332–339. doi:10.1016/S0002-9343(99)00235-1

Waylen, A., Stallard, N., & Stewart-Brown, S. (2008). Parenting and health in mid-childhood: A longitudinal study. *European Journal of Public Health, 18,* 300–305. doi:10.1093/eurpub/ckm131

Weidner, G., Hutt, J., Connor, S. L., & Mendell, N. R. (1992). Family stress and coronary risk in children. *Psychosomatic Medicine, 54,* 471–479.

White, J., & Halliwell, E. (2011). Family meal frequency and alcohol and tobacco use in adolescence: Testing reciprocal effects. *The Journal of Early Adolescence, 31,* 735–749. doi:10.1177/0272431610373104

Woodall, K. L., & Matthews, K. A. (1989). Familial environment associated with Type A behaviors and psychophysiological responses to stress in children. *Health Psychology, 8,* 403–426. doi:10.1037/0278-6133.8.4.403

Wright, R. J. (2007). Prenatal maternal stress and early caregiving experiences: Implications for childhood asthma risk. *Paediatric and Perinatal Epidemiology, 21,* 8–14. doi:10.1111/j.1365-3016.2007.00879.x

Yehuda, R. (1997). Sensitization of the hypothalamic–pituitary–adrenal axis in posttraumatic stress disorder. *Annals of the New York Academy of Sciences, 821,* 57–75. doi:10.1111/j.1749-6632.1997.tb48269.x

7

PEER RELATIONSHIPS AND HEALTH: FROM CHILDHOOD THROUGH ADULTHOOD

KATHLEEN S. BRYAN, YESMINA N. PUCKETT,
AND MATTHEW L. NEWMAN

The time people spend with their peers—those of roughly the same age or maturity level—provides a valuable source of information about how the world works outside the family environment. Peers can be a source of support in times of need, but they can just as easily be a source of angst for those who do not fit in (see Fehr, 1996, for a review). Peer relationships are unique in that they can be present regardless of whether someone is married or single, experiences a partner loss, or grows up in a supportive or critical family. Throughout the life span, individuals spend the majority of their time in groups, with peer group relationships and friendships representing a large portion of these group interactions (cf. Hartup & Stevens, 1999). Indeed, more time may be spent with peers than with one's spouse or family because they are the primary source of social interaction when at school or work.

With this in mind, an understanding of the relation between peer relationships and health can shed light on the general impact of social

DOI: 10.1037/14036-008
Health and Social Relationships: The Good, the Bad, and the Complicated, Matthew L. Newman
and Nicole A. Roberts (Editors)

relationships on health outcomes. Our focus in this chapter is on health connections and outcomes with respect to peer relationships at different life stages. By reviewing literature on a variety of examples of both "good" and "bad" peer relationships, this chapter highlights how peer relationships can affect, and be affected by, health outcomes in a variety of settings and at any age.

Much of the literature has made a distinction between overall *peer acceptance*, broadly defined as one's social standing within the overall peer group, and *friendships*, defined as relationships based on mutual respect, appreciation, and liking. These two constructs have been associated with overlapping, but slightly different, outcomes: Greater acceptance by the group is associated with increased feelings of belonging and with fewer behavioral problems (Brown & Lohr, 1987; Coie, Terry, Lenox, Lochman, & Hyman, 1995), whereas friendships are associated with reduced feelings of loneliness (Bukowski, Hoza, & Boivin, 1993), which is associated with a host of negative outcomes (e.g., Cacioppo et al., 2002). However, both of these are predictive of increased self-esteem and better psychological adjustment (Parker & Asher, 1993). For this reason, we cover both constructs here under the umbrella of *peer relationships*.

Our review of the connections between peer relationships and health is guided by the theoretical model shown in Figure 7.1. We argue that (a) there is a bidirectional relationship between peer relationships and health, with different mechanisms driving each direction and (b) the connections between relationships and health can be either positive or negative. As suggested in the top portion of Figure 7.1, we discuss how peer relationships can have a positive impact on health, through increased social support and/or encouraging positive health behaviors. We also discuss how peer relationships can have a negative impact on health, either because the relationships are a source of stress or because they encourage unhealthy behaviors.

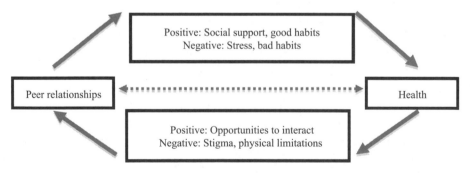

Figure 7.1. Proposed pathways linking peer relationships and health. This model suggests that (a) there is a bidirectional relationship between peer relationships and health, with different mechanisms driving each direction and (b) the connections between relationships and health can be either positive or negative.

As suggested in the bottom portion of Figure 7.1, an individual's physical and emotional health can also shape his or her peer relationships. For example, good emotional health can facilitate positive interactions, whereas poor physical health can limit ability to engage fully in social activities or can be associated with stigma that is damaging to forming new peer relationships. In the sections that follow, we review evidence for several examples of this bidirectional model at three different life stages—childhood, adolescence, and adulthood—highlighting the unique features of peer relationships within each stage.

CHILDHOOD

Unique Features of Childhood

The links between peer relationships and health in children can be distinguished from other age groups in several ways. Specifically, the health implications resulting from childhood peer relationships last long after the childhood years and well into adulthood. Furthermore, for children, the peer group is not yet the most influential or critical relationship, meaning that any positive or negative experiences with this group will interact with familial relationship outcomes to determine health implications. Although mothers and fathers are seen as the most frequent providers of support for children in the fourth grade, same-sex friends were perceived to be as supportive as parents by the seventh grade (Furman & Buhrmester, 1992). Furthermore, children with health problems struggle in their peer relationships, just as individuals in other age groups. However, as discussed later, only part of the struggle is due to stigmas that their peer groups assign to them; some children with illness place this stigma on themselves. This suggests insecurity and low self-worth, both of which are results of poor peer relationships. For this age group in particular, then, we see that the cyclical relationship between peer relationships and health is particularly relevant. However, it is important to note that many of the outcomes of peer relationships during this time do not lead to direct health outcomes during childhood; instead, many are associated with behaviors that predispose children to positive or negative health outcomes when they reach adolescence.

Effects of Peer Relationships on Health

Rubin, Coplan, Chen, Buskirk, and Wojslawowicz (2005) differentiated the construct of friendship from those of popularity, cliques, or peer groups on the basis of its emphasis on reciprocity. Friendships in particular play an important role in the lives of children (Hartup & Stevens, 1999). Newcomb and Bagwell (1995) focused specifically on defining the role of friendships and suggested that friendship in childhood serves four distinct purposes, each of which either directly or indirectly affects health outcomes. For children, friendship (a) provides the opportunity to learn and use skills effective for interpersonal communication; (b) provides a foundation for future relationships, including romantic, peer, and familial; (c) provides the opportunity to express emotion and gain experience in regulating emotions; and (d) provides the opportunity to share, cooperate, and help others (Newcomb & Bagwell, 1995).

Parker and Gottman (1989) suggested that friendships serve different purposes at different stages of childhood. Specifically, for the young child, friendship serves to maximize amusement and excitement during play activities and begins to teach the child how to organize behaviors during such excitement. In middle childhood, friendships help individuals learn behavioral norms and the skills required to meet and fit within those norms. These skills become critical during this stage because anxiety about peer relationships begins to develop. Finally, in late childhood (or the start of adolescence), individuals are in a period of self-exploration, and friendships provide an avenue through which they can do this (Parker & Gottman, 1989). Although these functions vary by age, each touches on skills necessary for adaptive and healthy development.

According to Berndt and Keefe (1995), during times of transition, friendship can promote positive adjustment during stressful experiences. As an example, as children transition into elementary school, those who enter school with a mutual friend report higher levels of school satisfaction and academic interest (Rubin et al., 2005). In addition, among preschool children, positive interactive play behavior was associated with active engagement in classroom learning, higher levels of competence motivation, attention, persistence, and a positive attitude toward learning (Coolahan, Fantuzzo, Mendez, & McDermott, 2000). Further, peer acceptance among 5-year-old children moderates the negative effects of family adversity, and friendship can moderate the negative effects of harsh discipline at home (Criss, Pettit, Bates, Dodge, & Lapp, 2002).

Children without friends, in contrast, report more loneliness and may lack social skills (Rubin et al., 2005). Specifically, regardless of their level of overall acceptance within their peer group, children without best friends were found to be lonelier than children with best friends (Parker & Asher, 1993). In addition to acceptance and lack of friends, the quality of children's friendships was also found to predict loneliness at a 1-month follow-up assessment. Parker and Asher (1993) found that children's feelings of loneliness arise from several sources that, taken together, can cause serious harm to children's feelings of well-being. The sources included being poorly accepted by peers, lacking a friend, or having a friend of poor quality. When looking at the long-term health implications of loneliness, Bagwell, Newcomb, and Bukowski (1998) found that not having a close, reciprocal friend in the fifth grade predicted negative feelings of self-worth during adulthood.

Although it is not surprising that children who are rejected and disliked tend to feel lonely and isolated, Rubin et al. (2005) found that rejected children incorporate the rejection into their self-concept. Specifically, they report feeling less competent, less effective, and less satisfied with their social skills and peer relationships than their more popular counterparts. This conclusion was found to be true, however, only for rejected children described as withdrawn, timid, or submissive. Rejected children who were described as aggressive, in contrast, tend to overestimate their social skills and acceptance. However, like rejected children described as withdrawn, rejected children who are aggressive also report feeling less competent and less effective.

Hymel, Rubin, Rowden, and LeMare (1990) further explored this topic by looking at whether social difficulties in early childhood predicted internalizing and externalizing problems in middle childhood. The authors found that early peer rejection was predictive of aggression and other externalizing difficulties later in childhood. In addition, early peer rejection was linked to internalizing problems in middle childhood, including feelings of poor peer acceptance, social isolation, and perceptions of social incompetence. Thus, social isolation, they found, is a significant risk factor in early child development (Hymel et al., 1990). After studying variations of peer rejection in terms of proximity and duration, DeRosier, Kupersmidt, and Patterson (1994) found that all levels of rejection were associated with greater absenteeism from school, whereas more chronic and proximal rejection was associated with higher levels of externalizing and internalizing behavior problems. Therefore, it becomes clear that peer rejection in childhood is associated with both internalizing and externalizing behavior problems that can last well into late childhood and beyond.

It has been found that during childhood, bullies and bully victims are more aggressive than their peers (Perren & Alsaker, 2006). Much of the research on bullying during childhood focuses on outcomes for the victims; however, the bullies have distinct and flawed peer relationships as well, which have various health implications. Overall, bullies are often preferred by classmates, particularly by other aggressive peers, belong to larger social groups, and possess more leadership skills. However, although they do not tend to experience peer rejection or victimization, they exhibit less prosocial behavior (Perren & Alsaker, 2006). As a result, they are likely to be influenced by their peer groups to maintain or even increase their aggressive behaviors, as well as to maintain nonprosocial behaviors, both of which increase the likelihood for negative health behaviors and outcomes.

Taken together, we see that during childhood, peer relationships can have a significant impact on health. However, many of these outcomes, positive or negative, occur in combination with other variables; this is particularly true of family situations. Many of the outcomes of peer relationships during this time do not lead to direct health outcomes during childhood; instead, childhood peer relationships are associated with behaviors that predispose children to positive or negative health outcomes when they reach adolescence.

Effects of Health on Peer Relationships

As pointed out in the previous section, support from close friends and positive peer relationships can minimize the negative impact of stressors—but peer rejection and other forms of negative peer relationships can exacerbate stress. This may be particularly true with respect to children with health conditions, which in turn influences peer relationships in a cyclical fashion. For example, children with chronic illnesses must adjust to having a disease and often undergo difficult medical treatments and procedures. Given that these children are faced with higher numbers and severity of stressors than other children their age, it would seem critical that they have close friends and positive peer relationships to help buffer these stressors. However, due to the stigmatizing nature of many chronic illnesses, it seems fair to expect that children with health issues are less likely to receive peer support. Surprisingly, however, children with chronic health conditions do not generally have more problems in peer relationships than children without any health issues (La Greca, Bearman, & Moore, 2002).

Although children with chronic health issues do not generally experience any setbacks in their peer relationships, those with stigmatizing medical conditions often do encounter some problems in relating to their peers. Specifically, children with cancer, asthma, and diabetes have generally not been found to have problems in their peer relationships, whereas children with cerebral palsy, central nervous system–related conditions, spina bifida, epilepsy, sickle cell disease, HIV infection, and cancers that involve brain tissue have demonstrated difficulties in their peer relationships (La Greca et al., 2002). The nature of the illness, therefore, is a critical predictor of whether children with health problems are able to develop positive peer relationships.

By the age of 7, children with attention-deficit/hyperactivity disorder (ADHD) are ranked lower on social preference, are less well liked, and are more often placed in the rejected social status category by their peer group (Hinshaw & Melnick, 1995; Hoza et al., 2005), and this stigma persists into young adulthood (Canu, Newman, Morrow, & Pope, 2008). Improving the peer relationships of children with ADHD is thought to have a significant effect on both long- and short-term health outcomes (Mrug, Hoza, & Gerdes, 2001). ADHD affects a child's ability to develop positive peer relationships because of a combination of hyperactivity and aggression (Mrug et al., 2001) and deficits in social skills (e.g., Mikami, Lerner, & Lun, 2010). Improving these relationships is considered important for health because the positive outcomes of peer relationships are thought to mitigate the severity of the disease (Mrug et al., 2001).

Children with autism often struggle with peer relationships, experiencing few close and stable friendships, few invitations to parties or other children's homes, and poor relationships with classmates (Kelly, Garnett, Attwood, & Peterson, 2008). However, there is a lack of relationship between peer support, or lack thereof, and autism symptomatology. This is not to say that no positive health outcomes result from peer relationships for children with autism, only that there are no positive direct effects on the disease itself that are derived from peer relationships (Kelly et al., 2008). Instead, peer support appears to influence potential mediators of symptom reduction.

An interesting group to consider is children who are obese. Not surprisingly, overweight and obese children (ages 11–16) are more likely to be the victims of bullying behaviors and peer victimization. Interestingly, these same children are also more likely to be the perpetrators of bullying behaviors and peer victimization (Janssen, Craig, Boyce, & Pickett, 2004). Although obese children are victimized because of their weight, they tend to bully other children on the basis of race, color, or religion. It is possible that after being victimized for their appearance, they internalize these criticisms and behave in a way that manifests these criticisms (Janssen et al., 2004). The negative effects, including loneliness, sadness, and nervousness, of peer victimization and poor peer relationships are the same for obese children as they are for other children (Janssen et al., 2004).

Part of the challenge in developing peer relationships for children with health conditions is not the stigma or the perceptions held by other children, but instead the perceptions of the children themselves. Many children with chronic medical problems express concern about the impact of their condition on their ability to fit in, and the possible disruption of their peer relationships. Children have even been found to forgo treatment to better fit in with peers (La Greca et al., 2002). It is possible, then, that one component of the stigmas attached to some illnesses exists in the mind of the child with the illness. In this way, it is possible that children with illness have fewer and lower quality peer relationships in part because of feelings of their peer group, but also in part as a result of their own negative feelings about their illness and themselves.

Understanding peer relationships for children with health problems is difficult, given that for some illnesses, health conditions do not affect peer relationships. For other conditions, peer relationships are negatively affected, and children with those illnesses experience greater rejection and peer victimization. It appears that the strongest negative impact on peer relationships comes from illnesses that are the most stigmatizing and illnesses with the greatest outward manifestation of symptoms.

ADOLESCENCE

Unique Features of Adolescence

Social status and interaction with peers increase in importance during adolescence, compared with the focus on parent and family involvement during childhood. Indeed, research has indicated that older youth interact with peers more frequently and for longer periods than do younger youth, both within school and outside of school (Larson & Richards, 1991). During high school and adolescence, same-sex friends become the most frequent providers of support, whereas romantic partners move up in importance during college, along with friends and mothers (Furman & Buhrmester, 1992).

Most relationships of any nature are based on a principle of propinquity, with adolescents connecting with those whom they see most often (Feld, 1981; McPherson, Smith-Lovin, & Cook, 2001), and the greatest portion of adolescent socialization takes place in an educational setting (Haas, Schaefer, & Kornienko, 2010). As discussed by Tobin, Slatcher, and Robles (Chapter 6, this volume), familial involvement in childhood has a clear impact on health outcomes during adolescence. Social interactions begin to play a highly influential role during this period as well.

One of the landmark social changes in adolescence is the development of physical and romantic relationships. Because of the onset of puberty and the beginning of significant differentiation of male and female roles, the health and social experience for each gender can vary significantly. In addition, the gap in societal and social expectation of males and females becomes more prominent at this stage of life (Haas et al., 2010; Worell, 1981). According to Worell (1981) and Galambos, Almeida, and Petersen (1990), boys have a social expectation to exhibit independent behaviors, whereas girls have the expectation to develop nurturing and expressive behaviors.

Although no longer the primary focus, relationships with adults continue to have relevance and influence during adolescence and can moderate the influence of peer relationships. The presence or absence of family members, particularly fathers, can have long-term impact on academic achievement in school for males (Nation, Vieno, Perkins, & Santinello, 2008) and can be used as a predictor of future occupational success for both males and females (Flouri & Buchanan, 2002, 2004). Positive interactions and perceived social support from adults—both parents and teachers—can improve perceived quality of life, reduce incidents of bullying and victimization in school, and lead to improved academic performance (Nation et al., 2008). In addition, DuBois and Karcher (2005) found that although adolescents put increased effort into their relationships with peers, maintaining positive secondary relationships with adults can make intervention into negative peer relationships more successful. For example, adolescents who eat dinner with their families for a majority of the week are less likely to participate in risk-taking behaviors, to experience depression or suicidal ideation, or to be overweight or obese.

Effects of Peer Relationships on Health

Multiple issues in peer relationships can have serious effects on the health and development of adolescents. In this section, we focus on four such factors: bullying and victimization, romantic involvement, sexual orientation, and obesity.

In many aspects of health and peer development in adolescents, there is a clear distinction between the male and female experience (Nishina, Juvonen, & Witkow, 2005). It is not a coincidence that this stage in development coincides with hormonal changes in males and menarche and hormonal shifts in females. All types of romantic interaction have the potential to either enhance positive social bonds and physical health or create a deleterious environment. Adolescents at this stage of life are beginning to adapt and conform to gender identity standards—a process referred to as *gender intensification*. The pressure to conform to traditional gender roles is much stronger for males than females (Galambos et al., 1990; Tolman, Striepe, & Harmon, 2003). Boys who are labeled not "man enough" face an increase in suicidal ideations, depressive symptoms, and decreased healthy social interactions (Swearer, Espelage, Vaillancourt, & Hymel, 2010). Kimmel and Mahler (2003) argued that nearly all of the incidents of school shootings between 1982 and 2001 were carried out by boys who had been frequently taunted for appearing gay, sexually inadequate, or being nonconformist with typical male culture.

Gender development at this stage of life has a major impact on adolescents' type, quality, and amount of social interaction and specifically on sexual health, sexual choices, and stability of sexual relationships (Tolman et al., 2003). Specifically, this research has suggested that adolescent girls with negative sexual experiences and negative or stunted gender development are more at risk of negative health outcomes such as domestic violence, sexually transmitted disease, or unwanted pregnancy. For heterosexual boys, there is a constant need to reject notions of homosexuality and appear "less gay" or risk being socially ostracized or physically harmed by their peers. Negative romantic relationships for both males and females can lead to a number of physical and psychological conditions such as depression, anxiety, substance abuse, or actual physical harm from a partner. A striking number of adolescents report some sort of domestic abuse from a partner, whether it is in the form of physical or emotional abuse, and this abuse is not limited to females (Muñoz-Rivas, Grana, O'Leary, & Gonzàlez, 2007). This research by Muñoz-Rivas et al. (2007) also suggested that males experience additional pressure to become sexually active at a young age and that there is a higher acceptance of multiple sexual partners.

Interpersonal and domestic relationship violence is not the only risk factor for adolescents. Bullying among adolescents, defined as chronic mistreatment by more-powerful peers, is one of the clearest and best-documented risks to adolescent health. The typical bullying scenario imagined by most is overt physical bullying. However, research has shown that other forms are equally psychologically harmful (e.g., Baldry, 2004). Verbal and relational bullying (e.g., having gossip spread, being purposely ignored) is more common among females and can lead to some of the same psychological and somatic conditions as overt physical bullying. Victims of bullying are often physically weaker, have a low self-concept, and have a lower level of social skill behaviors (Holt & Espelage, 2007). Adolescents with obvious physical or psychological conditions are more likely to have a smaller social network, become socially isolated, and have weaker social ties (Haas et al., 2010). Haas et al. (2010) also reported that students with weaker social ties report a more negative self-image, less connection with community, and lower self-worth. These students are at greater risk of becoming victims of bullying. Another important aspect of bullying victims is a low level of perceived social support (Rigby, 2000). An increase in the amount of perceived social support can buffer the negative psychological or somatic symptoms of being bullied (Cohen & Wills, 1985; Holt & Espelage, 2007). Consistent with this idea, Newman, Holden, and Delville (2005) found that bullying victims who reported greater amounts of support during adolescence were buffered from developing long-term high levels of stress.

Previous research on bullying (Newman, Holden, & Delville, 2011) has already demonstrated that victims of bullying are more likely to develop avoidant coping strategies. Homosexuality presents a unique set of additional issues. Swearer, Turner, Givens, and Pollack (2008) found that harassment based on sexual orientation is rarely viewed as bullying in a public school setting, and consequently, school administrators rarely intervene. Youth who identify as lesbian, bisexual, gay, transgender, or queer/questioning (LGBTQ) are more likely to be verbally harassed or threatened with violence, more likely to witness violence, and more likely to be injured by this violence than their heterosexual peers (Russell, Franz, & Driscoll, 2001). Members of the LGBTQ community are also more likely to attempt suicide, abuse drugs, and become truant from school because of fear (DuRant, Krowchuk, & Sinal, 1998). However, recent research has found that when compared with their heterosexual peers, LGBTQ youth showed increased stress and more negative self-image as well as avoidant coping strategies. This effect increases with the disparity between sex and gender—gay males who report having characteristics that are more feminine experience bullying at a higher rate than gay males who report more socially acceptable masculine characteristics (Puckett & Newman, 2011).

Bullying based on gender and sexual orientation is also less likely to be reported and less likely to be resolved than other types of bullying (Swearer et al., 2008). Even more alarming and concerning is the rate of suicide and suicidal ideation among the young gay community. Suicide attempts, successful suicides, and thoughts of suicide in the LGBTQ community are among the highest of any minority group (Garofalo, Wolf, Kessel, Palfrey, & DuRant, 1998). Gay youth also experience higher rates of depression, anxiety, and other psychological symptoms at a higher rate than their heterosexual peers (Kosciw, Greytak, Diaz, & Bartkiewicz, 2010).

Finally, on the positive side, DuBois and Karcher (2005) found that positive mentoring relationships in adolescents can increase the likelihood of positive health outcomes. A mentoring relationship can be with a parent, teacher, informal social support, or even a sibling. The increase in positive health outcomes includes a decrease in reported sexually transmitted diseases, a high rate of birth control use, and less frequent or severe substance use. DuBois and Karcher also found that positive mentorship influenced psychological factors such as presence of depression, anxiety, and self-esteem, which also correlate with health outcomes. Previous research (Berkman & Glass, 2000) found that individuals with meaningful and strong bonds with friends and family members have a longer life expectancy and report higher overall life satisfaction than those with a smaller or more poorly integrated social network.

Effects of Health on Peer Relationships

Preexisting physical health factors can also have a significant influence on the type of peer relationships an adolescent will experience. Lower levels of physical activity in adolescents shape the type of peer relationships one may have. Instead of having positive peer interactions, adolescents with lower physical activity are more likely to engage in risky or socially inappropriate behavior such as smoking, drug use, and truancy from school (Nelson, 2006). Furthermore, in an analysis of data from the National Longitudinal Study of Adolescent Health, Haas et al. (2010) found that adolescents in poor health tended to form smaller networks and to gravitate toward the periphery of these networks.

Another aspect of adolescent health that affects relationships and the quality of interaction is obesity. Janssen et al. (2004) found that adolescent obesity is a precursor for a range of health-related issues including, but not limited to, Type 2 diabetes, cardiovascular disease, shortened life expectancy, and risk of obesity in adulthood. The effect of obesity on peer relationships can be equally as deleterious. Adolescents who are obese experience negative social and psychological effects such as peer rejection, ostracism, and peer aggression (e.g., Griffiths, Wolke, Page, & Horwood, 2006; Janssen et al., 2004).

Overweight females are more likely to experience social isolation and victimization because of weight and are less likely to form bonds than their peers who are not overweight. As the population of overweight children and adolescents continues to rise, it is unclear whether this effect will shift or whether the perception of what constitutes being overweight will change (F. Johnson, Cooke, Croker, & Wardle, 2008; Paeratakul, White, Williamson, Ryan, & Bray, 2002; Warschburger & Kröller, 2009). Recent research has shown that fewer people have a true concept of whether they are actually overweight compared with the findings of a study published in 1999 (F. Johnson et al., 2008). In addition, mothers who looked at the silhouettes of preschool-aged overweight children tended to underestimate the health consequences of future obesity (Warschburger & Kröller, 2009). In some ethnic groups, the culture of obesity has changed, and what is considered overweight within that culture is also changing (Paeratakul et al., 2002). This raises questions and concerns of how the next generation of youth and adolescents will perceive themselves and others and whether this will lead to increased risk of heart disease or social consequences such as bullying or ostracism.

ADULTHOOD

Unique Features of Adulthood

Although many of the specific health outcomes for adults reflect experiences with peer relationships during childhood and adolescence (Bagwell et al., 1998; Bagwell, Schmidt, Newcomb, & Bukowski, 2001), health outcomes are also affected by adult peer relationships. This happens most frequently through positive and negative habits and through workplace relationships.

We see several unique relationships between peer relationships and health in adulthood, particularly in the avenues through which peer relationships influence health.

Effects of Peer Relationships on Health

Like the positive associations found between peer relationships and health for most children and adolescents, similar positive outcomes on health have been found for adult peer relationships. In particular, peer relationships affect health through the development and maintenance of positive and negative habits. Buller et al. (1999) found that peer groups can effectively influence adults' choice to increase fruit and vegetable intake. Similarly, Christakis and Fowler (2008), studying smoking cessation, found that people tended to quit in concert with their entire social group. Furthermore, although the chances of smoking decreased most drastically when a person's spouse quit (67%), the chances of smoking also decreased significantly when a person's friend (36%) or coworker (34%) quit (Christakis & Fowler, 2008, p. 2249). These findings suggest that although family relationships, and romantic relationships in particular, may be most influential in predicting health outcomes, peer relationships continue to influence health-related behaviors for adults. (See Chapter 5, this volume, for further discussion of these dynamics within the context of romantic relationships.)

Similar positive health outcomes have been found for older adults. Specifically, people with more types of social ties were found to be less susceptible to upper respiratory illness (Cohen, Doyle, Skoner, Rabin, & Gwaltney, 1997). In addition, adults 70 years old or older were found to have higher rates of survival over a 10-year period when their social network of peers was greater (Giles, Glonek, Luszcz, & Andrews, 2005). Although better social networks with friends and confidants predicted lower rates of mortality, there was no effect of familial social networks on survival. Therefore, in contrast to findings related to younger adults, friends rather than family deliver the most health benefits in the later stages of adulthood and life (Giles et al., 2004).

Health outcomes resulting from peer relationships can be negative for adults just as they are for children and adolescents. House, Landis, and Umberson (1988) found that people with low quantity, and even sometimes low quality, of social relationships experience an increased risk of death. Social isolation was found to be a major risk factor for death from a wide range of causes (House et al., 1988). In addition, just as loneliness has serious health ramifications for children and adolescents, loneliness in adults can affect health in several ways (Cacioppo et al., 2002). Specifically, people who report more loneliness have higher rates of sleep dysfunction and cardiovascular issues (Cacioppo et al., 2002).

Strained peer relationships are also associated with high levels of distress in adults, and women experience higher levels of distress than men do (Umberson, Chen, House, Hopkins, & Slaten, 1996). An interesting gender difference, however, is that if women did not have higher levels of social involvement than men, they might experience even higher levels of distress relative to men (Umberson et al., 1996). Furthermore, women may feel less support from their peer relationships, which may result in the higher levels of psychological distress (Kawachi & Berkman, 2001). Specifically, having more social connections may actually increase psychological distress for women with low resources, especially if such connections require strain to fulfill obligations to provide social support to others (Kawachi & Berkman, 2001). Taken together, it appears that although women require greater peer involvement than men, they are also more likely to experience distress because of those relationships.

Alcohol use is also influenced by peer relationships, demonstrating that physical health is affected in addition to the mental health outcomes discussed earlier. For persons in young adulthood (college age and slightly older), alcohol use is influenced by the quality of a person's peer relationships (Borsari & Carey, 2006). In particular, three elements of an individual's peer relationships affect alcohol use during young adulthood: (a) the lack of quality or deterioration in quality of peer relationships, (b) alcohol being a critical part of peer interactions, and (c) whether peers disapprove of alcohol use or do not drink (Borsari & Carey, 2006).

In a less obviously health-related area, peer relationships have been found to have an interesting effect on career outcomes, which may indirectly affect health through feelings of self-worth and stress levels. Dansky (1996) found that group mentoring, studied through professional associations, positively affects career outcomes. Specifically, of the four components of group mentoring (psychosocial support, inclusion, networking, and role modeling), inclusion predicted higher job attainment, and role modeling contributed to salary. Thus, the social aspects of professional associations significantly contribute to career advancement.

Kram and Isabella (1985) found that relationships with peers in the workplace can support psychosocial and career development at every career stage. Distinguished from mentoring relationships, peer support in the workplace can help individuals gain knowledge, gain recognition, learn about and prepare for advancement opportunities, feel a sense of competence, stay committed to the organization, and balance their work and family commitments (Kram & Isabella, 1985). Although peers in the workplace can affect an individual's health through positive or negative habits, it is also important to see that they can have a tremendous effect on career outcomes, which indirectly affect health as well.

Effects of Health on Peer Relationships

Similar to other age groups, the development and maintenance of peer relationships may be negatively affected by illness in adults, particularly for those illnesses to which stigmas are more readily attributed. In addition, individuals with illnesses that are viewed as more stigmatizing seek social support more frequently than individuals with illness without such stigmas (Davison, Pennebaker, & Dickerson, 2000). Specifically, when investigating support-seeking behaviors for individuals with any of 20 illnesses, support seeking is most common for individuals with AIDS, alcoholism, breast cancer, and prostate cancer, each of which is highly stigmatized. In contrast, support-seeking behaviors were least common for individuals with less embarrassing but equally devastating conditions, such as heart disease (Davison et al., 2000).

Other diseases found to be detrimental to peer relationships and that are based on stigmas include ADHD and posttraumatic stress disorder (PTSD). Among undergraduate college students, individuals have less desire to engage with individuals with ADHD (Canu et al., 2008). Interestingly, personality traits have an effect on how adult individuals judge people with ADHD. Specifically, college students who were higher in agreeableness and extraversion and lower in conscientiousness tended to make more positive judgments of fellow students with ADHD (Canu et al., 2008). There is a bias toward ADHD that contributes to rejection of people with the disorder, and personality traits of those making the judgments have an effect on this rejection (Canu et al., 2008). Similarly, Vietnam veterans with PTSD reported a steady decline in social support from before Vietnam to the present, whereas other veterans without PTSD experienced stable or improved social support over time (Keane, Scott, Chavoya, Lamparski, & Fairbank, 1985). One interpretation of these correlational data is that individuals with PTSD are judged negatively by their peers, and as a result, they receive less social support than individuals without their condition.

A study of women diagnosed with breast cancer found that after a 6-month peer-counseling intervention, the women showed significant improvement in trauma symptoms, emotional well-being, cancer self-efficacy, and desire for information on breast cancer resources (Giese-Davis et al., 2006). The authors found that women with breast cancer expressed the greatest need for peer counseling at the time of diagnosis and wanted to speak with someone who had the same cancer but who had lived through the treatment (Giese-Davis et al., 2006). This work suggests that women with breast cancer likely do not struggle to maintain existing peer relationships but are more concerned with developing relationships with women in similar positions.

The link between social support and improvements in disease outlook and maintenance exists for other illnesses as well. Among individuals with bipolar I disorder, those with low social support take longer to recover from episodes and are more symptomatic (S. L. Johnson, Winett, Meyer, Greenhouse, & Miller, 1999). It is notable that support influences depressive symptoms but not manic symptoms, which may lend further support to the findings relating to loneliness and peer relationships (S. L. Johnson et al., 1999). Similarly, in a study of people 65 years and older with acute myocardial infarction, prior emotional support was found to be significantly associated with risk of death in the first 6 months after the heart attack (Berkman, Leo-Summers, & Horwitz, 1992). Specifically, lack of emotional support prior to the heart attack negatively affected survival rates in the first 6 months after the attack (Berkman et al., 1992).

Taken together, we see that peer relationships in adulthood can affect mental and physical health. As with children and adolescents, this happens through, for example, the buffering nature of positive social support as well as the loneliness and other negative outcomes that result from peer rejection. Furthermore, the development of positive and negative habits is influenced by peer groups in adulthood and can affect health positively and negatively. Research has suggested that unlike children and adolescents, adults with stigmatizing illnesses will actively seek social support, but like children and adolescents, they are often rejected socially because of their conditions.

CONCLUSION

The links between peer relationships and health are complex and bi- (if not multi-) directional. At each of three major life stages—childhood, adolescence, and adulthood—peers can be a valuable source of support, setting positive examples and providing shoulders to cry on in times of need. However, peers can also be bad for our health, encouraging bad habits and passing judgment on stigmatizing conditions. In this chapter, we have reviewed a wide range of examples and have attempted to provide a framework for understanding when and why peer relationships can have both positive and negative associations with health. In a frequently quoted passage from *The Four Loves*, C. S. Lewis (1991) suggested, "Friendship is unnecessary, like philosophy, like art. . . . It has no survival value, rather it is one of those things that give value to survival" (p. 71). Although this quotation elegantly captures the intangible benefits of friendship, we of course know better now: Friendships can have enormous and concrete benefits for both survival and well-being—even if they sometimes make us sick.

REFERENCES

Bagwell, C. L., Newcomb, A. F., & Bukowski, W. M. (1998). Preadolescent friendship and peer rejection as predictors of adult adjustment. *Child Development, 69*, 140–153.

Bagwell, C. L., Schmidt, M. E., Newcomb, A. F., & Bukowski, W. M. (2001). Friendship and peer rejection as predictors of adult adjustment. *New Directions for Child and Adolescent Development, 91*, 25–49. doi:10.1002/cd.4

Baldry, A. C. (2004). The impact of direct and indirect bullying on the mental and physical health of Italian youngsters. *Aggressive Behavior, 30*, 343–355. doi:10.1002/ab.20043

Berkman, L. F., & Glass, T. (2000). Social integration, social networks, social support, and health. In L. F. Berkman & I. Kawachi (Eds.), *Social epidemiology* (pp. 137–173). New York, NY: Oxford University Press.

Berkman, L. F., Leo-Summers, L., & Horwitz, R. L. (1992). Emotional support and survival after myocardial infarction. *Annals of Internal Medicine, 117*, 1003–1009.

Berndt, T. J., & Keefe, K. (1995). Friends' influence on adolescents' adjustment to school. *Child Development, 66*, 1312–1329. doi:10.2307/1131649

Borsari, B., & Carey, K. B. (2006). How the quality of peer relationships influences college alcohol use. *Drug and Alcohol Review, 25*, 361–370. doi:10.1080/09595230600741339

Brown, B. B., & Lohr, M. J. (1987). Peer-group affiliation and adolescent self-esteem: An integration of ego-identity and symbolic-interaction theories. *Journal of Personality and Social Psychology, 52*, 47–55. doi:10.1037/0022-3514.52.1.47

Bukowski, W. M., Hoza, B., & Boivin, M. (1993). Popularity, friendship, and emotional adjustment during early adolescence. In W. Damon (Series Ed.) & B. Laursen (Vol. Ed.), *New directions for child development: Vol. 60. Close friendships in adolescence* (pp. 23–37). San Francisco, CA: Jossey-Bass.

Buller, D. B., Morrill, C., Taren, D., Aickin, M., Sennott-Miller, L., Buller, M. K., . . . Wentzel, T. M. (1999). Randomized trial testing the effect of peer education at increasing fruit and vegetable intake. *Journal of the National Cancer Institute, 91*, 1491–1500. doi:10.1093/jnci/91.17.1491

Cacioppo, J. T., Hawkley, L. C., Crawford, E., Ernst, J. M., Burleson, M. H., Kowalewski, R. B., . . . Berntson, G. G. (2002). Loneliness and health: Potential mechanisms. *Psychosomatic Medicine, 64*, 407–417.

Canu, W. H., Newman, M. L., Morrow, T. L., & Pope, D. L. (2008). Social appraisal of adult ADHD: Stigma and influences of the beholder's big five personality traits. *Journal of Attention Disorders, 11*, 700–710. doi:10.1177/1087054707305090

Christakis, N. A., & Fowler, J. H. (2008). The collective dynamics of smoking in a large social network. *The New England Journal of Medicine, 358*, 2249–2258. doi:10.1056/NEJMsa0706154

Cohen, S., Doyle, W. J., Skoner, D. P., Rabin, B. S., & Gwaltney, J. M. Jr. (1997, June 25). Social ties and susceptibility to the common cold. *JAMA, 277*, 1940–1944. doi:10.1001/jama.1997.03540480040036

Cohen, S., & Wills, T. A. (1985). Stress, social support, and the buffering hypothesis. *Psychological Bulletin, 98*, 310–357. doi:10.1037//0033-2909.98.2.310

Coie, J., Terry, R., Lenox, K., Lochman, J., & Hyman, C. (1995). Childhood peer rejection and aggression as predictors of stable patterns of adolescent disorder. *Development and Psychopathology, 7*, 697–713. doi:10.1017/S0954579400006799

Coolahan, K., Fantuzzo, J., Mendez, J., & McDermott, P. (2000). Preschool peer interactions and readiness to learn: Relationships between classroom peer play and learning behaviors and conduct. *Journal of Educational Psychology, 92*, 458–465. doi:10.1037/0022-0663.92.3.458

Criss, M. M., Pettit, G. S., Bates, J. E., Dodge, K. A., & Lapp, A. L. (2002). Family adversity, positive peer relationships, and children's externalizing behavior: A longitudinal perspective on risk and resilience. *Child Development, 73*, 1220–1237. doi:10.1111/1467-8624.00468

Dansky, K. H. (1996). The effect of group mentoring on career outcomes. *Group & Organization Management, 21*, 5–21. doi:10.1177/1059601196211002

Davison, K. P., Pennebaker, J. W., & Dickerson, S. S. (2000). Who talks? The social psychology of illness support groups. *American Psychologist, 55*, 205–217. doi:10.1037/0003-066X.55.2.205

DeRosier, M. E., Kupersmidt, J. B., & Patterson, C. J. (1994). Children's academic and behavioral adjustment as a function of the chronicity and proximity of peer rejection. *Child Development, 65*, 1799–1813. doi:10.2307/1131295

DuBois, D. L., & Karcher, M. J. (2005). *Handbook of youth mentoring*. Thousand Oaks, CA: Sage.

DuRant, R. H., Krowchuk, D. P., & Sinal, S. H. (1998). Victimization, use of violence, and drug use among male adolescents who engage in samesex sexual behavior. *Journal of Pediatrics, 133*, 113–118.

Fehr, B. (1996). *Friendship processes*. Thousand Oaks, CA: Sage.

Feld, S. L. (1981). The focused organization of social ties. *American Journal of Sociology, 86*, 1015–1035. doi:10.1086/227352

Flouri, E., & Buchanan, A. (2002). Life satisfaction in teenage boys: The moderating role of father involvement and bullying. *Aggressive Behavior, 28*, 126–133. doi:10.1002/ab.90014

Flouri, E., & Buchanan, A. (2004). Early father's and mother's involvement and child's later educational outcomes. *British Journal of Educational Psychology, 74*, 141–153. doi:10.1348/000709904773839806

Furman, W., & Buhrmester, D. (1992). Age and sex differences in perceptions of networks of personal relationships. *Child Development, 63*, 103–115. doi:10.2307/1130905

Galambos, N. L., Almeida, D. M., & Petersen, A. C. (1990). Masculinity, femininity, and sex role attitudes in early adolescence: Exploring gender intensification. *Child Development, 61*, 1905–1914. doi:10.2307/1130846

Garofalo, R., Wolf, R. C., Kessel, S., Palfrey, J., & DuRant, R. H. (1998). The association between health risk behaviors and sexual orientation among a school-based sample of adolescents. *Pediatrics, 101*, 895–902. doi:10.1542/peds.101.5.895

Giese-Davis, J., Bliss-Isberg, C., Carson, K., Star, P., Donaghy, J., Cordova, M. J., . . . Spiegel, D. (2006). The effect of peer counseling on quality of life following diagnosis of breast cancer: An observational study. *Psycho-Oncology, 15*, 1014–1022. doi:10.1002/pon.1037

Giles, L. C., Glonek, G. F. V., Luszcz, M. A., & Andrews, G. R. (2005). Effect of social networks on 10 year survival in very old Australians: The Australian longitudinal study of aging. *Journal of Epidemiology and Community Health, 59*, 574–579. doi:10.1136/jech.2004.025429

Griffiths, L. J., Wolke, D., Page, A. S., & Horwood, J. P. (2006). Obesity and bullying: Different effects for boys and girls. *Archives of Disease in Childhood, 91*(2), 121–125. doi:10.1136/adc.2005.072314

Haas, S. A., Schaefer, D. R., & Kornienko, O. (2010). Health and the structure of adolescent social networks. *Journal of Health and Social Behavior, 51*, 424–439. doi:10.1177/0022146510386791

Hartup, W. W., & Stevens, N. (1999). Friendships and adaptation across the life span. *Current Directions in Psychological Science, 8*, 76–79. doi:10.1111/1467-8721.00018

Hinshaw, S. P., & Melnick, S. M. (1995). Peer relationships in boys with attention-deficit hyperactivity disorder with and without comorbid aggression. *Development and Psychopathology, 7*, 627–647. doi:10.1017/S0954579400006751

Holt, M. K., & Espelage, L. D. (2007). Perceived social support among bullies, victims, and bully-victims. *Journal of Youth and Adolescence, 36*, 984–994. doi:10.1007/s10964-006-9153-3

House, J. S., Landis, K. R., & Umberson, D. (1988, July 29). Social relationships and health. *Science, 241*, 540–545. doi:10.1126/science.3399889

Hoza, B., Mrug, S., Gerdes, A. C., Bukowski, W. M., Kraemer, H. C., Wigal, T., . . . Arnold, L. E. (2005). What aspects of peer relationships are impaired in children with attention-deficit/hyperactivity disorder? *Journal of Consulting and Clinical Psychology, 73*, 411–423. doi:10.1037/0022-006X.73.3.411

Hymel, S., Rubin, K. H., Rowden, L., & LeMare, L. (1990). Children's peer relationships: Longitudinal prediction of internalizing and externalizing problems from middle to late childhood. *Child Development, 61*, 2004–2021.

Janssen, I., Craig, W. M., Boyce, W. F., & Pickett, W. (2004). Associations between overweight and obesity with bullying behaviors in school-aged children. *Pediatrics, 113*, 1187–1194. doi:10.1542/peds.113.5.1187

Johnson, F., Cooke, L., Croker, H., & Wardle, J. (2008). Changing perceptions of weight in Great Britain: Comparison of two population surveys. *BMJ, 337,* a494. doi:10.1136/bmj.a494

Johnson, S. L., Winett, C. A., Meyer, B., Greenhouse, W., & Miller, I. (1999). Social support and the course of bipolar disorder. *Journal of Abnormal Psychology, 108,* 558–566. doi:10.1037/0021-843X.108.4.558

Kawachi, I., & Berkman, L. F. (2001). Social ties and mental health. *Journal of Urban Health, 78,* 458–467. doi:10.1093/jurban/78.3.458

Keane, T. M., Scott, W. O., Chavoya, G. A., Lamparski, D. M., & Fairbank, J. A. (1985). Social support in Vietnam veterans with posttraumatic stress disorder: A comparative analysis. *Journal of Consulting and Clinical Psychology, 53,* 95–102. doi:10.1037/0022-006X.53.1.95

Kelly, A. B., Garnett, M. S., Attwood, T., & Peterson, C. (2008). Autism spectrum symptomatology in children: The impact of family and peer relationships. *Journal of Abnormal Child Psychology, 36,* 1069–81. doi:10.1007/s10802-008-9234-8

Kimmel, M. S., & Mahler, M. (2003). Adolescent masculinity, homophobia, and violence. *American Behavioral Scientist, 46,* 1439–1458. doi:10.1177/0002764203046010010

Kosciw, J. G., Greytak, E. A., Diaz, E. M., & Bartkiewicz, M. J. (2010). *The 2009 National School Climate Survey: The experiences of lesbian, gay, bisexual and transgender youth in our nation's schools.* New York, NY: GLSEN.

Kram, K. E., & Isabella, L. A. (1985). Mentoring alternatives: The role of peer relationships in career development. *Academy of Management Journal, 28,* 110–132. doi:10.2307/256064

La Greca, A. M., Bearman, K. J., & Moore, H. (2002). Peer relations of youth with pediatric conditions and health risks: Promoting social support and healthy lifestyles. *Journal of Developmental and Behavioral Pediatrics, 23,* 271–280. doi:10.1097/00004703-200208000-00013

Larson, R., & Richards, M. H. (1991). Daily companionship in late childhood and early adolescence: Changing developmental contexts. *Child Development, 62,* 284–300. doi:10.2307/1131003

Lewis, C. S. (1991). *The four loves.* New York, NY: Houghton Mifflin Harcourt.

McPherson, M., Smith-Lovin, L., & Cook, J. M. (2001). Birds of a feather: Homophily in social networks. *Annual Review of Sociology, 27,* 415–444. doi:10.1146/annurev.soc.27.1.415

Mikami, A. Y., Lerner, M. D., & Lun, J. (2010). Social context influences on children's rejection by their peers. *Child Development Perspectives, 4,* 123–130. doi:10.1111/j.1750-8606.2010.00130.x

Mrug, S., Hoza, B., & Gerdes, A. C. (2001). Children with attention-deficit/hyperactivity disorder: Peer relationships and peer-oriented interventions. *New Directions for Child and Adolescent Development, 2001*(91), 51–77. doi:10.1002/cd.5

Muñoz-Rivas, M. J., Grana, J. L., O'Leary, K. D., & Gonzàlez, M. P. (2007). Aggression in adolescent dating relationships: Prevalence, justification, and health consequences. *Journal of Adolescent Health*, *40*, 298–304. doi:10.1016/j.jadohealth.2006.11.137

Nation, M., Vieno, A., Perkins, D. D., & Santinello, M. (2008). Bullying in school and adolescent sense of empowerment: An analysis of relationships with parents, friends, and teachers. *Journal of Community & Applied Social Psychology*, *18*, 211–232. doi:10.1002/casp.921

Nelson, M. C. (2006). Physical activity and sedentary behavior patterns are associated with selected adolescent health risk behaviors. *Pediatrics*, *117*, 1281–1290. doi:10.1542/peds.2005-1692

Newcomb, A. F., & Bagwell, C. L. (1995). Children's friendship relations: A meta-analytic review. *Psychological Bulletin*, *117*, 306–347. doi:10.1037/0033-2909.117.2.306

Newman, M. L., Holden, G. W., & Delville, Y. (2005). Isolation and the stress of being bullied. *Journal of Adolescence*, *28*, 343–357. doi:10.1016/j.adolescence.2004.08.002

Newman, M. L., Holden, G. W., & Delville, Y. (2011). Coping with the stress of being bullied: Consequences of coping strategies among college students. *Social Psychological and Personality Science*, *2*, 205–211. doi:10.1177/1948550610386388

Nishina, A., Juvonen, J., & Witkow, M. R. (2005). Sticks and stones may break my bones, but names will make me feel sick: The psychosocial, somatic, and scholastic consequences of peer harassment. *Journal of Clinical Child and Adolescent Psychology*, *34*, 37–48. doi:10.1207/s15374424jccp3401_4

Paeratakul, S., White, M. A., Williamson, D. A., Ryan, D. H., & Bray, G. A. (2002). Sex, race/ethnicity, socioeconomic status, and BMI in relation to self-perception of overweight. *Obesity Research*, *10*, 345–350. doi:10.1038/oby.2002.48

Parker, J. G., & Asher, S. R. (1993). Friendship and friendship quality in middle childhood: Links with peer group acceptance and feelings of loneliness and social dissatisfaction. *Developmental Psychology*, *29*, 611–621. doi:10.1037/0012-1649.29.4.611

Parker, J. G., & Gottman, J. M. (1989). Social and emotional development in a relational context: Friendship interaction from early childhood to adolescence. In T. J. Berndt & G. W. Ladd (Eds.), *Peer relations in child development* (pp. 95–131). New York, NY: Wiley.

Perren, S., & Alsaker, F. D. (2006). Social behavior and peer relationships of victims, bully-victims, and bullies in kindergarten. *Journal of Child Psychology and Psychiatry*, *47*, 45–57. doi:10.1111/j.1469-7610.2005.01445.x

Puckett, Y., & Newman, M. L. (2011, October). *Long-term impacts of bullying in the LGBTQ community*. Paper presented at the meeting of the International Association for Relationships Research, Tucson, AZ.

Rigby, K. (2000). Effects of peer victimization in schools and perceived social support on adolescent well-being. *Journal of Adolescence, 23*, 57–68. doi:10.1006/jado.1999.0289

Rubin, K. H., Coplan, R., Chen, X., Buskirk, A. A., & Wojslawowicz, J. C. (2005). Peer relationships in childhood. In M. H. Bornstein & M. E. Lamb (Eds.), *Developmental science: An advanced textbook* (5th ed., pp. 469–512). Mahwah, NJ: Erlbaum.

Russell, S. T., Franz, B. T., & Driscoll, A. K. (2001). Same-sex romantic attraction and experiences of violence in adolescence. *American Journal of Public Health, 91*, 903–906. doi:10.2105/AJPH.91.6.903

Swearer, S. M., Espelage, D. L., Vaillancourt, T., & Hymel, S. (2010). What can be done about school bullying? *Educational Researcher, 39*, 38–47. doi:10.3102/0013189X09357622

Swearer, S. M., Turner, R. K., Givens, J. E., & Pollack, W. S. (2008). "You're so gay!": Do different forms of bullying matter for adolescent males? *School Psychology Review, 37*, 160–173.

Tolman, D. L., Striepe, M. I., & Harmon, T. (2003). Gender matters: Constructing a model of adolescent sexual health. *Journal of Sex Research, 40*, 4–12. doi:10.1080/00224490309552162

Umberson, D., Chen, M. D., House, J. S., Hopkins, K., & Slaten, E. (1996). The effect of social relationships on psychological well-being: Are men and women really so different? *American Sociological Review, 61*, 837–857. doi:10.2307/2096456

Warschburger, P., & Kröller, K. (2009). Maternal perception of weight status and health risks associated with obesity in children. *Pediatrics, 124*, e60–e68. doi:10.1542/peds.2008-1845

Worell, J. (1981). Life-span sex roles: Development, continuity and change. In R. M. Lerner & N. A. Busch-Rossnagel (Eds.), *Individuals as producers of their development: A life-span perspective* (pp. 313–347). New York, NY: Academic Press.

8

THE ROLE OF CULTURAL FIT IN THE CONNECTION BETWEEN HEALTH AND SOCIAL RELATIONSHIPS

JOSÉ A. SOTO, YULIA CHENTSOVA-DUTTON, AND ELIZABETH A. LEE

Humans have evolved to both shape and adapt to their social environments. Our brains support and prioritize the processing of social information, enabling our minds to construct sophisticated models of social interactions (e.g., Adolphs, 1999). The chapters in this volume have thus far highlighted how enacting these models in the context of social relationships relates to mental and physical health outcomes. An important consideration that has not been emphasized thus far is that these models of social interactions are embedded in a cultural context that serves to foster and normalize our interpersonal motives, values, norms, beliefs, and behaviors.

Cultural contexts constrain the infinite set of possible social motives and behaviors to help us navigate complex interpersonal tasks such as noticing subtle social cues, sharing our thoughts and feelings with others, or offering and extending help. We propose that the ability to successfully handle

We thank Andrew Ryder and Nicole Roberts for their comments on earlier drafts of this chapter.

DOI: 10.1037/14036-009
Health and Social Relationships: The Good, the Bad, and the Complicated, Matthew L. Newman and Nicole A. Roberts (Editors)

these and myriad other relationship tasks (already shown to contribute to well-being) partially depends on being able to do so in a manner consistent with cultural prescriptions—what we refer to as *cultural fit*. The concept of cultural fit borrows from traditions in social psychology and anthropology demonstrating that a match between an individual's behavior/personal standards and cultural behavioral standards is associated with certain psychological and health benefits (Dressler & Bindon, 2000; Higgins, 2005). This constant, dynamic interaction between an individual's social behavior and culture arguably places culture at the forefront of the relationship between health and social relationships.

In this chapter, we highlight two examples from recent research on how cultural fit in interpersonal functioning influences the link between relationships and well-being. First, we focus on cultural shaping of social support practices and their health and well-being outcomes. Second, we explore how cultural differences in how emotions should transpire in interpersonal settings (i.e., emotion regulation) lead to divergent outcomes in health and well-being. Taken together, these examples challenge assumptions of decades-old research and illustrate that the links between interpersonal behavior and psychological and physical well-being cannot be fully understood without considering the broader role of culture. We then present possible mechanisms for the examples given, before concluding with a discussion about additional factors that can affect our understanding of the interplay between culture, social relationships, and health.

KEY CONCEPTS

Culture and Cultural Scripts

Culture is a notoriously complex and difficult-to-define concept. Although no definition of culture is complete, we favor definitions that move away from equating culture with fixed and stable categories, such as ethnic and cultural groups. When we talk about *culture*, we refer to shared systems of values, norms, behaviors, and products that shape the mind and the brain in a cycle of mutual constitution (Markus & Kitayama, 1991; Ryder, Ban, & Chentsova-Dutton, 2011; Shweder, 1990). Although these systems can operate at a macro level where they are often shared among members of groups, our focus is on how culture is manifested within individuals in the form of implicit and explicit knowledge, values, norms, and behavior. For example, a person living in North America is likely to have internalized the norm that it is both appropriate and desirable to experience and express one's emotions, particularly positive emotions (Eid & Diener, 2001; Wierzbicka, 1999). This person can therefore be said to be engaging with North American culture based on having internalized the norms that compose the meaning system that is shared among others in the culture.

Culture is also manifested in the world in the form of cultural products or practices that are directly observable and that provide tangible reminders of what is desirable and moral in this context. One of the authors recently discovered a handwritten sign in a university office that read, "Did you remember to smile today?" This experience is by no means unusual—the norms to express positive emotions can be gleaned from North American TV commercials and children's books (Kim & Markus, 1999; Tsai, Louie, Chen, & Uchida, 2007). They can also be observed in emotional behavior, such as smiling (Tsai, Chentsova-Dutton, Freire-Bebeau, & Przymus, 2002). *Cultural scripts* are one element of culture that reflect this dual view of culture as something that exists in the head (i.e., the "cognitive" component of culture) and in the world. Cultural scripts function as shared guides for encoding and enacting culturally salient information (see DiMaggio, 1997). They guide and constrain individuals' repertoires of interpersonal behavior, allowing for easy retrieval, identification, and interpretation of one's own and others' behavior. These guides may be implicit or explicit in nature, and they are dynamic, responding to changes in the cultural environment.

Although no person holds a complete set of cultural scripts, most salient ones will be recognized by most individuals within a group (see Dressler & Bindon, 2000, for an example of identifying shared cultural scripts). Inevitably, each person is exposed to a cultural context and its associated scripts. However, people react with a range of responses, ranging from acceptance to rejection of the scripts. Such explicit or implicit responses are especially meaningful within interpersonal contexts, where culturally normative and counternormative behavior can elicit different responses from others.

Cultural Scripts and Health Outcomes

Cultural scripts pertaining to social relationships and their maintenance likely evolved to aid communication and optimize survival of cultural groups in their ecological niches. Thus, it is no surprise that some of these scripts may also affect personal health and well-being both directly and indirectly. As examples of this influence, consider the way that adherence to cultural values and practices offers benefits for healthy weight and cardiac health among Japanese in Japan (Schwingel et al., 2007) and for breastfeeding among Hispanic American mothers (Guendelman & Siega-Riz, 2002). In both examples, the results have been ascribed in part to culturally sanctioned scripts about maintaining stable networks of close relationships that provide support at the time of stress or ties to breastfeeding role models. Conversely, cultural scripts may impair physical or psychological health. For example, cultural scripts of early marriage and sexual intercourse in the context of these marriages promote early pregnancy and childbearing in sub-Saharan Africa (Zabin & Kiragu, 1998), whereas cultural scripts linking socializing with binge drinking promote problematic alcohol consumption in Russia (see Cockerham, 2000). In all of these cases, cultural models of relationships affect health and well-being outcomes by directly or indirectly promoting or inhibiting aspects of healthy lifestyles, such as healthy diet or effective management of stress, which are assumed to function similarly across cultural contexts.

Our focus in this chapter is on how adherence to cultural models of interpersonal interactions provides additional benefits for health and well-being that are not explained by changes in lifestyle. Acting, feeling, and thinking in culturally normative ways may benefit a person's health and well-being above and beyond the impact of these norms on a person's ability and willingness to maintain a healthy lifestyle. We present two areas of research (social support and emotion regulation) that demonstrate how cultural fit in interpersonal functioning influences the link between relationships and well-being.

CULTURE AND SOCIAL SUPPORT

Social support has been defined as "an exchange of resources . . . perceived by the provider or the recipient to be intended to enhance the well-being of the recipient" (Shumaker & Brownell, 1984, p. 13). As reviewed elsewhere in this volume (see Chapters 1, 2, 3), the relationship between social support and psychological and physical well-being is far from straightforward. Although social support can act as a powerful buffer from the harmful effects of stress, it can also be ineffective and even harmful. A number of factors—ranging from the style of support delivered to the match between offered support and the recipient's needs—influence its effectiveness. One limitation of the prior research is that it has not systematically accounted for the role of culture in shaping the association between social support and emotional and physical well-being. This omission is striking because of the centrality of cultural scripts in providing a template for balancing individual well-being and interpersonal connectedness (Adams, Anderson, & Adonu, 2004; Jacobson, 1987; Markus & Kitayama, 1991).

A handful of studies that have examined social support across cultural contexts indicate that cultural values and practices shape social support scripts. Most of these studies have compared participants from European American and East Asian cultures. These cultures differ in their emphases on autonomy and competency, self-expression, interpersonal harmony, and face-saving (i.e., the extent to which people are expected to maintain face). European American cultural contexts privilege the importance of personal autonomy, competency, and self-expression (Fiske, Kitayama, Markus, & Nisbett, 1998; Kim & Sherman, 2007). In contrast, East Asian cultural contexts privilege the importance of preserving interpersonal harmony and maintaining face (Chang & Holt, 1994; Ting-Toomey et al., 1991). These values are readily used for interpreting social behavior and guiding social support scripts. Indeed, accumulating studies suggest that people from European American and East Asian cultural contexts differ in many aspects of social support, ranging from their willingness to seek support to their preferences for the type of help that is desired.

In the United States, the script for effective support scaffolds the recipient's sense of competence. The person providing support is expected to pay attention to whether the recipient wants help (Chentsova-Dutton & Vaughn, 2011; Horowitz et al., 2001) and worry about "butting in" (Goldsmith, 2000; Goldsmith & Fitch, 1997). One way to address these concerns is to delegate the initiative to support recipients. After all, the act of asking for support gives control to the recipients and allows them to preserve their sense of autonomy while openly expressing their concerns. These benefits are particularly salient in the European American cultural context. Of course, asking for support also has its costs. It can undermine the face of the recipient, place inappropriate demands on others, and by doing so can disrupt harmony. These costs of support seeking are more salient in East Asian cultural contexts. Indeed, cultural differences in social support-seeking reflect concerns with these values. People in European American cultural contexts endorse and seek emotional and informational support more than those in East Asian cultural contexts (Kim, Sherman, Ko, & Taylor, 2006; Taylor et al., 2004) and find support seeking to be more effective. Moreover, because concerns about threatening face of others and maintaining harmony of valued relationships are not as salient in their cultural context, European Americans are equally willing to seek support from close others as they are from those with whom they do not feel particularly close. In contrast, Asian Americans are less willing to seek support from individuals who are closer to them (Kim et al., 2006), reflecting an effort to protect these valued relationships.

Cultural differences in seeking social support provide an excellent example of how biological and contextual influences can interact to shape interpersonal behavior. For instance, genetic predisposition can affect an individual's sensitivity to socioemotional or interpersonal cues, such as support or rejection. Interpersonal contexts can, in turn, shape the how this sensitivity (genotype) is manifested (phenotype). Moreover, these effects can become heritable without affecting the DNA in a phenomenon known as *epigenetics* (e.g., Champagne, 2009). Thus, cultural contexts can potentially shape the expression of genes relevant to interpersonal functioning. Emerging studies provide initial support for this model. For example, in the European American cultural context, the tendency to seek support is a product of an interaction between a genetic predisposition to be particularly affiliation prone and motivation to alleviate distress (Kim et al., 2010). In fact, European Americans and acculturated Korean Americans with an oxytocin receptor allele that has been linked to socioemotional sensitivity are particularly likely to seek support from others during times of stress, whereas this pattern is not evident for Koreans living in Korea. This may suggest that a cultural script discouraging support seeking minimizes the effect of the genetic predisposition on support seeking. Taken together, these findings suggest that social support seeking is a response that is jointly shaped by the genetic predisposition to be affiliative, levels of psychological distress, and cultural scripts. Moreover, these factors likely shape each other. For instance, cultural scripts regarding social relationships may provide advantages to individuals with certain genotypes.

In addition to scripts regarding the seeking of social support, cultural differences emerge in preferences for types of support. There are different ways in which people support each other, ranging from trying to cheer someone up to offering practical assistance. Emotional support (i.e., help that aims to make the recipient feel better) allows for self-expression and self-validation. It does not imply indebtedness or threaten the autonomy of the recipient as strongly as instrumental and informational support (i.e., practical help or advice from others), especially when the emotional support is voluntarily solicited. Although people across various cultural contexts value emotional support, European American cultural contexts are particularly likely to foster it relative to practical and informational help (Adams & Plaut, 2003). Indeed, married adults in the United States report receiving more emotional support and less informational support from their spouses than do their counterparts in China (Xu & Burleson, 2001).

It is notable that at least one study provides evidence that the psychological and physical well-being benefits of emotional support among European Americans may occur indirectly rather than directly (Uchida, Kitayama, Mesquita, Reyes, & Morling, 2008). When modest beneficial effects were observed, they could be attributed to the impact of emotional support on recipients' self-esteem, which is highly valued in North American cultural contexts (Heine, 2001). In contrast, emotional support was more directly beneficial for emotional and physical well-being in the context of East Asian interdependent relationships (Uchida et al., 2008). Thus, cultural scripts regarding social support differ in European American and East Asian cultural contexts, translating into culturally specific benefits.

Diverse Scripts of Social Support in Collectivistic Contexts

The comparison of social support in European American and East Asian contexts invites the question of whether cultural differences in social support are best explained by global dimensions, such as individualism and collectivism, rather than specific cultural scripts. After all, these dimensions do predict perceived support from close others (Goodwin & Plaza, 2000). Yet, the patterns of cross-cultural differences observed in the literature are not easily explained by these dimensions alone. Instead, it appears that scripts of social support reveal that there are many ways to be collectivistic. Given culturally salient concerns with openly seeking support, East Asian cultural contexts foster a discreet form of support known as implicit support (i.e., being present for another person without addressing the problem). This type of support fits with East Asian values because it does not require explicit acknowledgement of the problem or requests for help. Indeed, it is not only common but also effective in ameliorating psychological and physiological stress. When facing a stressor, Asian Americans benefitted more from thinking about receiving implicit rather than explicit support, whereas the opposite was true for European Americans (Taylor, Welch, Kim, & Sherman, 2007).

In contrast to the East Asian preference for discreet implicit support, other collectivistic contexts foster assertive and visible support. For example, kibbutz-dwelling Israelis (Nadler, 1986) and Russians (Jose et al., 1998) feel comfortable with seeking help and comfort from others. Despite fostering interdependent models of the self similar to those in East Asian cultural contexts (Realo & Allik, 1999), Russians offer more positive interpretations of imposed support and are less concerned with whether or not the intended recipients want help than are European Americans (Chentsova-Dutton, 2012; Chentsova-Dutton & Vaughn, 2012). This pattern is in line with the specific values that scaffold Russian interdependence. Unlike East Asian cultural contexts, Russian context deemphasizes face and interpersonal harmony (Michailova & Hutchings, 2006; Rathmayr, 2008) and emphasizes mutual responsibility for solving problems (Rose, 2000). As a result, East Asian and Russian contexts engender similar levels of relational interdependence but different styles of connecting to and helping them.

These empirical examples illustrate that the impact of social support on health and well-being is culturally embedded and depends on the interaction of cultural values regarding the self and social relationships. After all, social support is particularly effective when it matches the needs of the recipients (Cohen, 1992; Cutrona, 1990), which are themselves culturally shaped. Forms of social support that match cultural scripts are more likely to be effective in protecting the health and well-being of the recipients, affecting a wide range of health indicators ranging from blood pressure (Dressler,

Mata, Chavez, Viteri, & Gallagher, 1986) to life satisfaction (Uchida et al., 2008). These benefits can even affect the next generation. One study observed that higher levels of perceived social support during early pregnancy uniquely predicted birth weight for the infants of foreign-born Latina mothers, a cultural group placing value on maintaining close relationships (Campos et al., 2008). However, forms of social support that violate cultural scripts are likely to generate stress and tension and may come with health costs, such as increased blood pressure (see Dressler, 2011). In turn, deterioration of physical and emotional health may further impair individuals' abilities to obtain culturally normative forms of support, triggering a dysfunctional cycle.

The work on culture and social support has focused on variables such as support satisfaction, well-being, and emotional adjustment. By regulating negative emotions, social support is likely to prevent the immune and endocrine dysregulation that is associated with emotional distress and, by doing so, protect physical health (see Kiecolt-Glaser, McGuire, Robles, & Glaser, 2002). Indeed, culturally congruent social support benefits health (Uchida et al., 2008; Dressler et al., 1986). Future work should increasingly focus on physical health and identify pathways linking cultural scripts of social support to physical health and well-being.

In summary, effective social support takes on different forms. Scaffolding autonomy and competency is an effective support strategy in North American contexts (Coyne, Ellard, & Smith, 1990; Goldsmith, 2004). Scripts for support provision in clinical and educational settings are steeped in these values. Clinicians and teachers are encouraged to soften or withhold imposed support and help their patients or students feel competent (Buetow, 1999; Reeve & Jang, 2006; Stott & Pill, 1990). These autonomy-supporting efforts may not transfer well to cultural contexts that deemphasize autonomy and may backfire and indicate lack of caring in these contexts. Effective social support provision in a wide variety of settings, ranging from online support from website forums to support from caregiving and educational and healthcare settings, may be enhanced by exploring the key stakeholders' cultural scripts of social support.

CULTURE, EMOTION REGULATION, AND HEALTH

The regulation of emotion across different cultural contexts provides a second example of how fit between behavior and cultural scripts can influence the connection between health and social relationships. From this perspective, emotions are crucial to social relationships. They can both threaten (e.g., jealousy undermining trust) and strengthen (e.g., happiness reinforcing intimacy) relationships. And although emotions may be ubiquitous and important to social relationships in all societies, the ways in which they are valued can be highly variable across cultures (Ekman & Friesen, 1969; Markus & Kitayama, 1991; Triandis, 1990). Because the experience (or lack thereof) of certain emotions can have direct implications for health and well-being (Catalino & Fredrickson, 2011; Dickerson, Gruenewald, & Kemeny, 2004; Moskowitz, 2003; Moskowitz & Epel, 2006), understanding cultural differences in how emotions are experienced and regulated in the service of relationships is a critical aspect of the connection between social relationships and health.

Theoretical and empirical arguments for the existence of cultural differences in emotion regulation have existed for over 4 decades (Ekman, 1972; Markus & Kitayama, 1991; Matsumoto, 1990; Matsumoto, Yoo, & Nakagawa, 2008; Mesquita & Frijda, 1992; Triandis, 1993). Less discussed, however, is that this expectation of cultural variability is ultimately grounded in different cultural scripts about how individuals within a culture should approach social relationships. For example, the collectivistic or interdependent focus of many Asian cultures emphasizes a reliance on others and highlights the primacy of social relationships relative to individual needs (Cole & Tamang, 1998; Markus & Kitayama, 1991; Matsumoto, 1990). Within this frame, Chinese traditional values view emotions as potentially threatening and unhealthy (Klineberg, 1938) because they can disrupt interpersonal harmony by drawing unwanted attention to the individual. It is not surprising that this focus has been associated with emotional restraint or emotional control among Chinese and other Asian cultures (Kleinman, 1986; Tsai, 2007; Tsai, Miao, Seppala, Fung, & Yeung, 2007). The reverse is true about members of American and many Western cultures in which individual needs take precedence over social relationships and emotional expression is seen as a part of personal expression (Bellah, Madsen, Sullivan, Swindler, & Tipton, 1985).

Numerous studies have now empirically documented a clear tendency for Asians and Easterners to report using *expressive suppression* (i.e., not showing one's emotions outwardly) as a regulation strategy more often than European Americans and other Westerners (Butler, Lee, & Gross, 2007; Gross & John, 2003; Matsumoto, 2006; Matsumoto et al., 2008; Soto, Perez, Kim, Lee, & Minnick, 2011). These opposing philosophical approaches about how emotions should be expressed in the context of social relationships lead to different predictions about the types of emotion regulation strategies that would be desirable, healthy, and adaptive within each culture. In many Western or individualistic contexts, free expression should be associated with positive health outcomes, and expressive suppression with negative outcomes. In collectivistic or East Asian contexts, the open expression of emotion should not fit with Asian cultural scripts of emotional restraint and should therefore be associated with negative outcomes, whereas the suppression of emotions may actually be beneficial for one's health. Empirical studies examining emotion regulation and culture have provided some support for each of these ideas.

Expression, Suppression, and Health and Well-Being

Western tradition has long asserted that expression is an adaptive strategy for managing health. This perspective traces back to Freud's psychodynamic theory about healing through catharsis (Breuer & Freud, 1957; Hokanson, Willers, & Koropsak, 1968; Pennebaker & Beall, 1986). Expression can be thought of as an emotion regulation strategy characterized by allowing one to display one's emotions freely. Perhaps the most well-known work on the expression–health link has been conducted by Pennebaker and colleagues, who suggested that the benefits of expression are mediated by enhancement of our immune system (Esterling, Antoni, Fletcher, Margulies, & Schneiderman, 1994; Pennebaker & Seagal, 1999). In studies in which participants were encouraged to express themselves in writing, particularly about the negative emotions associated with traumatic events, these acts of expression led to enhanced immune system functioning and decreased pain, stress, and depression (Pennebaker & Francis, 1996; Petrie, Booth, & Pennebaker, 1998). In addition, self-expression (through the creation of personal narratives) assists with the memory processing of past aversive events and the management of the distress associated with those events (Pennebaker & Francis, 1996). Thus, studies conducted primarily in an American/Western context demonstrated that expression facilitates adaptive coping behaviors, immune system functioning, and cognitive processing.

However, expressive suppression or inhibition has typically been associated with negative health and well-being outcomes for those in a Western context. These negative outcomes include increased physiological arousal, delayed physiological recovery, increased risk of depression, impaired memory, disrupted interpersonal functioning, diminished expression and experience of positive emotion, decreased immune system functioning, and decreased satisfaction with life (Butler et al., 2003; Demaree et al., 2006; Dorr, Brosschot, Sollers, & Thayer, 2007; Gross & John, 2003; Gross & Levenson, 1993; Krantz & Manuck 1984; Petrie et al., 1998; Richards & Gross, 2000; Roberts, Levenson, & Gross, 2008; Wenzlaff, Rude, Taylor, Stultz, & Sweatt, 2001). Research has even shown that habitual suppression is correlated with the progression of cancer (Garssen & Goodkin, 1999) and a continuous weakening of the immune system (Petrie et al., 1998). Pennebaker and colleagues argued that the negative health outcomes associated with suppression may result from increasing stress and ruminative thoughts (Pennebaker & Francis, 1996; Spera, Buhrfeind, & Pennebaker, 1994). Studies comparing explicit (effortful) and implicit (automatic) use of suppression have found that the latter is less problematic in terms of negative outcomes for the individual, suggesting that effortful suppression in a Western context may come with an increased cognitive and physiological load (Mauss et al., 2007). These findings are consistent with the idea outlined earlier that in Western contexts—where the cultural script prioritizes individuals over social relationships—individual expression is healthier than emotional suppression.

Although studies focusing on emotion regulation in Western contexts have dominated the research landscape, recent work has highlighted the importance of considering other cultural contexts (Butler & Gross, 2009; Consedine, Magai, & Bonanno, 2002; Consedine, Magai, Cohen, & Gillespie 2002; Consedine, Magai, & Horton, 2005). Of particular interest are findings pertaining to the effects of suppression among collectivistic cultures, where greater weight is given to the needs of others, relative to individual needs, elevating the role of social relationships. For example, an investigation of Southeast Asian immigrants in Canada found that the association between discrimination and depression was weaker among those endorsing suppression of emotional behavior to cope with discrimination, particularly if they identified more with their Asian ethnicity (Noh, Beiser, Kaspar, Hou, & Rummens, 1999). Also along these lines, Butler et al. (2007) found that Asian American and European American individuals endorsing more "Asian" values (regardless of ethnicity) showed attenuated adverse effects of suppression during a social interaction task than individuals with more Western or European values. These examples in the literature highlight the need for further consideration of cultural fit in studies of emotion regulation's consequences for social relationships and health.

An implicit assumption of most of these studies is that group differences are driven by the extent to which emotional restraint or control is endorsed by individuals from Eastern or Western cultures. Mauss and Butler (2010) demonstrated this expected difference in their comparison of European Americans and Asian Americans by showing that the latter group reported valuing emotional restraint more than the former. More important, the relationship between valuing emotional restraint and the physiological consequences of suppression differed between the two groups. For Asian Americans, who value a cultural script that promotes suppression in the service of social relationships, suppression was associated with a physiological *challenge response*— a response characteristic of individuals responding to external demands they feel well-equipped to handle—rather than a physiological stress response (Mauss & Butler, 2010). Thus, these findings suggest that Asian Americans endorsing values consistent with Asian culture (emotional control) did not experience suppression negatively. Furthermore, in a recent study examining the relationship between suppression and psychological functioning, suppression was associated with greater depression symptoms and less life satisfaction among European Americans but not among Hong Kong Chinese (Soto et al., 2011). The converse has also been found in that the benefits of expression observed in European Americans (through writing) are not seen among Asian Americans (Knowles, Wearing, & Campos, 2011). Thus, not only have Asians shown a preference for coping strategies, such as suppression, that focus on internal changes in response to a stressor (Lam & Zane, 2004), but they also seem to either benefit from its use (e.g., Noh et al., 1999) or, at the very least, not show the same adverse effects exhibited by European Americans (Mauss & Butler, 2010; Soto et al., 2011).

Evidence within clinical psychology has further suggested that the cultural norm for Easterners and Westerners with respect to suppression of emotions in interpersonal contexts can lead to different outcomes for these groups. The *cultural norm hypothesis* argues that the ability to act in accordance with cultural norms of emotion is a marker of health (Chentsova-Dutton et al., 2007; Chentsova-Dutton, Tsai, & Gotlib, 2010); the converse of this supposition is that those with mental illness are therefore prone to enact culturally incongruent behaviors. Chentsova-Dutton et al. (2007, 2010) tested whether depression would interfere with the ability to experience and/or express emotions in culturally consistent ways. Their findings showed that Asian Americans with depression actually expressed their positive or negative emotions more than Asian Americans without depression. Likewise, European Americans with depression suppressed their positive or negative emotions compared with European Americans without depression. The forces affecting this relationship can be bidirectional. For instance, failing to adhere to cultural scripts can engender negativity from others (and/or oneself) in a manner that precipitates depression. This depression, in turn, can make it even harder to enact cultural scripts, thereby increasing distress in a negative cycle. Ultimately, these studies suggest that a crucial link exists between one's capacity to enact culturally normative emotion regulation behaviors and mental health.

The studies reviewed here provide one illustration of how conflicting norms regarding how and when emotions should unfold within relationships can be associated with different consequences for individual health. Although a comprehensive review of these cultural variations is outside of the scope of this chapter, research on emotion regulation and health has documented similar context-dependent health outcomes among other cultures. For example, research on self-reported physical health has demonstrated that the typically positive correlation between negative health outcomes (e.g., arthritis, hypertension) and emotion suppression appears to be attenuated among certain Eastern European immigrant populations (Consedine et al., 2005), another cultural group that values and practices suppression more than European Americans (Matsumoto et al., 2008). Thus, there is mounting evidence that cultural scripts pertaining to emotions and emotion regulation figure prominently in the connection between health and social relationships.

HOW CULTURAL FIT CAN INFLUENCE HEALTH OUTCOMES

One limitation of much of the research presented here is that these studies do not address the precise mechanism by which enacting (or not enacting) cultural scripts can lead to differential health outcomes. Although this has not been empirically studied in the literature, we suggest several theoretically based alternatives for why these effects might exist. In so doing, we hope that future research might begin to examine these issues more closely.

First, adherence to culturally normative ways of acting, attending, thinking, and feeling in interpersonal contexts is likely to infuse people's daily life with a sense of purpose and meaning. We know that the ability to derive meaning from experience fosters adaptive coping with stressful life events (Davis, Nolen-Hoeksema, & Larson, 1998; Hilbert, 1984; Urcuyo, Boyers, Carver, & Antoni, 2005; see also Baumeister & Vohs, 2002, and Park, 2010, for reviews). For example, Graham et al. (2009) showed that people who used words suggestive of meaning making when discussing a conflict with their spouses showed attenuated inflammatory responses to physical and psychological stress. Although people can and do engage in meaning making even when violating cultural scripts, culturally normative behavior is likely to cue in "ready-made" meanings, ensuring that moment-to-moment interpersonal behavior is infused with deeper meaning.

Second, adherence to cultural scripts is likely to minimize social disapproval, tension, and misunderstanding, thereby lowering stress levels. Culturally normative behavior can be readily interpreted through the prism of the shared meaning system and is, therefore, less likely to stand out or be misconstrued by others. From this perspective, greater fit between one's behavior and the prevailing cultural scripts can not only prevent the experience of dissonance with the surrounding environment (and therefore negative health outcomes) but also possibly promote a sense of being in synchrony with those around us (and therefore social rewards). Higgins (2005) described this "value from fit" between enactment of a script and a person's values and beliefs regarding this script as a sense that the enactment of scripts "feels right." For example, Uskul, Sherman, and Fitzgibbon (2009) demonstrated that people were more persuaded by health messages that were framed in culturally congruent ways. Increased persuasion was due to a match between the persuasion message and participants' culturally shaped tendency to preferentially attend to gains or losses.

Third, adherence to cultural scripts is likely to result in behaviors that are well practiced. Many cultural scripts, such as greetings or discussing problems, are ubiquitous in our daily lives. As such, they are likely to require less conscious effort than deviations from cultural norms (see Bargh & Chartrand, 1999, on the effects of automaticity). A related argument has certainly been advanced in regards to emotion regulation. For example, Engebretson, Matthews, and Scheier (1989) proposed that the physiological consequences of emotion regulation (e.g., suppression) depend on how habitually the strategy is practiced. To the extent that cultural scripts represent or lead to normative behavioral practices, it would follow that these behaviors become well rehearsed over time. The implementation of these practiced behaviors can influence health by requiring less cognitive or physical effort (which may adversely affect health over the long term). In sum, following cultural scripts can imbue our behavior with meaning, minimize feelings of dissonance and social tension, maximize feelings of engaging in socially appropriate behaviors, and be relatively effortless. Taken together, all of these factors can endow culturally congruent behavior with social, physical, and psychological benefits and represent exciting directions for future research endeavors. Focusing on cultural fit will allow researchers to examine specific factors that may drive different health and well-being outcomes (e.g., social approval).

ADDITIONAL CONSIDERATIONS

Thus far, the discussion of match or fit between behaviors and cultural scripts with respect to social relationships has been rather simplified for the sake of presentation (e.g., a behavior is consistent or inconsistent with cultural script X). In actuality, this process is likely to be far more complicated as individuals must navigate between multiple cultural scripts derived from their membership in more than one meaningful social group. For example, an elderly Tamang woman living in Nepal might have to pay attention to cultural scripts associated with Eastern tradition but also cultural scripts that delineate appropriate behavior for females, Buddhists, and the functions of elders within a community (Cole & Tamang, 1998). In many instances, these cultural scripts might be mutually informative and therefore largely consistent. For example, Buddhist philosophy is consistent with Asian values and traditions. However, there is also likely to be instances where two or more cultural scripts specify contradictory or competing behaviors. For example, Asian American children may be socialized to value moderation of emotion at home but open emotional expression in school. Moreover, even within a single cultural context, such as a European American context, these children may be exposed to inconsistent or context-specific norms (e.g., encouraged to be more deferential to some teachers, calling them Mr. or Mrs., and less deferential with others, referring to them by their first names). Thus, competing cultural scripts are important to factor into the equation when evaluating whether individual social behavior is consistent with norms.

Two cultural scripts in particular may be especially relevant when discussing health and social relationships: those pertaining to gender and minority status. Many cultures outline appropriate and inappropriate behaviors for how men and women interact with others within a society (see Best & Williams, 2001). These can include prescriptions about help seeking and emotional displays but can also pertain to courting, aggressiveness, nurturance, and a host of other behaviors. The same is true for individuals who also belong to minority groups within a particular society. Minority individuals (e.g., ethnic, sexual, religious) typically exist within a power structure that enables majority group members to withhold resources or privileges to the detriment of minority group members (Hanna, Talley, & Guindon, 2000). Thus, minority group membership can be associated with a unique set of cultural scripts that guide behavior within the confines of this inequitable social reality. These can include taking care to not confirm existing stereotypes of an already marginalized group, being deferent to members of the dominant group, or showing a favorable bias toward other ingroup members.

In addition to these considerations, it is important to keep in mind that many individuals are in the midst of negotiating cultural transitions. This is true of immigrants, refugees, visitors, and others who find themselves undergoing some degree of acculturation to a new environment (Berry, 1990). These individuals may be in the position of having to decide which of two cultural scripts (e.g., host culture vs. culture of origin) to follow and then dealing with the ensuing consequences of that choice, such as potential alienation from the culture whose scripts are not enacted. For example, different scripts for romantic relationships between American culture and Mexican culture may lead to intergenerational conflict among immigrant families where children choose to follow the American script, but the parents do not. Although a full treatment of how acculturation might affect cultural fit is outside of the scope of this chapter, considering the potential for overlapping cultural realities adds yet another layer of complexity in thinking about cultural fit between scripts and behaviors and the ensuing consequences of this fit.

CONCLUSION

Social relationships (and our internal representations of these relationships) are inextricably embedded within a rich cultural context that determines many of the parameters for how individuals approach others or comport themselves in relation to others. These parameters, or cultural scripts, provide a method by which individuals sharing a culture can operate efficiently and successfully within the social domain. The considerable variation across cultures in what constitutes successful social functioning inevitably means that culture plays a substantial part in the relation between social relationships and health. Emerging research in this arena should focus on improving our understanding of precisely how culture exerts its effect on this association. One domain particularly in need of such work is the clinical application of what is understood to be adaptive expectations within social relationships. By providing clinicians with the knowledge to make culturally competent suggestions to their clients experiencing difficulties in social functioning, such research can promote the health and well-being for diverse populations. Our hope with this chapter was to provide a glimpse into the importance of this line of exploration and highlight the complexities that result when culture is properly considered.

REFERENCES

Adams, G., Anderson, S. L., & Adonu, J. K. (2004). The cultural grounding of closeness and intimacy. In D. Mashek & A. Aron (Eds.), *The handbook of closeness and intimacy* (pp. 321–339). Mahwah, NJ: Erlbaum.

Adams, G., & Plaut, V. C. (2003). The cultural grounding of personal relationship: Friendship in North American and West African worlds. *Personal Relationships, 10,* 333–347. doi:10.1111/1475-6811.00053

Adolphs, R. (1999). Social cognition and the human brain. *Trends in Cognitive Sciences, 3,* 469–479. doi:10.1016/S1364-6613(99)01399-6

Bargh, J. A., & Chartrand, T. L. (1999). The unbearable automaticity of being. *American Psychologist, 54,* 462–479. doi:10.1037/0003-066X.54.7.462

Baumeister, R. F., & Vohs, K. D. (2002). The pursuit of meaningfulness in life. In C. R. Snyder & S. J. Lopez (Eds.), *Handbook of positive psychology* (pp. 608–618). New York, NY: Oxford University Press.

Bellah, R. N., Madsen, R., Sullivan, W. M., Swindler, A., & Tipton, S. M. (1985). *Habits of the heart: Individualism and commitment in American life.* New York, NY: Harper & Row.

Berry, J. W. (1990). Psychology of acculturation: Understanding individuals moving between cultures. In R. W. Brislin (Ed.), *Applied cross-cultural psychology* (pp. 232–253). Newbury Park, CA: Sage.

Best, D. L., & Williams, J. E. (2001). Gender and culture. In D. Matsumoto (Ed.), *Handbook of culture and psychology* (pp. 195–219). New York, NY: Oxford University Press.

Breuer, J., & Freud, S. (1957). *Studies on hysteria.* Oxford, England: Basic Books.

Buetow, S. A. (1999). Unsolicited GP advice against smoking: To give or not to give? *Journal of Health Communication, 4,* 67–74. doi:10.1080/108107399127101

Butler, E. A., Egloff, B., Wilhelm, F. H., Smith, N. C., Erikson, E. A., & Gross, J. J. (2003). The social consequences of expressive suppression. *Emotion, 3*, 48–67. doi:10.1037/1528-3542.3.1.48

Butler, E. A., & Gross, J. J. (2009). Emotion and emotion regulation: Integrating individual and social levels of analysis. *Emotion Review, 1*, 86–87. doi:10.1177/1754073908099131

Butler, E. A., Lee, T. L., & Gross, J. J. (2007). Emotion regulation and culture: Are social consequences of emotion suppression culture-specific? *Emotion, 7*, 30–48. doi:10.1037/1528-3542.7.1.30

Campos, B., Schetter, C. D., Abdou, C. M., Hobel, C. J., Glynn, L. M., & Sandman, C. A. (2008). Familialism, social support, and stress: Positive implications for pregnant Latinas. *Cultural Diversity and Ethnic Minority Psychology, 14*, 155–162. doi:10.1037/1099-9809.14.2.155

Catalino, L. I., & Fredrickson, B. L. (2011). A Tuesday in the life of a flourisher: The role of positive emotional reactivity in optimal mental health. *Emotion, 11*, 938–950. doi:10.1037/a0024889

Champagne, F. A. (2009). Nurturing nature: Social experiences and the brain. *Journal of Neuroendocrinology, 21*, 867–868. doi:10.1111/j.1365-2826.2009.01901.x

Chang, H. C., & Holt, G. R. (1994). A Chinese perspective on face as inter-relational concern. In S. Ting-Toomey (Ed.), *The challenge of facework: Cross-cultural and interpersonal issues* (pp. 95–132). Albany, NY: State University of New York Press.

Chentsova-Dutton, Y. E. (2012). Butting in vs. being a friend: Cultural differences and similarities in the evaluation of imposed social support. *Journal of Social Psychology, 52*, 493–509.

Chentsova-Dutton, Y. E., Chu, J. P., Tsai, J. L., Rottenberg, J., Gross, J. J., & Gotlib, I. H. (2007). Depression and emotional reactivity: Variation among Asian Americans of East Asian descent and European Americans. *Journal of Abnormal Psychology, 116*, 776–785. doi:10.1037/0021-843X.116.4.776

Chentsova-Dutton, Y. E., Tsai, J. L., & Gotlib, I. H. (2010). Further evidence for the cultural norm hypothesis: Positive emotion in depressed and control European American and Asian American women. *Cultural Diversity and Ethnic Minority Psychology, 16*, 284–295. doi:10.1037/a0017562

Chentsova-Dutton, Y. E., & Vaughn, A. (2012). Let me tell you what to do: Cultural differences in advice-giving. *Journal of Cross-Cultural Psychology, 43*, 687–703. doi:10.1177/0022022111402343

Cockerham, W. C. (2000). Health lifestyles in Russia. *Social Science & Medicine, 51*, 1313–1324.

Cohen, S. (1992). Stress, social support and disorder. In H. Veiel & U. Baumann (Eds.), *The meaning and measurement of social support* (pp. 109–124). New York, NY: Hemisphere Press.

Cole, P. M., & Tamang, B. L. (1998). Nepali children's ideas about emotional displays in hypothetical challenges. *Developmental Psychology, 34*, 640–646. doi:10.1037/0012-1649.34.4.640

Consedine, N. S., Magai, C., & Bonanno, G. A. (2002). Moderators of the emotion inhibition–health relationship: A review and research agenda. *Review of General Psychology, 6*, 204–228. doi:10.1037/1089-2680.6.2.204

Consedine, N. S., Magai, C., Cohen, C., & Gillespie, M. (2002). Ethnic variation in the impact of negative emotion and emotion inhibition on the health of older adults. *The Journals of Gerontology: Series B. Psychological Sciences and Social Sciences, 57*, P396–P408. doi:10.1093/geronb/57.5.P396

Consedine, N. S., Magai, C., & Horton, D. (2005). Ethnic variation in the impact of emotion and emotion regulation on health: A replication and extension. *The Journals of Gerontology: Series B. Psychological Sciences and Social Sciences, 60*, P165–P173. doi:10.1093/geronb/60.4.P165

Coyne, J. C., Ellard, J. H., & Smith, D. A. F. (1990). Social support, interdependence, and the dilemmas of helping. In B. R. Sarason & I. G. Sarason (Eds.), *Social support: An interactional view* (pp. 129–149). Oxford, England: Wiley.

Cutrona, C. E. (1990). Stress and social support—In search of optimal matching. *Journal of Social and Clinical Psychology, 9*, 3–14. doi:10.1521/jscp.1990.9.1.3

Davis, C. G., Nolen-Hoeksema, S., & Larson, J. (1998). Making sense of loss and benefiting from the experience: Two construals of meaning. *Journal of Personality and Social Psychology, 75*, 561–574. doi:10.1037/0022-3514.75.2.561

Demaree, H. A., Schmeichel, B. J., Robinson, J. L., Pu, J., Everhart, D. E., & Berntson, G. G. (2006). Up- and down-regulating facial disgust: Affective, vagal, sympathetic, and respiratory consequences. *Biological Psychology, 71*, 90–99. doi:10.1016/j.biopsycho.2005.02.006

Dickerson, S. S., Gruenewald, T., & Kemeny, M. (2004). When the social self is threatened: Shame, physiology, and health. *Journal of Personality, 72*, 1191–1216. doi:10.1111/j.1467-6494.2004.00295.x

DiMaggio, P. (1997). Culture and cognition. *Annual Review of Sociology, 23*, 263–287.

Dorr, N., Brosschot, J. F., Sollers, J. J., III, & Thayer, J. F. (2007). Damned if you do, damned if you don't: The differential effect of expression and inhibition of anger on cadiovascular recovery in Black and White males. *International Journal of Psychophysiology, 66*, 125–134. doi:10.1016/j.ijpsycho.2007.03.022

Dressler, W. W. (2011). Culture and the stress process. In M. Singer and P. Erickson (Eds.), *A companion to medical anthropology* (pp. 119–134). New York, NY: Wiley-Blackwell.

Dressler, W. W., & Bindon, J. R. (2000). The health consequences of cultural consonance: Cultural dimensions of lifestyle, social support, and arterial blood pressure in an African American community. *American Anthropologist, 102*, 244–260. doi:10.1525/aa.2000.102.2.244

Dressler, W. W., Mata, A., Chavez, A., Viteri, F. E., & Gallagher, P. (1986). Social support and arterial pressure in a Central Mexican community. *Psychosomatic Medicine, 48*, 338–350.

Eid, M., & Diener, E. (2001). Norms for experiencing emotions in different cultures: Inter- and intranational differences. *Journal of Personality and Social Psychology, 81,* 869–885. doi:10.1037/0022-3514.81.5.869

Ekman, P. (1972). Universals and cultural differences in facial expressions of emotion. In J. Cole (Ed.), *Nebraska symposium on motivation, 1971* (pp. 207–283). Lincoln, NE: University of Nebraska Press.

Ekman, P., & Friesen, W. V. (1969). Nonverbal leakage and clues to deception. *Psychiatry, 32,* 88–106.

Engebretson, T. O., Matthews, K. A., & Scheier, M. F. (1989). Relations between anger expression and cardiovascular reactivity: Reconciling inconsistent findings through a matching hypothesis. *Journal of Personality and Social Psychology, 57,* 513–521. doi:10.1037/0022-3514.57.3.513

Esterling, B. A., Antoni, M. H., Fletcher, M. A., Margulies, S., & Schneiderman, N. (1994). Emotional disclosure through writing or speaking modulates latent Epstein-Barr virus antibody titers. *Journal of Consulting and Clinical Psychology, 62,* 130–140. doi:10.1037/0022-006X.62.1.130

Fiske, A. P., Kitayama, S., Markus, H. R., & Nisbett, R. E. (1998). The cultural matrix of social psychology. In D. Gilbert, S. Fiske, & G. Lindzey (Eds.), *The handbook of social psychology* (4th ed., pp. 915–981). San Francisco, CA: McGraw-Hill.

Garssen, B., & Goodkin, K. (1999). On the role of immunological factors as mediators between psychosocial factors and cancer progression. *Psychiatry Research, 85,* 51–61. doi:10.1016/S0165-1781(99)00008-6

Goldsmith, D. J. (2000). Soliciting advice: The role of sequential placement in mitigating face threat. *Communication Monographs, 67,* 1–19. doi:10.1080/03637750009376492

Goldsmith, D. J. (2004). *Communicating social support: Advances in personal relationships.* Cambridge, England: Cambridge University Press.

Goldsmith, D. J., & Fitch, K. (1997). The normative context of advice as social support. *Human Communication Research, 23,* 454–476. doi:10.1111/j.1468-2958.1997.tb00406.x

Goodwin, R., & Plaza, H. (2000). Perceived and received social support in two cultures: Collectivism and support among British and Spanish students. *Journal of Social and Personal Relationships, 17,* 282. doi:10.1177/0265407500172007

Graham, J. E., Glaser, R., Loving, T. J., Malarkey, W. B., Stowell, J. R., & Kiecolt-Glaser, J. K. (2009). Cognitive word use during marital conflict and increases in proinflammatory cytokines. *Health Psychology, 28,* 621–630. doi:10.1037/a0015208

Gross, J. J., & John, O. P. (2003). Individual differences in two emotion regulation processes: Implications for affect, relationships, and well-being. *Journal of Personality and Social Psychology, 85,* 348–362. doi:10.1037/0022-3514.85.2.348

Gross, J. J., & Levenson, R. W. (1993). Emotional suppression: Physiology, self-report, and expressive behavior. *Journal of Personality and Social Psychology, 64,* 970–986. doi:10.1037/0022-3514.64.6.970

Guendelman, S., & Siega-Riz, A. M. (2002). Infant feeding practices and maternal dietary intake among Latino immigrants in California. *Journal of Immigrant Health, 4*, 137–146. doi:10.1023/A:1015698817387

Hanna, F. J., Talley, W. B., & Guindon, M. H. (2000). The power of perception: Toward a model of cultural oppression and liberation. *Journal of Counseling & Development, 78*, 430–441.

Heine, S. J. (2001). Self as cultural product: An examination of East Asian and North American selves. *Journal of Personality, 69*, 881–905. doi:10.1111/1467-6494.696168

Higgins, E. T. (2005). Value from regulatory fit. *Current Directions in Psychological Science, 14*, 209–213. doi:10.1111/j.0963-7214.2005.00366.x

Hilbert, R. A. (1984). The acultural dimensions of chronic pain: Flawed reality construction and the problem of meaning. *Social Problems, 31*, 365–378. doi:10.1525/sp.1984.31.4.03a00010

Hokanson, J. E., Willers, K. R., & Koropsak, E. (1968). The modification of autonomic responses during aggressive interchange. *Journal of Personality, 36*, 386–404.

Horowitz, L. M., Krasnoperova, E. N., Tatar, D. G., Hansen, M. B., Person, E. A., Galvin, K. L., & Nelson, K. L. (2001). The way to console may depend on the goal: Experimental studies of social support. *Journal of Experimental Social Psychology, 37*, 49–61. doi:10.1006/jesp.2000.1435

Jacobson, D. (1987). The cultural context of social support and support networks. *Medical Anthropology Quarterly, 1*, 42–67. doi:10.1525/maq.1987.1.1.02a00030

Jose, P. E., D'Anna, C. A., Cafasso, L. L., Bryant, F. B., Chiker, V., Gein, N., & Zhezmer, N. (1998). Stress and coping among Russian and American early adolescents. *Developmental Psychology, 34*, 757–769. doi:10.1037/0012-1649.34.4.757

Kiecolt-Glaser, J. K., McGuire, L., Robles, T. F., & Glaser, R. (2002). Emotions, morbidity, and mortality: New perspectives from psychoneuroimmunology. *Annual Review of Psychology, 53*, 83–107. doi:10.1146/annurev.psych.53.100901.135217

Kim, H., & Markus, H. R. (1999). Deviance or uniqueness, harmony or conformity? A cultural analysis. *Journal of Personality and Social Psychology, 77*, 785–800. doi:10.1037/0022-3514.77.4.785

Kim, H. S., & Sherman, D. K. (2007). "Express yourself": Culture and the effect of self-expression on choice. *Journal of Personality and Social Psychology, 92*, 1–11. doi:10.1037/0022-3514.92.1.1

Kim, H. S., Sherman, D. K., Ko, D., & Taylor, S. E. (2006). Pursuit of comfort and pursuit of harmony: Culture, relationships, and social support seeking. *Personality and Social Psychology Bulletin, 32*, 1595–1607. doi:10.1177/0146167206291991

Kim, H. S., Sherman, D. K., Sasaki, J. Y., Xu, J., Chu, T. Q., Ryu, C., . . . Taylor, S. E. (2010). Culture, distress and oxytocin receptor polymorphism (OXTR) interact to influence emotional support seeking. *Proceedings of the National Academy of Sciences of the United States of America, 107*, 15717–15721. doi:10.1073/pnas.1010830107

Kleinman, A. (1986). *Social origins of distress and disease: Depression, neurasthenia, and pain in modern China*. New Haven, CT: Yale University Press.

Klineberg, O. (1938). Emotional expression in Chinese literature. *The Journal of Abnormal and Social Psychology, 33*, 517–520. doi:10.1037/h0057105

Knowles, E., Wearing, J., & Campos, B. (2011). Culture and the health benefits of expressive writing. *Social Psychological and Personality Science, 2*, 408–415. doi:10.1177/1948550610395780

Krantz, D. S., & Manuck, S. B. (1984). Acute psychophysiological reactivity and risk of cardiovascular disease: A review and methodological critique. *Psychological Bulletin, 96*, 435–464. doi:10.1037/0033-2909.96.3.435

Lam, A. G., & Zane, N. W. S. (2004). Ethnic differences in coping with interpersonal stressors: A test of self-construals as cultural mediators. *Journal of Cross-Cultural Psychology, 35*, 446–459. doi:10.1177/0022022104266108

Markus, H. R., & Kitayama, S. (1991). Culture and the self: Implications for cognition, emotion, and motivation. *Psychological Review, 98*, 224–253. doi:10.1037/0033-295X.98.2.224

Matsumoto, D. (2006). Are cultural differences in emotion regulation mediated by personality traits? *Journal of Cross-Cultural Psychology, 37*, 421–437. doi:10.1177/0022022106288478

Matsumoto, D., Yoo, S. H., & Nakagawa, S. (2008). Culture, emotion regulation, and adjustment. *Journal of Personality and Social Psychology, 94*, 925–937. doi:10.1037/0022-3514.94.6.925

Mauss, I. B., Bunge, S. A., Gross, J. J., Mauss, I. B., Bunge, S. A., & Gross, J. J. (2007). Automatic emotion regulation. *Social and Personality Psychology Compass, 1*, 146–167. doi:10.1111/j.1751-9004.2007.00005.x

Mauss, I. B., & Butler, E. A. (2010). Cultural context moderates the relationship between emotion control values and cardiovascular challenge versus threat responses. *Biological Psychology, 84*, 521–530. doi:10.1016/j.biopsycho.2009.09.010

Mesquita, B., & Frijda, N. H. (1992). Cultural variations in emotions: A review. *Psychological Bulletin, 112*, 179–204. doi:10.1037/0033-2909.112.2.179

Michailova, S., & Hutchings, K. (2006). National cultural influences on knowledge sharing: A comparison of China and Russia. *Journal of Management Studies, 43*, 383–405. doi:10.1111/j.1467-6486.2006.00595.x

Moskowitz, J. T. (2003). Positive affect predicts lower risk of AIDS mortality. *Psychosomatic Medicine, 65*, 620–626. doi:10.1097/01.PSY.0000073873.74829.23

Moskowitz, J. T., & Epel, E. S. (2006). Benefit finding and diurnal cortisol slope in maternal caregivers: A moderating role for positive emotion. *The Journal of Positive Psychology, 1*, 83–91. doi:10.1080/17439760500510510

Nadler, A. (1986). Help seeking as a cultural phenomenon: Differences between city and kibbutz dwellers. *Journal of Personality and Social Psychology, 51*, 976–982. doi:10.1037/0022-3514.51.5.976

Noh, S., Beiser, M., Kaspar, V., Hou, F., & Rummens, A. (1999). Perceived racial discrimination, depression, and coping: A study of Southeast Asian refugees in Canada. *Journal of Health and Social Behavior, 40*, 193–207. doi:10.2307/2676348

Park, C. L. (2010). Making sense of the meaning literature: An integrative review of meaning making and its effects on adjustment to stressful life events. *Psychological Bulletin, 136*, 257–301. doi:10.1037/a0018301

Pennebaker, J. W., & Beall, S. K. (1986). Confronting a traumatic event: Toward an understanding of inhibition and disease. *Journal of Abnormal Psychology, 95*, 274–281. doi:10.1037/0021-843X.95.3.274

Pennebaker, J. W., & Francis, M. E. (1996). Cognitive, emotional, and language processes in disclosure. *Cognition and Emotion, 10*, 601–626. doi:10.1080/026999396380079

Pennebaker, J. W., & Seagal, J. D. (1999). Forming a story: The health benefits of narrative. *Journal of Clinical Psychology, 55*, 1243–1254. doi:10.1002/(SICI)1097-4679(199910)55:10<1243::AID-JCLP6>3.0.CO;2-N

Petrie, K. J., Booth, R. J., & Pennebaker, J. W. (1998). The immunological effects of thought suppression. *Journal of Personality and Social Psychology, 75*, 1264–1272. doi:10.1037/0022-3514.75.5.1264

Rathmayr, R. (2008). Intercultural aspects of new Russian politeness. *WU Online Papers in International Business Communication, 4*, 2–7.

Realo, A., & Allik, J. (1999). A cross-cultural study of collectivism: A comparison of American, Estonian, and Russian students. *The Journal of Social Psychology, 139*, 133–142. doi:10.1080/00224549909598367

Reeve, J., & Jang, H. (2006). What teachers say and do to support students' autonomy during a learning activity. *Journal of Educational Psychology, 98*, 209. doi:10.1037/0022-0663.98.1.209

Richards, J. M., & Gross, J. J. (2000). Emotion regulation and memory: The cognitive costs of keeping one's cool. *Journal of Personality and Social Psychology, 79*, 410–424. doi:10.1037/0022-3514.79.3.410

Roberts, N. A., Levenson, R. W., & Gross, J. (2008). Cardiovascular costs of emotion suppression cross ethnic lines. *International Journal of Psychophysiology, 70*, 82–87. doi:10.1016/j.ijpsycho.2008.06.003

Rose, R. (2000). Getting things done in an antimodern society: Social capital networks in Russia. In P. Dasgupta & I. Serageldin (Eds.), *Social capital: A multifaceted perspective* (pp. 147–172). Washington, DC: The World Bank.

Ryder, A. G., Ban, L. M., & Chentsova-Dutton, Y. E. (2011). Towards a cultural–clinical psychology. *Social and Personality Psychology Compass, 5*, 960–975. doi:10.1111/j.1751-9004.2011.00404.x

Schwingel, A., Nakata, Y., Ito, L., Chodzko-Zajko, W., Erb, C., Shigematsu, R., . . . Tanaka, K. (2007). Central obesity and health-related factors among middle-aged men: A comparison among Native Japanese and Japanese-Brazilians residing in Brazil and Japan. *Journal of Physiological Anthropology, 26*, 339–347. doi:10.2114/jpa2.26.339

Shumaker, S. A., & Brownell, A. (1984). Toward a theory of social support: Closing conceptual gaps. *Journal of Social Issues, 40*, 11–36. doi:10.1111/j.1540-4560.1984. tb01105.x

Shweder, R. A. (1990). Cultural psychology: What is it? In J. W. Stigler, R. A. Shweder, & G. Herdt (Eds.), *Cultural psychology: Essays on comparative human development* (pp. 1–4). Cambridge, England: Cambridge University Press.

Soto, J. A., Perez, C. R., Kim, Y.-H., Lee, E. A., & Minnick, M. R. (2011). Is expressive suppression always associated with poorer psychological functioning? A cross-cultural comparison between European Americans and Hong Kong Chinese. *Emotion, 11*, 1450–1455. doi:10.1037/a0023340

Spera, S. P., Buhrfeind, E. D., & Pennebaker, J. W. (1994). Expressive writing and coping with job loss. *Academy of Management Journal, 37*, 722–733. doi:10.2307/256708

Stott, N. C. H., & Pill, R. M. (1990). "Advise yes, dictate no." Patients' views on health promotion in the consultation. *Family Practice, 7*, 125–131. doi:10.1093/fampra/7.2.125

Taylor, S. E., Sherman, D. K., Kim, H. S., Jarcho, J., Takagi, K., & Dunagan, M. S. (2004). Culture and social support: Who seeks it and why? *Journal of Personality and Social Psychology, 87*, 354–362. doi:10.1037/0022-3514.87.3.354

Taylor, S. E., Welch, W. T., Kim, H. S., & Sherman, D. K. (2007). Cultural differences in the impact of social support on psychological and biological stress responses. *Psychological Science, 18*, 831–837. doi:10.1111/j.1467-9280.2007.01987.x

Ting-Toomey, S., Gao, G., Trubisky, P., Yang, Z., Kim, H. S., Lin, S. L., & Nishida, T. (1991). Culture, face maintenance, and styles of handling interpersonal conflict: A study in five cultures. *International Journal of Conflict Management, 2*, 275–296. doi:10.1108/eb022702

Triandis, H. C. (1990). Cross-cultural studies of individualism–collectivism. In J. Berman (Ed.), *Nebraska Symposium on Motivation 1989* (Vol. 37, pp. 41–133). Lincoln, NE: University of Nebraska Press.

Triandis, H. C. (1993). Collectivism and individualism as cultural syndromes. *Cross-Cultural Research, 27*, 155–180. doi:10.1177/106939719302700301

Tsai, J. L. (2007). Ideal affect: Cultural causes and behavioral consequences. *Perspectives on Psychological Science, 2*, 242–259. doi:10.1111/j.1745-6916.2007.00043.x

Tsai, J. L., Chentsova-Dutton, Y., Freire-Bebeau, L., & Przymus, D. E. (2002). Emotional expression and physiology in European Americans and Hmong Americans. *Emotion, 2*, 380–397. doi:10.1037/1528-3542.2.4.380

Tsai, J. L., Louie, J. Y., Chen, E. E., & Uchida, Y. (2007). Learning what feelings to desire: Socialization of ideal affect through children's storybooks. *Personality and Social Psychology Bulletin, 33*, 17. doi:10.1177/0146167206292749

Tsai, J. L., Miao, F. F., Seppala, E., Fung, H. H., & Yeung, D. Y. (2007). Influence and adjustment goals: Sources of cultural differences in ideal affect. *Journal of Personality and Social Psychology, 92*, 1102–1117. doi:10.1037/0022-3514.92.6.1102

Uchida, Y., Kitayama, S., Mesquita, B., Reyes, J. A. S., & Morling, B. (2008). Is perceived emotional support beneficial? Well-being and health in independent and interdependent cultures. *Personality and Social Psychology Bulletin, 34*, 741–754. doi:10.1177/0146167208315157

Urcuyo, K. R., Boyers, A. E., Carver, C. S., & Antoni, M. H. (2005). Finding benefit in breast cancer: Relations with personality, coping, and concurrent well-being. *Psychology & Health, 20*, 175–192. doi:10.1080/08870440512331317634

Uskul, A. K., Sherman, D. K., & Fitzgibbon, J. (2009). The cultural congruency effect: Culture, regulatory focus, and the effectiveness of gain- vs. loss-framed health messages. *Journal of Experimental Social Psychology, 45*, 535–541. doi:10.1016/j.jesp.2008.12.005

Wenzlaff, R. M., Rude, S. S., Taylor, C. J., Stultz, C. H., & Sweatt, R. A. (2001). Beneath the veil of thought suppression: Attentional bias and depression risk. *Cognition and Emotion, 15*, 435–452.

Wierzbicka, A. (1999). *Emotions across languages and cultures: Diversity and universals*. New York, NY: Cambridge University Press.

Xu, Y., & Burleson, B. R. (2001). Effects of sex, culture, and support type on perceptions of spousal social support: An assessment of the "support gap" hypothesis in early marriage. *Human Communication Research, 27*, 535–566. doi:10.1111/j.1468-2958.2001.tb00792.x

Zabin, L. S., & Kiragu, K. (1998). The health consequences of adolescent sexual and fertility behavior in sub-Saharan Africa. *Studies in Family Planning, 29*, 210–232. doi:10.2307/172160

IV
PRACTICAL IMPLICATIONS

9

RESILIENCE: A FRAMEWORK FOR UNDERSTANDING THE DYNAMIC RELATIONSHIP BETWEEN SOCIAL RELATIONS AND HEALTH

ANNE AREWASIKPORN, MARY C. DAVIS, AND ALEX ZAUTRA

We face challenges every day, some mundane and some tragic, and our capacity to be resilient in the face of difficult circumstances is inexorably linked with the quality of our social bonds. Strong social bonds can help us get through difficult times, and weak ones can make those times all the more difficult. In the cases of Judith and Sarah (described later), both women faced extraordinary adversity in the past, but the response of important people in their lives to their experience was quite different. As a result, Judith and Sarah dealt with the adversity in different ways that continue to affect how they perceive and interact within their social worlds now, these many years later.

The authors contributed equally in this work and are listed in alphabetical order. This work is supported in part by a grant from the National Institute on Aging (R01 AG 026006; principal investigator: Alex Zautra). In addition, the authors wish to acknowledge St. Luke's Charitable Trust and the Arizona State University Office of the Vice President for Research for their support.

DOI: 10.1037/14036-010
Health and Social Relationships: The Good, the Bad, and the Complicated, Matthew L. Newman and Nicole A. Roberts (Editors)

Judith, a corrections officer, was completing a routine cell check when a large, aggressive male inmate maneuvered her into the corner of his jail cell. Concerned for her safety, Judith called for backup. Though her fellow officers became aware of the situation, they did not act. The other prisoners called for help as well, and when the other guards did not come to Judith's aid, the nearby prisoners engaged the inmate themselves and helped her escape. Afterward, the incident remained largely unaddressed—none of the other corrections officers on duty were reprimanded, and no procedures were changed. After that, Judith recalled feeling isolated and found it difficult to connect with others and impossible to sustain meaningful relationships. She fell into a deep depression with thoughts of suicide and sought counseling. Judith and her husband were unable to keep their marriage together under the strain, and they divorced. These changes made it impossible for Judith to find fulfillment in her work, which had previously given her life purpose and meaning. She ultimately left her 20-year career as a corrections facility officer.

Years later, Judith now operates under the assumption that she cannot depend on others for her safety and well-being. Survival requires her to be self-reliant. In the face of adversity, it is a common response to revert to this type of mind-set, especially after one's safety is compromised as a result of misplaced trust in others. Learning to depend on oneself is a valuable lesson, but in the extreme, it limits our capacity to be resilient.

Judith's story comes from a study we are conducting of people in midlife who are asked to report on the most stressful experience in their lives. Her story represents one kind of response to a difficult situation. Here is a different story involving a violent encounter, taken from the same study. When Sarah was 16 years old, a stranger broke into her home and sexually assaulted her at knifepoint. Sarah said that she was able to recover with the help of support groups and counseling. Her family and friends supported her without judgment or blame, and Sarah attributes much of her recovery to the support she received. Despite the physical and emotional pain, she was able to continue to pursue the goals that gave her life meaning—she continued to socialize with her peers and to be an industrious student. Beyond recovering from this traumatic experience and sustaining purpose in her life, Sarah has transformed her experience into work in rape crisis counseling, helping others who also have survived sexual assault. One could reasonably assume that Sarah would harbor feelings of anger and resentment toward the man who assaulted her, but in an interview some 40 years later, she expresses feelings of forgiveness and compassion for her attacker, who himself experienced a life of violence and abuse.

Both Judith and Sarah faced threats of physical harm, yet both came away from these experiences—the most stressful event of their lives—with different perspectives. Though Judith reports having mostly recovered from the experience, feeling abandoned by the people she depended on for her safety has left an indelible mark on her ability to connect with and depend on others. Her narrative contains what McAdams, Reynolds, Lewis, Patten, and Bowman (2001) termed *contamination sequences*, in which the storyteller describes an episode that shifts from a good, affectively positive life scene to one that becomes contaminated and turns into an affectively negative one.

In contrast, Sarah also endured incredible emotional distress, but instead of feeling isolated and alone, she described being buoyed by the support of her family, friends, and church. Sarah's narrative was composed of *redemption sequences*, in which an affectively negative life scene is transformed into a positive one (McAdams et al., 2001). She has strengthened her existing relationships and formed new ones. Not only was Sarah able to recover from the physical and emotional trauma, but she was also able to find meaning and purpose in the experience. Research has suggested that individuals like Sarah, who in recounting their life stories use benefit-finding strategies in the face of adversity, tend to report enhanced psychological well-being, whereas individuals like Judith, who recount contamination sequences, tend to report lower levels of well-being (McAdams et al., 2001).

As the stories of Judith and Sarah illustrate, life narratives are jointly authored by the individuals themselves and by the social context in which they live. In this chapter, we offer a resilience framework to conceptualize the individual- and social-level strengths and vulnerabilities that influence how individuals facing adversity fare over time.

RESILIENCE: ADAPTING TO ADVERSITY

To observe resilience processes, the object of study must undergo some sort of stress or threat to homeostasis. Resilient responding cannot emerge otherwise, because it can only be elicited in response to stressful experiences (Zautra, Arewasikporn, & Davis, 2010). Had Sarah not been assaulted, she might never have known her capacity for drawing strength from adversity. Likewise, if Judith had not undergone her stressful ordeal, her vulnerabilities might not have emerged. *Allostasis*, the ability to maintain homeostasis through change and adaptation (Ganzel, Morris, & Wethington, 2010), is fundamental to the study of resilience. Indeed, resilience emerges when the organism changes as it adapts to a stressor. How resilient the organism is depends on the success of that adaptive response.

A focus on risk continues to be a driving force in the study of human behavior. The use of a risk-based approach allows us to examine the contexts in which people fall apart. Though this is a valuable avenue of inquiry, it is also limiting. Distress often but not always accompanies stressful times, and it does not last long for most people. Individuals do not typically fall apart; recovery is the norm (Bonanno, 2004; Masten, 2001). Resilience research and commentary examines under which conditions successful adaptation to stress is most likely to occur and which forms of adaptation are healthiest. They also can identify which conditions, though successful for recovery in the short term, fail to strengthen the person's capacities to endure hardship in the long term (Zautra et al., 2010).

Under a risk-based model, one might focus on the extent and intensity of the distress that Judith and Sarah had felt as an immediate response to the stressful events, whereas a resilience approach would also include consideration of how long and how fully Judith and Sarah recovered. Furthermore, the study of resilience extends beyond the distress experienced during stress and recovery. We also ask about how well Judith and Sarah were able to sustain their interest in the aspects of life that gave meaning and purpose despite the presence of stressors. Last, we pose questions about positive changes in life brought about by adversity that allow an individual to grow stronger. For example, though Sarah's rape was difficult to overcome, it became a transformative experience that led her to seek a career connecting with and aiding other survivors of sexual assault. She has not only adjusted to life after the trauma but now also thrives and finds greater meaning in her life because of it. Judith, in contrast, was unable to maintain a connection with the aspects of her life that mattered to her. Her focus narrowed, and her social world became smaller. In sum, Judith and Sarah both had violent encounters and consider themselves to have mostly recovered from their experience, yet subtleties emerge in how they responded when one considers how each was able to endure and learn from what happened.

One person can learn and grow from a stressful experience, yet not fully recover. Another can fully recover, yet not learn or grow from the experience. Following a stressful experience, such as divorce, some people carry on with work and maintain meaningful relationships even as they continue to grieve for the loss of a marriage. Still others will focus their attention on alleviating their suffering but neglect to sustain activities that give their lives value and purpose. When viewed as an outcome, resilience encompasses three domains: *recovery*—the ability to bounce back fully from stressors (Masten, 2001; Rutter, 1987), *sustainability*—the capacity to endure and sustain positive engagements in the face of stress (Reich, Zautra, & Hall, 2010), and *growth*—the process of learning from and cultivating new capacities from these stressful experiences (Zautra & Reich, 2010).

RESILIENCE IS SOCIAL

It should come as no surprise that humans are social (Cacioppo, Reis, & Zautra, 2011). Individuals naturally connect with others—we seek out lifelong partners and form family units, and we tend to cluster together in small communities or cities rather than live in complete isolation. These emergent social structures can be complex and abstract, ranging from dyads to global communities (Murray & Zautra, 2011). The propensity for creating social structures comes from the innate tendency of our species to seek out and maintain intimate and meaningful relationships (Baumeister & Leary, 1995).

Judith and Sarah's stories provide valuable insight into the power of relationships. The outcomes of these stories differ, but one theme weaves through both narratives: We are social beings greatly affected by the people around us. For Judith, the absence of social support caused considerable emotional pain, whereas for Sarah, the affirmation of existing relationships facilitated her recovery and growth. We all have the capacity to feel pain in the face of social isolation as Judith did and to be strengthened by our bonds with others in times of stress, as was the case for Sarah. We also have the capacity to feel *empathy*—that is, to experience another's social pain as if it were our own. These intrinsically human qualities help define our social nature, though their expression varies greatly from person to person (Lavigne, Vallerand, & Crevier-Braud, 2011).

Even in the worst of times, and maybe especially then, people seek to connect. When an explosion caused the Upper Big Branch Mine to collapse and trap four West Virginian miners in 2010, the men left notes of reassurance for their loved ones: "Tell them I'll see them on the other side. . . . It wasn't bad, I just went to sleep. . . . I love you." As it became clear that rescue would not reach them in time, their instinct to affirm existing relationships overruled potential messages of pain, anxiety, fear, or anger. New Yorkers, standing on the ledge of one of the Twin Towers on 9/11 did the same. Knowing they had to jump to their deaths, many texted those they loved to say goodbye for the last time. Our relationships inform nearly all our motivations and our emotions, and we must consider how these relationships fit into our conceptualization of resilience.

CHRONIC PAIN AND RESILIENCE

The chronic pain experience can be one fraught with stresses related to health and functioning. Because pain is ongoing, the potential for chronic stress is high. Studying individuals with chronic pain, as well as their families, provides

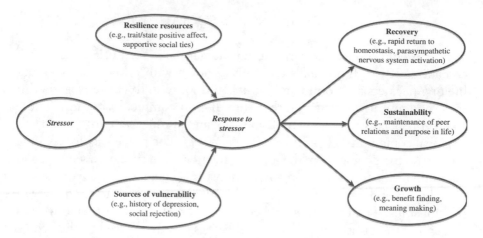

Figure 9.1. Resilience resources and outcomes. Key factors influencing resilient responding.

a unique opportunity to study both stress and resilience. Sturgeon and Zautra (2010) presented an expanded resilience framework for chronic pain that incorporates a two-dimensional framework with resilience resources and outcomes. This framework includes both resilience resources and vulnerability traits, which affect coping responses to stress and which in turn affect resilient outcomes (see Figure 9.1). Resilience resources such as trait positive affect and strong social ties represent capacities for resilient responding. Alternately, vulnerability traits, such as a history of depression or trauma, may predispose an individual to respond in a manner detrimental to his or her health and well-being.

We have found that positive experiences are most salient under conditions of heightened stress, and perhaps it is the seeking of these experiences during difficult times that best characterizes the resilient response. In a sample of women with osteoarthritis and fibromyalgia, our multilevel modeling analyses revealed that weekly reports of positive affect had their most powerful effects in deterring negative affects in weeks when the patients' bodily pain was highest (Zautra, Johnson, & Davis, 2005).

The value of positive emotion was not confined to times of heightened pain, however. Interpersonal stressors also waxed and waned through the 12 weeks of the study, leading to an analysis of whether positive emotion played a role in reducing affective distress in weeks of interpersonal conflict. We had these patients also report weekly on the occurrence of interpersonal events in four domains: family, friendships, work life, and spouse relations. Items included events such as "Had an argument with spouse," "Friend did not show up for a scheduled meeting," and "Criticized a family member," using the Inventory of Stressful Life Events (Zautra, Guarnaccia, & Dohrenwend, 1986). An interpersonal stress measure was formed as the average of four ratings of the stressfulness of relationships across the four domains that followed inquiries into the weekly frequency of stressful events. As with pain exacerbations, when interpersonal stress was highest, positive emotions deterred negative affective states. In sum, for these patients with chronic pain, having higher levels of positive affect limited the negative impact of pain and stress.

The unique contribution of positive emotion was also found in another of our studies of patients with rheumatic illness, which examined the effects of depression history on pain reports during stress induction in patients with rheumatoid arthritis (RA; Zautra et al., 2007). Stress was induced in a laboratory setting using two tasks. In the first stress induction task, each participant prepared and presented a 5-minute speech describing their best and worst qualities (Davis, Zautra, & Reich, 2001), and for the second task, the participant was asked to recall and reflect on a recent conflict with someone close to them (Davis, Twamley, Hamilton, & Swan, 1999; Davis et al., 2001). Perceived stress increased in response to the tasks, as expected. It is noteworthy that merely thinking about an interpersonal conflict can induce stress. Also, as expected, depressive symptoms, negative affect, perceived stress, and a history of multiple depressive episodes predicted increases in reports of joint pain and bodily pain (Zautra et al., 2007). Changes in positive affect did not affect pain reports for everyone. It was the subset of participants with a history of multiple depressive episodes who benefited most from positive affect. For these individuals with an additional affective vulnerability, changes in positive affect were protective against stress-related increases in pain.

In chronically stressed groups, one common issue is a dampened awareness of positive emotional resources, including an oversimplification of affective experience (Zautra et al., 2010). In essence, these individuals experience emotions as black or white, either negative or positive, and show limited capacity to experience emotional complexity. It is not difficult to understand how individuals under stress tend to focus their attention on the negative experiences that characterize their stressful situation while minimizing the positive, considering our natural bias toward negative stimuli. We (Zautra, Davis, et al., 2008) developed a mindfulness-based intervention for patients with RA that targeted affective dysfunction. The intervention was created to promote effective regulation of negative emotional responses to stress and to encourage positive emotional experience on a daily basis (Zautra, Davis, et al., 2008). In a head-to-head comparison with a standard cognitive behavior therapy for pain and education placebo control, the mindfulness group reported increased positive affect, decreased negative affect, and decreased physician-reported swelling and joint tenderness. Follow-up analyses suggested the mindfulness group evidenced better emotion regulation under stress. The mindfulness group was less reactive to daily interpersonal stressors compared with the pain management and education groups (Davis, Zautra, & Kratz, 2010). This intervention is one example of enhancing resilience capacities by cultivating emotional complexity, especially by promoting positive emotional experience.

Positive emotion serves an important function by helping individuals regulate their inner negative affective states, which in turn may promote more social engagement and stronger social bonds. Positive emotions alone do not make for a resilient person, but they do emerge as a key resilience resource that people draw on when in pain. The parallels between physical pain and social pain are particularly striking and have drawn us to envision ways of strengthening social resilience for its own sake.

SOCIAL PAIN

When people describe social stressors such as social isolation, social conflict, social losses, and social rejection, they often refer to those experiences as painful ones (MacDonald & Leary, 2005). The end of a romantic relationship or divorce is described as painful, and hurt feelings abound in the vernacular of friendships that have turned sour. Beyond similarities in linguistic descriptors, recent studies have found behavioral and neural evidence supporting a shared neurobiological system for physiological and social pain (e.g. MacDonald & Jensen-Campbell, 2011). DeWall et al. (2010) examined the overlap between social pain and physical pain processes in two studies by testing the effectiveness of acetaminophen, a physical pain suppressant that acts through central neural mechanisms, in reducing social pain. The investigators hypothesized that acetaminophen would reduce both behavioral and neural responses to social rejection. In the first experiment, individuals who took acetaminophen reported in daily diary reports that they had fewer instances of hurt feelings compared with those who took the placebo. Moreover, region-of-interest and whole brain analyses of the neuroimaging data in the second experiment revealed that participants in the acetaminophen versus placebo condition demonstrated less activity in the dorsal anterior cingulate cortex and anterior insula—regions of the brain previously shown to be associated with social pain (Eisenberger, Lieberman, & Williams, 2003)—in response to social exclusion over inclusion. These participants also showed significantly less activity in brain regions associated with affective processes (bilateral posterior insula, right amygdala) than did those in the placebo condition. The reduction in self-report feelings of social rejection coupled with neuroimaging data in this study and others (see MacDonald & Jensen-Campbell, 2011) provides a compelling case for a common neural network for social and physical pain.

Social pain is often accompanied by feelings of sadness and loneliness. These emotions are signals that tell us something is amiss and needs attention if we are to avoid harm to our social world, much like acute physical pain is a signal of potential harm to the body. We can conceptualize loneliness as an evolutionary mechanism that serves to promote the essential need to connect to others (Cacioppo, Hawkley, & Correll, in press). Feeling socially excluded induces pain, and repeated episodes of social isolation and disregard have adverse health and mental health consequences as well (House, Landis, & Umberson, 1988; see also Chapter 7, this volume). For instance, loneliness has been associated with depressive symptomatology (Kawachi & Berkman, 2001), suicidal ideation and behavior (Rudatsikira, Muula, Siziya, & Twa-Twa, 2007), and a variety of poor health outcomes from reduced immunocompetence (e.g., Kiecolt-Glaser, Gouin, & Hantsoo, 2010) to increased mortality (Cacioppo et al., in press).

Likewise, positive social connection is associated with better psychological well-being, mental health, and physical health outcomes. For example, strong relationships with romantic partners confer health benefits, as has been shown in previous chapters in this volume (see Chapters 3, 4, 5, this volume). It is not difficult to see that positive interactions with those who are closest to us—our intimate friends and partners—can change a taciturn and grumpy mood into a happier one. Over time, the accumulation of these interactions may serve as a buffer against stressors and build an individual's capacity to be resilient in the face of stress, both acute and chronic.

Reviewing our interviews with community members telling their stories of the most stressful experience in their lives, we have found that the seeds of chronicity may begin early in the person's response to the stressor and in the adequacy of the response of those close at hand at the time. The successes and failures of oneself and important others felt early on can continue to affect the person for decades afterward. These defining narratives are powerful influences over the person's sense of their own capacities and vulnerabilities as well as the perceptions of the extent to which others can be counted on. For individuals caught in narratives of contamination, a key to restoring resilience may be in finding a way to rewrite these narratives. Social scientists could not go wrong in directing some of their attention to these stories when investigating the social processes underlying successful adaptations to personal crises as well as failures of resilience.

SOCIAL FITNESS

Most human adaptation challenges are organized around the self. In Western culture especially, we assign the work of adjustment—of resilience—to each individual, laying responsibility on the person, not his or her social world. To do so may seem the best approach in a society built on the notion that freedom and responsibility are vested in each citizen. However, a snapshot of resilience that focuses solely on the individual is narrow and incomplete. Indeed, virtually all of the conditions in which people live involve participation in a group culture that exerts a strong influence on the capacity of individuals to adapt, recover from adversity, sustain their sense of purpose, and learn from those experiences.

The earliest and most intimate source of social influence on resilience is kith and kin, and as one's social world expands over development, sources of social influence expand as well (see Chapter 6, this volume). Some important clues regarding the social environmental factors that promote resilience can be gleaned from a seminal study that followed children facing tremendous adversity, such as parental psychopathology and family poverty, as they matured into adults (Werner, 1993). Among the most surprising findings was that, by adulthood, the majority of children exposed to hardship were indistinguishable from children reared in circumstances that were more benign. That is, most of the children were resilient. What contributed to resilience? Being in contact with caring adults who valued them as individuals during their childhood contributed to the capacity of these children to thrive over time. So, too, did engaging in activities that allowed the children to be part of a cooperative enterprise, such as a 4-H club, and that required them to perform helpful acts for others in their family and community. In adulthood, resilience was fostered by involvement in the military service and church activities, which embedded these individuals in groups that valued connection, provided meaning, and fostered growth. As they looked back over their early lives, the adults who were exposed to socially resilient environments over their development described their past in ways that were compassionate toward others' emotional pain and dysfunction, and they were optimistic and hopeful about the future (i.e., they relayed redemption narratives).

The evidence gleaned from studying families facing adversity has suggested that a socially resilient environment is one that promotes connectedness by providing a shared sense of commitment and meaning and by encouraging individuals to reach out to and help others, share a range of feelings, and foster hope (Walsh, 2003). Aspects of social resilience evident in family networks are likely to have relevance for other stable, closely knit groups that face adversity, including units of military personnel, firefighters, and emergency medical professionals. Many of the key challenges faced by these groups are social in nature. For example, in military and firefighting units, individuals can become disconnected from the unit because of personal stresses and/or their own failure to pull their weight in the group. Not all individuals have difficulty, but those who do stand out in stark contrast to the rest and become a source of concern for the health and safety of not only those who are disconnected but also the unit as a whole. Isolation also can occur when people form groups on the basis of ethnicity, age, gender, or similar groupings and exclude those who are different from themselves (Galinsky & Moskowitz, 2000).

To date, no empirically tested interventions have targeted social resilience for intact groups beyond families. However, much like family-based treatment, a "social fitness" program may prove useful to promote social resilience for groups facing adversity. Social connection within these groups may be strengthened by increasing group members' awareness of group dynamics and identifying actions to improve social fitness. In Table 9.1, we highlight the key components that can serve as a foundation for a program to maximize social resilience in intact groups. Among the central themes are (a) the role of emotions in sustaining strong social connections, (b) the effects of social isolation within a group, (c) the benefits of constructive resolution of conflict, and (d) the role each member plays in building the social fitness of the group. Within each component, targeted outcomes include increased knowledge and awareness, as well as improved skills to promote strong social bonds. The brief framework included here is meant to invite further development along these lines.

COMMUNITY RESILIENCE

Thus far, we have emphasized the resilience capacities observed in relationships between individuals and also in closely knit groups, but the concept of social resilience is inherently multidimensional. Individual resilience, except in rare circumstances, is embedded within a larger social context. For example, the way in which a person typically responds to challenge is dependent on the social context. Cultural norms guide key interpersonal behaviors, such as the provision of financial assistance and social support from neighbors, the sustainability of social ties, and the responsiveness of whole communities in times of crisis (Murray & Zautra, 2011). Characteristics of a community such as diversity, efficient public programs, and infrastructure can affect an individual's daily life (Zautra, Hall, Murray, & the Resilience Solutions Group, 2008). When we speak of an individual's social resilience, we conceptualize his or her capacity to be resilient in relation to another entity. This other entity may be another individual, a group of a few, a community, or system of many. This connection between one organism and another—or several—contributes to socially resilient processes. Social resilience is the study of relationships across multiple levels of analysis.

Communities can be thought of as entities, like individuals, that are influenced by their history and have unique characteristics, including differing

TABLE 9.1
Social Fitness Training

Theme	Awareness components	Action components
(a) Bolstering the foundations of social connection	Seeing emotion in self and other as a source of information. Recognizing clues to identifying others' emotions.	Sharing one's own positive experiences. Being responsive to the positive stories others tell.
(b) Reducing social isolation	Recognizing pain of isolation in others due to disconnection from family and friends. Understanding the social outcasts in the group.	Showing empathy and acceptance; learning to listen. Learning to be flexible in response to others' emotions; showing new members the "ropes." Identifying how the group and outcast can each demonstrate "reciprocity": viewing human relations as a "two-way street."
(c) Mitigating social conflict	Understanding the underlying causes of conflict, including perceptions of unfairness, distrust of intentions, social sensitivity, and differences in conflict-resolution styles.	Engaging in perspective-taking. Interrupting of one's own cultural stereotypes, false assumptions, and quick and harsh judgments. Identifying one's own best method of resolving conflict.
(d) Promoting social integration	Understanding wisdom of the group—collective wisdom. Identifying unique talents of each person (including oneself) in contributing to the social life of the group. Identifying ways that social fitness knowledge and skills can be integrated with the existing values of the community.	Recording and sharing plans for teaching elements of social wisdom to others. Preparing a plan of action for self-improvement in social fitness going forward.

capacities for resilience to the challenges they may face (Zautra, Hall, & Murray, 2008). Not only can communities affect individual health and well-being, but they can also be resilient in their own right. Tragedy and adversity befall communities too. Events such as the West Virginia Upper Big Branch mine disaster, the 9/11 terrorist attack, and the 2011 Tōhoku, Japan, earthquake and tsunami affected families and communities in addition to the individuals that comprise these groups. The three aspects of resilience—recovery, sustainability, and growth—apply to community resilience, just as they do to individual resilience. For example, communities may differ in the empathetic concern that residents display for one another. This resilience resource may predict how the community recovers and how rapidly it returns to the normal pace of community life following disaster. The capacity for democratic decision making may relate to a community's ability to sustain trust in governance of community resources. Community growth, as measured in transformative social relations, may vary as a function of the community's openness to opposing views.

CULTIVATING COMMUNITY RESILIENCE

We have begun to understand the qualities that make a community resilient. Some communities have created opportunities to promote resilience by expanding opportunities for positive social interaction between community members (Zautra et al., 2010). Okvat and Zautra (2011) highlighted community gardening as a resilience-building activity that promotes individual, community, and ecological well-being. Community gardening has been found to elicit cognitive and affective benefits for individuals, promoting social cohesion and feelings of connectedness (Okvat & Zautra, 2011). This type of intervention works on many levels—individuals within the community benefit, as does the community as a whole. It may also be a first step in the development of social ties among neighbors, which then fosters a greater collective capacity to address larger social–community problems that affect the well-being of the community at large (Tidball & Krasny, 2007).

Another example of an intervention that works across multiple levels is Experience Corps, a national program that enlists older volunteers within a community to tutor and mentor elementary school children, assist children within the classroom, and facilitate after-school enrichment programs (http://www.experiencecorps.org). A pilot study evaluating generativity and health promotion of older adult volunteers ages 60 to 86 years in Experience Corps found that compared with controls, volunteers benefited in the realms of physical health, cognitive activity, and social engagement (Fried et al., 2004). Volunteers demonstrated increased physical activity and reported strength, more cognitive activity, and an increase in the number of people they could turn to for help. Fried and colleagues (2004) discovered that the number of social connections did not increase, suggesting that the quality, not the quantity, of relationships between important people in the volunteers' lives had improved. The Experience Corps pilot also appeared to improve student reading achievement, and children's classroom behavior improved as well, as evidenced by a significant decrease in the number of principal office referrals, lessening the burden of school staff responsibilities (Rebok et al., 2004). Although community indicators were not addressed in these studies, we may surmise that the community is strengthened, for example, through the development and strengthening of relationships among community members, through the growth of feelings of connectedness, and through the development of social capital.

CONCLUSION

Using a resilience framework allows us to conceptualize how humans adapt to adversity and in so doing provides a rich venue in which we may examine how individuals recover, sustain positive engagements, and even benefit because of (not in spite of) the difficulties that are encountered. Studies of resilience have allowed us to identify who is resilient and what characteristics resilient individuals tend to espouse (i.e., meaningful relationships, optimism, purpose in life). We have also begun to understand how resilience emerges—that is, what the mechanisms are that underlie resilient processes (i.e. benefit finding, active coping). Identifying these key variables and constructs facilitates the development of interventions aimed at building resilience capacities. We have given examples of interventions that promote resilience in individuals, and we have described programs that cultivate resilient responding for communities and small units. Some interventions directly target changing how an individual communicates or relates to others, such as in interventions for assertive communication or social skills. Other interventions, like our intervention to promote emotional complexity in patients with chronic pain and like community-based interventions such as Experience Corps, emphasize the importance of making and maintaining connections with others. This volume underscores the importance of relationships in influencing resilient outcomes. "No man is an island" (John Donne, "Meditation XVII"), and we are greatly influenced by the relationships in our lives. These positive social connections not only promote better health outcomes but may also bring meaning and purpose to life.

REFERENCES

Baumeister, R. F., & Leary, M. R. (1995). The need to belong: Desire for interpersonal attachments as a fundamental human motivation. *Psychological Bulletin*, *117*, 497–529. doi:10.1037/0033-2909.117.3.497

Bonanno, G. A. (2004). Loss, trauma, and human resilience: Have we underestimated the human capacity to thrive after extremely aversive events? *American Psychologist*, *59*, 20–28. doi:10.1037/0003-066X.59.1.20

Cacioppo, J. T., Hawkley, L. C., & Correll, J. (in press). Perceived social isolation within personal and evolutionary timescales. In C. N. DeWall (Ed.), *Oxford handbook of social exclusion*. New York, NY: Oxford University Press.

Cacioppo, J. T., Reis, H. T., & Zautra, A. J. (2011). Social resilience: The value of social fitness with an application to the military. *American Psychologist, 66*, 43–51. doi:10.1037/a0021419

Davis, M. C., Twamley, E. W., Hamilton, N. A., & Swan, P. D. (1999). Body fat distribution and hemodynamic stress responses in premenopausal obese women: A preliminary study. *Health Psychology, 18,* 625–633. doi:10.1037/0278-6133.18.6.625

Davis, M. C., Zautra, A. J., & Kratz, A. (2010). *Resilience to daily pain and stress: Effects of mindfulness-based and cognitive–behavioral interventions for chronic pain.* Unpublished manuscript.

Davis, M. C., Zautra, A. J., & Reich, J. W. (2001). Vulnerability to stress among women in chronic pain from fibromyalgia and osteoarthritis. *Annals of Behavioral Medicine, 23,* 215–226. doi:10.1207/S15324796ABM2303_9

DeWall, C. N., MacDonald, G., Webster, G. D., Masten, C. L., Baumeister, R. F., Powell, C., & Combs Tice, D. M. (2010). Acetaminophen reduces social pain. *Psychological Science, 21,* 931–937. doi:10.1177/0956797610374741

Eisenberger, N. I., Lieberman, M. D., & Williams, K. D. (2003, October 10). Does social rejection hurt? An fMRI study of social exclusion. *Science, 302,* 290–292. doi:10.1126/science.1089134

Fried, L. P., Carlson, M. C., Freedman, M., Frick, K. D., Glass, T. A., Hill, J., . . . Tielsch, J. (2004). A social model for health promotion for an aging population: Initial evidence on the experience corps model. *Journal of Urban Health, 81,* 64–78. doi:10.1093/jurban/jth094

Galinsky, A. D., & Moskowitz, G. B. (2000). Perspective-taking: Decreasing stereotype expression, stereotype accessibility, and in-group favoritism. *Journal of Personality and Social Psychology, 78,* 708–724. doi:10.1037/0022-3514.78.4.708

Ganzel, B. L., Morris, P. A., & Wethington, E. (2010). Allostasis and the human brain: Integrating models of stress from the social and life sciences. *Psychological Review, 117,* 134–174. doi:10.1037/a0017773

House, J. S., Landis, K. R., & Umberson, D. (1988, July 29). Social relationships and health. *Science, 241,* 540–545. doi:10.1126/science.3399889

Kawachi, I., & Berkman, L. F. (2001). Social ties and mental health. *Journal of Urban Health, 78,* 458–467. doi:10.1093/jurban/78.3.458

Kiecolt-Glaser, J. K., Gouin, J., & Hantsoo, L. (2010). Close relationships, inflammation, and health. *Neuroscience and Biobehavioral Reviews, 35,* 33–38. doi:10.1016/j.neubiorev.2009.09.003

Lavigne, G. L., Vallerand, R. J., & Crevier-Braud, L. (2011). The fundamental need to belong: On the distinction between growth and deficit-reduction orientations. *Personality and Social Psychology Bulletin.* Advance online publication. doi:10.1177/0146167211405995

MacDonald, G., & Jensen-Campbell, L. A. (Eds.). (2011). *Social pain: Neuropsychological and health implications of loss and exclusion*. Washington, DC: American Psychological Association. doi:10.1037/12351-000

MacDonald, G., & Leary, M. R. (2005). Why does social exclusion hurt? The relationship between social and physical pain. *Psychological Bulletin, 131*, 202–223. doi:10.1037/0033-2909.131.2.202

Masten, A. S. (2001). Ordinary magic: Resilience processes in development. *American Psychologist, 56*, 227–238. doi:10.1037/0003-066X.56.3.227

McAdams, D. P., Reynolds, J., Lewis, M., Patten, A. H., & Bowman, P. J. (2001). When bad things turn good and good things turn bad: Sequences of redemption and contamination in life narrative and their relation to psychosocial adaptation in midlife adults and in students. *Personality and Social Psychology Bulletin, 27*, 474–485. doi:10.1177/0146167201274008

Murray, K., & Zautra, A. J. (2011). Community resilience: Fostering recovery, sustainability, and growth. In M. Ungar (Ed.), *The social ecology of resilience: A handbook of theory and practice* (p. 26). New York, NY: Springer. doi:10.1007

Okvat, H. A., & Zautra, A. J. (2011). Community gardening: A parsimonious path to individual, community, and environmental resilience. *American Journal of Community Psychology, 47*, 374–387. doi:10.1007/s10464-010-9404-z

Rebok,G.W.,Carlson,M.C.,Glass,T.A.,McGill,S.,Hill,J.,Wasik,B.A., . . . Rasmussen, M. D. (2004). Short-term impact of experience corps participation on children and schools: Results from a pilot randomized trial. *Journal of Urban Health, 81*, 79–93. doi:10.1093/jurban/jth095

Reich, J. W., Zautra, A., & Hall, J. S. (2010). *Handbook of adult resilience*. New York, NY: Guilford Press.

Rudatsikira, E., Muula, A. S., Siziya, S., & Twa-Twa, J. (2007). Suicidal ideation and associated factors among school-going adolescents in rural Uganda. *BMC Psychiatry, 7*(67). doi:10.1186/1471-244X-7-67

Rutter, M. (1987). Psychosocial resilience and protective mechanisms. *American Journal of Orthopsychiatry, 57*, 316–331. doi:10.1111/j.1939-0025.1987.tb03541.x

Sturgeon, J. A., & Zautra, A. J. (2010). Resilience: A new paradigm for adaptation to chronic pain. *Current Pain and Headache Reports, 14*, 105–112. doi:10.1007/s11916-010-0095-9

Tidball, K. G., & Krasny, M. E. (2007). From risk to resilience: What role for community greening and civic ecology in cities? In A. Wals (Ed.), *Social learning toward a more sustainable world* (149–164). Wagengingen, Netherlands: Wagengingen Academic Press.

Walsh, F. (2003). Family resilience: A framework for clinical practice. *Family Process, 42*, 1–18. doi:10.1111/j.1545-5300.2003.00001.x

Werner, E. (1993). Risk, resilience, and recovery: Perspectives from the Kauai Longitudinal Study. *Development and Psychopathology, 5*, 503–515. doi:10.1017/S095457940000612X

Zautra, A. J., Arewasikporn, A., & Davis, M. C. (2010). Resilience: Promoting well-being through recovery, sustainability, and growth. *Research in Human Development, 7,* 221–238. doi:10.1080/15427609.2010.504431

Zautra, A. J., Davis, M. C., Reich, J. W., Nicassario, P., Tennen, H., Finan, P., . . . Irwin, M. R. (2008). Comparison of cognitive behavioral and mindfulness meditation interventions on adaptation to rheumatoid arthritis for patients with and without history of recurrent depression. *Journal of Consulting and Clinical Psychology, 76,* 408–421. doi:10.1037/0022-006X.76.3.408

Zautra, A. J., Guarnaccia, C., & Dohrenwend, D. P. (1986). The measurement of small events. *American Journal of Community Psychology, 14,* 629–655. doi:10.1007/BF00931340

Zautra, A. J., Hall, J. S., Murray, K. E., & the Resilience Solutions Group. (2008). Resilience: A new integrative approach to health and mental health research. *Health Psychology Review, 2,* 41–64. doi:10.1080/17437190802298568

Zautra, A. J., Johnson, L. M., & Davis, M. C. (2005). Positive affect as a source of resilience for women in chronic pain. *Journal of Consulting and Clinical Psychology, 73,* 212–220. doi:10.1037/0022-006X.73.2.212

Zautra, A. J., Parrish, B. P., Van Puymbroeck, C. M., Tennen, H., Davis, M. C., Reich, J. W., & Irwin, M. (2007). Depression history, stress, and pain in rheumatoid arthritis patients. *Journal of Behavioral Medicine, 30,* 187–197. doi:10.1007/s10865-007-9097-4

Zautra, A. J., & Reich, J. W. (2010). Resilience: The meanings, methods, and measures of a fundamental characteristic of human adaptation. In S. Folkman (Ed.), *The Oxford handbook of stress, health, and coping* (pp. 173–185). New York, NY: Oxford University Press.

10

RELATING FOR HEALTH: CLINICAL PERSPECTIVES

NICOLE A. ROBERTS

One of the best-known discoveries in clinical psychology is that the relationship between therapist and client is among the most reliable predictors of therapy outcome (Flückiger, Del Re, Wampold, Symonds, & Horvath, 2012; Horvath & Symonds, 1991). When the finding first emerged that common factors, such as therapist–client relationship, potentially mattered more than techniques specific to distinct therapies, it was both contentious and obvious (Luborsky et al., 2002; Rosenzweig, 1936). After all the work that went into carefully crafting theoretical models and therapeutic techniques, how could it be that what mattered most in therapy was simply a warm, caring relationship? Given the fundamental importance of relationships for everything in our lives—and the fact that clients often enter therapy because of relationship troubles—perhaps this should not have been such a surprise.

This volume discusses relationships from family of origin to peer influences to spousal-type relationships to cultures and their role in promoting

DOI: 10.1037/14036-011
Health and Social Relationships: The Good, the Bad, and the Complicated, Matthew L. Newman and Nicole A. Roberts (Editors)

positive physical and emotional health. It also considers how dysfunctional families, peer rejection, social evaluative threat, and the end of one's marriage may undermine health. Finally, it considers how individuals may be resilient despite these maladaptive relationships and situations. Although this volume reviews the importance of relationships for emotional and physical health and discusses many of the moderators and mechanisms through which relationships confer health advantages, some key pieces of the puzzle are missing: What constitutes a good relationship? How do we find such relationships in the first place, and once found, how do we cultivate and sustain them to achieve maximum health benefits? This chapter summarizes characteristics of good and bad relationships, discusses some of the strategic ways that the therapy relationship—a cornerstone of mental health treatment efficacy—can be a model for promoting healthy relationships, and revisits the volume's key themes and their implications.

WHAT IS A GOOD RELATIONSHIP—AND HOW DO WE FIND ONE?

What Constitutes a Good Relationship?

We now know that although there may be some benefits to simply having relationships, if they are not "unambivalently" good ones, the benefits are reduced and the relationships potentially detrimental (Holt-Lunstad, Uchino, Smith, & Hicks, 2007; Uchino, Holt-Lunstad, Uno, & Flinders, 2001). This, of course, raises the question, What is a good relationship? As outlined in this volume, a good relationship is one that provides and allows for the provision of support (see Chapter 2), minimizes a sense of being harshly evaluated (Chapter 1), promotes a sense of connection and meaning (Chapter 9), encourages health-enhancing behaviors and regulatory strategies (Chapter 5), provides opportunities for long-term partnership and even physical affection (Chapter 3), and acts as a buffer in the face of other bad relationships (Chapter 7). Moreover, a good relationship does all of this with consideration for each individual's sense of what support means (Chapter 8).

In one sense, finding and/or maintaining a relationship with all of these qualities seems reasonable enough. After all, humans are hardwired to form attachments, and cognitive and emotional resources are directed toward those attachments (Balas et al., 2010; Bowlby, 1988; Coan, 2010; Iacoboni, 2007). One of our earliest neural accomplishments is face processing (Balas et al., 2010); a smile is easier to detect from a distance than any other emotional expression (Darwin & Ekman, 1998). A passionate romantic relationship is associated with changes in the brain similar to those associated with addiction (Reynaud, Karila, Blecha, & Benyamina, 2010), compelling us to seek proximity to the object of our affections. The "caregiver system" described in Chapter 2 (this volume) gives us the desire to provide nurturance as well as to receive it. Fortunately, then, in many, if not most, ways our biology directs us toward relationships and the health benefits we can receive from them.

At the same time, bad relationship habits can be hard to break. In addition to our own established patterns of relating to others (Hazan & Shaver, 1987; Levenson & Strupp, 2007; Wile, 1995), day-to-day factors such as work stress or the exhaustion of child rearing can sabotage even the seemingly strongest of relationships (Cowan & Cowan, 1992; Gottman & Levenson, 1992; Karney & Bradbury, 2005; Repetti, Wang, & Saxbe, 2009; Story & Repetti, 2006). Knowing how to be appropriately supportive and responsive to others can be challenging (Maisel & Gable, 2009; see also Chapter 8, this volume), and implementing this knowledge perhaps even more so. Given the demands of modern society and the many pulls on individuals' time and psychological resources, it may be difficult to muster cognitive and emotional (i.e., self-regulatory) resources to listen attentively to a friend or partner or to play energetically with one's child (Baumeister, Bratslavsky, Muraven, & Tice, 1998; Maslach & Jackson, 1981; Repetti et al., 2009; Roberts & Levenson, 2001). At times of stress, withdrawing socially—such as staying in one's room watching television—may seem like the most obvious course of action, particularly to men (Lavee & Ben-Ari, 2007; Repetti et al., 2009). Avoidance or suppression of negative feelings may backfire longer term, however, by creating emotional distance and dissatisfaction in relationships, particularly for women (Roberts, Leonard, Butler, Levenson, & Kanter, in press). More remains to be learned about when the potential health benefits of a relationship become outweighed by its costs (see Chapter 3, this volume). Nevertheless, identifying how to maximize the good and minimize the bad within the constraints of one's relationships is important for maintaining all parties' mental and physical health, especially when leaving the relationship is not an option (e.g., as in the case of one's children).

How Do We Find a Good Relationship?

On hearing the question "How do I meet someone?" two answers that may quickly come to mind are "by going out on the town" and "by searching on the Internet." Statistics support these notions, with surveys of couples in the United States showing that meeting one's spouse or partner in a bar or restaurant and meeting online have been on the rise for several decades (meeting one's partner through friends—although still the top method among heterosexual couples—is on the decline; Rosenfeld & Thomas, in press). The advent of the Internet certainly has made it easier to find relationships, especially for underrepresented groups; close to 70% of same-sex couples surveyed in 2010 reported meeting online, versus 25% of heterosexual couples (meeting on the Internet also is a key method for mid-aged heterosexual couples; Rosenfeld & Thomas, in press). Finding a good relationship, however—namely, one that embodies the characteristics described earlier—may be more challenging. In fact, on the basis of an experiment in which participants viewed varied numbers of online dating profiles, having more relationship options does not yield better relationship choices and instead predicts choices that are more discrepant from one's relationship ideals (Wu & Chiou, 2009).

One obvious strategy with respect to finding a good relationship is to seek out others with similar backgrounds, values, and beliefs. After all, these shared characteristics promote strong ingroup bonds even among brand new acquaintances (Brewer, Weber, & Carini, 1995) and may predict relationship longevity among married couples (although this is a source of debate; Karney & Bradbury, 1995).

Perhaps, though, there is no easy answer to the million-dollar question "How do I find a good relationship?" because such a question implies a static process in which we select the right mate (or friend, mentor, gym partner) and a good relationship ensues. We now know, of course, that relationships are dynamic processes and that our own behavior influences the course of a relationship as much as that of the other person or persons (see, e.g., Chapter 5, this volume). Our perceptions also are quite influential in shaping and reflecting the quality of our relationships: Longitudinal research by John Gottman and colleagues (Carrére, Buehlman, Gottman, Coan, & Ruckstuhl, 2000) revealed that how couples meet is not nearly as important in predicting relationship success as their subsequent accounts of this meeting, where these events have the opportunity to be colored by partners' present view of their relationship. An important starting point for finding a good relationship, therefore, may be to develop our own good health and relationship behavior.

How Do We Avoid Bad Relationships?

Before focusing on how we can cultivate and maximize good relationships, it is essential to consider how to avoid potentially bad ones. Although, as discussed in the previous section, relationship patterns involve both parties, and one's own behaviors influence whether a relationship is "good" or "bad," there admittedly are certain individuals who lack empathy or have other traits that simply make them undesirable relationship partners. Furthermore, some of our arguably most important relationships—those with primary caregivers and other family members—are beyond our control. In other words, as peace activist Desmond Tutu said, "You don't choose your family." Other relationships as well, such as with bosses and coworkers, may not be by choice. Nevertheless, to some extent we can influence how and how frequently we engage with these "mandatory" yet problematic others. On the one hand, just one bad or ambivalent relationship may come with considerable health costs (Holt-Lunstad et al., 2007). On the other hand, minimizing emotional investment in these relationships, or offsetting them with positive relationships, may counteract the negative impact of these relationships on health. Fortunately, there are many important relationships we can in fact select (in most cultures), most notably romantic partners and friends. Having supportive, well-regulated relationships, such as friendships (see Chapter 7, this volume) may offset potentially negative consequences of other relationships over which we have less control. Nevertheless, people may find themselves in bad relationships, to the dismay of the supportive relationships they do have.

Certainly, relationships of any kind that are characterized by high levels of conflict and that are abusive, violent, and hostile—especially in the presence of children or directly involving children—have potentially devastating, long-lasting consequences (Oberlander, 2006; Repetti, Taylor, & Seeman, 2002; see also Chapter 6, this volume). Abuse and neglect of children can have a lasting adverse impact on health and well-being, as well as on brain development (De Bellis, Baum, et al., 1999; DeBellis, Keshavan, et al., 1999; Glaser, 2000). Clinical disorders associated with early childhood trauma, such as posttraumatic stress disorder and major depression, are associated with altered perceptions of social stimuli, such as perceptions of neutral or ambiguous cues as threatening (Dearing & Gotlib, 2009; Kanai, Sasagawa, Chen, Shimada, & Sakano, 2010; Pole, Neylan, Best, Orr, & Marmar, 2003).

As reviewed in this volume, even less extreme examples may nevertheless be linked to adverse health outcomes. As outlined earlier, attributes of a bad relationship may be opposite those of a good relationship, meaning partners (or triads or groups or communities) are unwilling to accept or give support, harshly evaluate one another, fail to provide a sense of connection or meaning, are poorly regulated and collude in health-compromising behaviors, are rejecting, and disregard the value system of the other member(s) of the relationship. A bad relationship also may be defined or foreshadowed by the absence of some of the emotional characteristics of a good relationship (e.g., affection; see Chapter 3, this volume). In a marriage, for example, an abundance of emotional neutrality can indicate "a devitalized, essentially affectless marriage" that places couples on a trajectory for divorce (Gottman & Levenson, 2002, p. 92).

Why, then, do people find themselves in relationships that are ridden with conflict and doomed to failure at worst or lack in providing support at best? Conditioning processes are powerful forces in relationships. As described by Selcuk, Zayas, and Hazan (2010); Sbarra and Hazan (2008); and discussed in Chapter 3 (this volume), patterns of relationship attachment are a powerful force. If we learn bad relationship habits through years of dysfunctional or risky family environments (see, e.g., Chapter 6, this volume), these habits can be incredibly difficult to break. Just as children learn how to ride a bicycle, they learn how to feel and behave in relationships. This is nothing new: For decades, therapists and researchers have known that we learn both directly and vicariously, and are more likely to enact a behavior that has been observed than one that has not (Bandura, Ross, & Ross, 1961). What we now know is that there are widespread physical health consequences, in addition to emotional ones, when individuals grow up with poor relationship models and continue to choose the wrong person to rely on as their source of "support." As discussed in the next section, awareness of relationship patterns may be an important starting point. Then, as with any new skill, practicing new relationship behaviors is vital.

CULTIVATING HEALTHY RELATIONSHIPS

Western-based psychotherapies, although diverse in theory and perspective, share the important goal of improving how an individual relates to others. This in turn can facilitate good relationship selection and improved interactions in those relationships. This section focuses on therapies that make use of the client–therapist relationship to help clients create the types of well-regulated, give-and-take interactions and sense of connection that may buffer stress while boosting immune, cardiovascular, and neuroendocrine function and, ultimately, mitigating disease outcome (Hawkley & Cacioppo, 2010; Robles & Kiecolt-Glaser, 2003).

Therapist–Client Relationship

Original therapies, most notably psychoanalysis, believed the therapist could and should be a neutral blank slate onto which clients would project their thoughts and feelings. For example, the therapist would not answer personal questions (e.g., "How long have you been practicing?" "Are you married?") and would sit silently or deflect questions back to the client. Whereas in other relationships it is customary to answer someone's questions, in a psychodynamic therapy relationship the client's curiosity about the therapist is viewed as an opportunity to continue exploring the client's issues. Although this typically is still the case for practicing psychoanalytic or psychodynamic therapists to some extent, it now is more widely believed that being a neutral therapist is not possible (e.g., Jones, 1997; Levenson, 2003). Instead, psychotherapy theorists and researchers point out that two (or more) people are indeed physically present in the room and therefore cannot avoid having a "real" (vs. transference-based) relationship. Current therapies make use of the real therapist–client relationship and in-session (in vivo) client behaviors in strategic ways. Such an approach is discussed next because it provides an opportunity to see how therapy can reverberate in nontherapy relationships and how during interpersonal interactions we have the potential to shape one another's behaviors in ways that ultimately may maximize relationship-related health benefits.

Behavior Change in Action

Functional analytic psychotherapy-enhanced behavioral activation is a type of therapy with a complicated name but a basic behavioral premise: Just as we can give pigeons pellets of food to teach them to play the piano, we can use reinforcement to shape humans' behavior in relationships. This may be simplifying things a bit, but not as much as one would think given the complexities of human relationship behavior. In this therapeutic method (Kanter, Manos, Busch, & Rusch, 2008; Kohlenberg & Tsai, 1991; Manos et al., 2009), the therapist ignores or discourages behaviors the client needs to change and reinforces ones that are more effective. Problem behaviors may include difficulties with intimacy, lack of assertiveness, or ruminating rather than acting according to a goal or plan (Kanter et al., 2008). It is notable that such behaviors may be counter to achieving resiliency, as described in Chapter 9 (this volume). As an illustration of how simple behavioral changes during therapy can add up to more enduring patterns of improved relating to others, Kanter and colleagues (2008) described a scenario in which "a therapist notices a client seems uncomfortable on a warm day and has glanced at the window." In response, the therapist says, "If you are warm, did you consider asking me to change the temperature or open a window?" (p. 791). Even small moments such as this may be opportunities for intervention.

How does such a simple example help elucidate the links between relationships and health? There may be many ways that, without realizing it, we undermine our ability to maximize the health benefits that can come from a good-quality relationship (e.g., Levenson & Strupp, 2007). Of course, relationships are dynamic systems whereby behavior change in one partner affects the other partner, sometimes in unexpected ways (Manos et al., 2009; see also Chapter 5, this volume). It is important to recognize, therefore, that promoting health may involve retooling an entire couple or family system, which is not always an easy task (see Chapters 5 and 6, this volume).

Lessons From Dialectical Behavior Therapy

To a large extent, we cannot control those around us. How do we adjust to current relationships, our family of origin, the independent minds of our own children, and cultural norms constantly influencing us, yet beyond our control? One solution is to express feelings in ways that are constructive. Dialectical behavior therapy (DBT), the first-line treatment for borderline personality disorder (often conceptualized as an emotion dysregulation disorder) is useful in offering strategies for constructive expression of feelings. This includes evaluating the goal of any interpersonal interaction and determining whether it is more important to be "right" (i.e., what the individual thinks is correct behavior) or be "effective" (i.e., a strategy that allows for successful resolution of the problem at hand; Linehan, 1993). A mentality of compromise and doing what works—rather than what may be an ideal scenario for only one of the individuals involved—can be particularly useful in promoting healthy relationships (Cowan & Cowan, 1992; Linehan, 1993). Similarly, DBT encourages *mindfulness*, or paying attention to one's experiences in the moment instead of bringing forward concerns from the past or attempting forecast into the future (Langer, 1989; Linehan, 1993).

Based on these philosophies, DBT and related therapies offer concrete strategies that can be applied to help mitigate difficult social interactions. For example, during an argument (or at least afterward, and prior to the next one) it can be useful to take a moment and ask oneself: Is this a meaningful relationship that I want to maintain? Is there a way to compromise in this situation? What are my goals in this situation? Am I behaving in a way that is consistent with these goals? Am I giving the relationship full but not undue consideration in making my choices? Cowan and Cowan (1992) suggested that couples often think one or the other partner has to completely change, when in fact small changes by one or both partners can go a long way.

An important future direction for researchers is to determine the extent to which small behavioral changes during interpersonal interactions map onto health. Are small, moment-to-moment compromises health saving or health costing, or is there a certain threshold for good or bad relationship behavior that must be crossed to yield the respective health benefits or decrements? As reviewed in this volume, we are getting closer to such answers, particularly in the context of couple relationships (see Chapter 3) and to some extent in parent–child and family relationships (see Chapter 6) as well as friendships (see Chapter 7). Answers to these questions have yet to be determined with respect to a range of other relationships, from acquaintances to coworkers. Some individuals spend more time with their coworkers than their spouses, for example, and therefore studying the intricacies of these relationships may be fruitful as well.

CONCLUDING THEMES

It has almost become cliché to say social relationships are important for health. As the chapters in this volume so poignantly illustrate, social relationships and individual health are inextricably linked. The brain is hardwired for social interaction, and our thought processes themselves, which we may view as products of our own minds, are indeed shaped by our social environment (e.g., Cacioppo & Patrick, 2008; Gazzaniga, 2011). We cannot remove the social world even from our innermost private selves, and we are connected even in the most individualistic cultures. It is not surprising that how we relate to others has such profound implications for our individual survival. The nuances of how this occurs, however, may be less obvious. The following is a review of the volume's key themes and their implications for policy, society, and everyday life.

Relationships Matter

Although it may seem obvious that relationships matter for health and well-being, trends in mental health have suggested it may be time to offer some reminders. In a 1990 article, Seligman presented data documenting a sharp increase in depression in the United States since World War II and argued that the country was experiencing an epidemic of depression. He further argued that societal trends that have "exalted the self" and "weakened the . . . 'commons'" contributed to this epidemic (p. 1). This theme of heightened self-focus, or "societal rises in individualism, self-esteem, and narcissism" has been echoed throughout more recent research (reviewed in Chapter 2, this volume, p. 49; see also Twenge, Konrath, Foster, Campbell, & Bushman, 2008). It is ironic that this type of self-focus may occur at the expense of individual health. Excessive self-focus can not only be alienating, which in turn increases the likelihood for poor health outcomes (Hawkley & Cacioppo, 2010), but it also may have more direct adverse effects on health. As noted in Chapter 2 (this volume, p. 50), "self-focus need not be too extreme to be costly to health." The authors offer as one example an experiment in which older adults were simply informed of self-oriented motivations for volunteering (e.g., to learn something new) in addition to their own other-oriented reasons (e.g., compassion); simply making participants aware of potential self-oriented motivations negated the decreases in mortality that were otherwise observed among the volunteers. The trend of increasing self-focus is a fascinating phenomenon, in part because it goes against extensive evidence presented in this volume and elsewhere that we should—and in many ways are hardwired to (e.g., Coan, 2008)—focus on cultivating supportive networks and, in turn, the health benefits they afford (Cohen & Janicki-Deverts, 2009).

Perceptions Matter

Perceptions are powerful in shaping and reflecting the quality of our relationships. For example, longitudinal research has revealed that spouses' perceptions of their partners and their marriages, as described during narrative interviews (their "how-we-met" story), predicted marital success or failure with 87% accuracy 4 to 6 years later and 81% accuracy 7 to 9 years later (Carrére et al., 2000). One of the most profound findings in the area of relationships and health is that one's experience—or perception—of loneliness matters more in terms of influencing health than whether one is actually alone (Hawkley & Cacioppo, 2010). In Chapter 7 of this volume, Bryan and colleagues discuss that self-stigma can be as influential as actual peer rejection among children with illness. It is important to acknowledge, however, that in some cases, reality is influential in place of or in addition to perceptions. For example, as reviewed in Chapter 3 (this volume), affectionate touch predicts healthier cardiovascular and endocrine responses to stress and reduces neural markers of pain responding, with marital quality moderating some of these effects (e.g., Coan, Schaefer, & Davidson, 2006).

In addition to perceptions, emotions matter considerably in mediating and moderating paths between social relationships and health. Emotion and emotion regulation are important themes in most chapters of this volume, which is not surprising given the centrality of emotion to social relationships and to physical and mental health.

Context Matters

Relationships and health shape one another in a reciprocal fashion. Advances in statistical techniques (e.g., multilevel modeling) have made it possible to begin to capture the bi- and multidirectional nature of health–relationship links, including their mediators and moderators (Butler, 2011). These methods can account for the "nesting" of individuals within dyads within groups and allow behavior to be tracked over time so that mutual influences can be characterized (e.g., Butler, 2011; Caspi, Bolger, & Eckenrode, 1987). Some of the key moderators highlighted in this volume include age and developmental stage (e.g., impact of peer relationships for children vs. adolescents vs. adults; see Chapter 7), gender (e.g., effects of marital quality on health in men vs. women; Chapter 3), and psychological functioning (e.g., self-esteem in moderating the influence of social evaluative threat on physiological reactivity; Chapter 1; or psychological well-being prior to the onset of a relationship loss; Chapter 4). There also are several fundamental processes that may serve as mediators in the relationship–health link across a variety of contexts, such as physiological processes (e.g., immune functioning, hypothalamic–pituitary–adrenal axis reactivity, and cardiovascular reactivity, highlighted in Chapter 6, on family functioning and child health), emotion regulation (e.g., highlighted in Chapter 5, on spousal/partner influences on health behavior), and relationship quality (e.g., highlighted in Chapter 3, on marriage and health).

More broadly, relationships and health exert their influence in cultural context. Soto and colleagues show in Chapter 8 (this volume) that "social support" may not be perceived as supportive at all and, rather, may be distressing if one's culture or own value system do not prescribe accepting help or accepting it in the particular way it is offered. As another illustration of the power of cultural context, suppressing feelings is shown to have detrimental physiological, cognitive, and relationship consequences in Western culture, even across ethnic groups (e.g., Roberts, Levenson, & Gross, 2008), but in cultures where emotion suppression is the norm, it is not nearly as costly (see Chapter 8).

Extending beyond this volume, research shows that cultural context has a considerable impact on health. For example, individuals in developing nations (e.g., India) show better recovery from severe mental illness such as schizophrenia than do individuals in developed nations (e.g., the United States), which is attributed to family and community structures with built-in social support and acceptance for the ill individual (Stanhope, 2002). Family members of individuals with schizophrenia also show less "expressed emotion" (i.e., as demonstrated by hostile, critical, or overly enmeshed families) and greater embeddedness in communities in developing versus developed countries (Stanhope, 2002). Within the United States, among Mexican American families but not Anglo American families, greater familial warmth is associated with considerably lower likelihood of schizophrenia relapse (López et al., 2004). These are powerful examples of how families and communities can act as buffers for an individual and how cross-cultural work can reveal some of these important processes. Cultures and countries with maximal effectiveness in providing support perhaps can serve as models when developing health care plans and systems in the United States, which admittedly is where much of the focus of the present volume lies.

Resilience Matters

One goal of this volume was to present both the good and the bad of relationship effects on health. The topic of stress has historically lent itself to a focus on the bad, with such a theme also reflected by chapters in this volume on social evaluative threat (Chapter 1), family dysfunction (Chapter 6), and loss (Chapter 4). However, the field has moved toward a focus on positive emotion and resiliency. For several years, research by Zautra, Davis, and colleagues has involved developing and testing models of resilience in a variety of contexts (see Chapter 9). The results of this research have yielded recommendations for a "social fitness" training program with the goal of bolstering social connection and integration and buffering social isolation and conflict within and between groups (see Chapter 9).

Currently, joint task forces under the auspices of the National Institute of Mental Health and the American Psychiatric Association are reevaluating and revising the *Diagnostic and Statistical Manual of Mental Disorders* (American Psychiatric Association, 2000). For health care in the United States, the DSM contains the decisive criteria for detection and diagnosis of mental disorders. Under consideration is a profound change—a shift away from symptom lists and categories (e.g., five specific symptoms are required to meet criteria for major depressive disorder) to descriptions of underlying physiological, psychological, and social processes (e.g., neurochemistry, emotion, attention, cognition, social interaction). The biopsychosocial processes outlined in this volume, including those related to resiliency, are prime candidates for inclusion in such a shift. Symptoms of depression could, for example, be framed in terms of loneliness, an excess of social-evaluative threat, peer rejection, or an emotionally impoverished family environment. Mental health also could be evaluated within the context of a client's potential for empathy, compassion, and an ability to form and sustain social relationships. Given what we now know about relationship effects on health, this is bound to be a leap forward.

REFERENCES

American Psychiatric Association. (2000). *Diagnostic and statistical manual of mental disorders* (4th ed., text rev.). Washington, DC: Author.

Balas, B. J., Nelson, C. A., Westerlund, A., Vogel-Farley, V., Riggins, T., & Kuefner, D. (2010). Personal familiarity influences the processing of upright and inverted faces in infants. *Frontiers in Human Neuroscience, 4*(1). doi:10.3389/neuro.09.001.2010

Bandura, A., Ross, D., & Ross, S. A. (1961). Transmission of aggression through imitation of aggressive models. *The Journal of Abnormal and Social Psychology, 63,* 575–582. doi:10.1037/h0045925

Baumeister, R. F., Bratslavsky, E., Muraven, M., & Tice, D. M. (1998). Ego-depletion: Is the active self a limited resource? *Journal of Personality and Social Psychology, 74,* 1252–1265. doi:10.1037/0022-3514.74.5.1252

Bowlby, J. (1988). *A secure base: Parent–child attachment and healthy human development.* New York, NY: Basic Books.

Brewer, M. B., Weber, J. G., & Carini, B. (1995). Person memory in intergroup contexts: Categorization versus individuation. *Journal of Personality and Social Psychology, 69,* 29–40. doi:10.1037/0022-3514.69.1.29

Butler, E. A. (2011). Temporal interpersonal emotion systems. *Personality and Social Psychology Review, 15*, 367–393. doi:10.1177/1088868311411164

Cacioppo, J. T., & Patrick, W. (2008). *Loneliness: Human nature and the need for social connection.* New York, NY: Norton.

Carrére, S., Buehlman, K. T., Gottman, J. M., Coan, J. A., & Ruckstuhl, L. (2000). Predicting marital stability and divorce in newlywed couples. *Journal of Family Psychology, 14*, 42–58. doi:10.1037/0893-3200.14.1.42

Caspi, A., Bolger, N., & Eckenrode, J. (1987). Linking person and context in the daily stress process. *Journal of Personality and Social Psychology, 52*, 184–195. doi:10.1037/0022-3514.52.1.184

Coan, J. A. (2008). Toward a neuroscience of attachment. In J. Cassidy & P. R. Shaver (Eds.), *Handbook of attachment: Theory, research, and clinical applications* (2nd ed., pp. 241–265). New York, NY: Guilford Press.

Coan, J. A. (2010). Adult attachment and the brain. *Journal of Social and Personal Relationships, 27*, 210–217. doi:10.1177/0265407509360900

Coan, J. A., Schaefer, H. S., & Davidson, R. J. (2006). Lending a hand. *Psychological Science, 17*, 1032–1039. doi:10.1111/j.1467-9280.2006.01832.x

Cohen, S., & Janicki-Deverts, D. (2009). Can we improve our physical health by altering our social networks? *Perspectives on Psychological Science, 4*, 375–378. doi:10.1111/j.1745-6924.2009.01141.x

Cowan, P. A., & Cowan, C. P. (1992). *When partners become parents: The big life change for couples.* New York, NY: Basic Books.

Darwin, C., & Ekman, P. (1998). *The expression of the emotions in man and animals* (3rd ed.). New York, NY: Oxford University Press.

Dearing, K. F., & Gotlib, I. H. (2009). Interpretation of ambiguous information in girls at risk for depression. *Journal of Abnormal Child Psychology, 37*, 79–91. doi:10.1007/s10802-008-9259-z

De Bellis, M. D., Baum, A. S., Birmaher, B., Keshavan, M. S., Eccard, C. H., Boring, A. M., . . . Ryan, N. D. (1999). Developmental traumatology: I. Biological stress systems. *Biological Psychiatry, 45*, 1259–1270. doi:10.1016/S0006-3223(99)00044-X

De Bellis, M. D., Keshavan, M. S., Clark, D. B., Casey, B. J., Giedd, J. N., Boring, A. M., . . . Ryan, N. D. (1999). Developmental traumatology: Part II. Brain development. *Biological Psychiatry, 45*, 1271–1284. doi:10.1016/S0006-3223(99)00045-1

Flückiger, C., Del Re, A. C., Wampold, B. E., Symonds, D., & Horvath, A. O. (2012). How central is the alliance in psychotherapy? A multilevel longitudinal meta-analysis. *Journal of Counseling Psychology, 59*, 10–17. doi:10.1037/a0025749

Gazzaniga, M. S. (2011). *Who's in charge? Free will and the science of the brain.* New York, NY: HarperCollins.

Glaser, D. (2000). Child abuse and neglect and the brain—A review. *Journal of Child Psychology and Psychiatry, 41*, 97–116. doi:10.1017/S0021963099004990

Gottman, J. M., & Levenson, R. W. (1992). Marital processes predictive of later dissolution: Behavior, physiology, and health. *Journal of Personality and Social Psychology, 63*, 221–233. doi:10.1037/0022-3514.63.2.221

Gottman, J. M., & Levenson, R. W. (2002). A two-factor model for predicting when a couple will divorce: Exploratory analyses using 14-year longitudinal data. *Family Process, 41*, 83–96. doi:10.1111/j.1545-5300.2002.40102000083.x

Hawkley, L. C., & Cacioppo, J. T. (2010). Loneliness matters: A theoretical and empirical review of consequences and mechanisms. *Annals of Behavioral Medicine, 40*, 218–227. doi:10.1007/s12160-010-9210-8

Hazan, C., & Shaver, P. (1987). Romantic love conceptualized as an attachment process. *Journal of Personality and Social Psychology, 52*, 511–524. doi:10.1037/0022-3514.52.3.511

Holt-Lunstad, J., Uchino, B. N., Smith, T. W., & Hicks, A. (2007). On the importance of relationship quality: The impact of ambivalence in friendships on cardiovascular functioning. *Annals of Behavioral Medicine, 33*, 278–290. doi:10.1007/BF02879910

Horvath, A., & Symonds, B. (1991). Relation between working alliance and outcome in psychotherapy: A meta-analysis. *Journal of Counseling Psychology, 38*, 139–149. doi:10.1037/0022-0167.38.2.139

Iacoboni, M. (2007). Face to face: The neural basis of social mirroring and empathy. *Psychiatric Annals, 37*, 236–241.

Jones, E. E. (1997). Modes of therapeutic action. *The International Journal of Psychoanalysis, 78*, 1135–1150.

Kanai, Y., Sasagawa, S., Chen, J., Shimada, H., & Sakano, Y. (2010). Interpretation bias for ambiguous social behavior among individuals with high and low levels of social anxiety. *Cognitive Therapy and Research, 34*, 229–240. doi:10.1007/s10608-009-9273-7

Kanter, J. W., Manos, R. C., Busch, A. M., & Rusch, L. (2008). Making behavioral activation more behavioral. *Behavior Modification, 32*, 780–803. doi:10.1177/0145445508317265

Karney, B. R., & Bradbury, T. N. (1995). The longitudinal course of marital quality and stability: A review of theory, method, and research. *Psychological Bulletin, 118*, 3–34. doi:10.1037/0033-2909.118.1.3

Karney, B. R., & Bradbury, T. N. (2005). Contextual influences on marriage: Implications for policy and intervention. *Current Directions in Psychological Science, 14*, 171–174. doi:10.1111/j.0963-7214.2005.00358.x

Kohlenberg, R. J., & Tsai, M. (1991). *Functional analytic psychotherapy: Creating intense and curative therapeutic relationships*. New York, NY: Plenum Press.

Langer, E. J. (1989). *Mindfulness*. Cambridge, MA: Perseus.

Lavee, Y., & Ben-Ari, A. (2007). Relationship of dyadic closeness with work-related stress: A daily diary study. *Journal of Marriage and Family, 69*, 1021–1035. doi:10.1111/j.1741-3737.2007.00428.x

Levenson, H. (2003). Time-limited dynamic psychotherapy: An integrative approach. *Journal of Psychotherapy Integration, 13*, 300–333. doi:10.1037/1053-0479.13.3-4.300

Levenson, H., & Strupp, H. H. (2007). Cyclical maladaptive patterns: Case formulation in time-limited dynamic psychotherapy. In T. D. Eells (Ed.), *Handbook of psychotherapy case formulation* (pp. 164–197). New York, NY: Guilford Press.

Linehan, M. (1993). *Skills training manual for treating borderline personality disorder.* New York, NY: Guilford Press.

López, S. R., Hipke, K. N., Polo, A. J., Jenkins, J. H., Karno, M., Vaughn, C., & Snyder, K. S. (2004). Ethnicity, expressed emotion, attributions, and course of schizophrenia: Family warmth matters. *Journal of Abnormal Psychology, 113*, 428–439. doi:10.1037/0021-843X.113.3.428

Luborsky, L., Rosenthal, R., Diguer, L., Andrusyna, T. P., Berman, J. S., Levitt, J. T., . . . Krause, E. D. (2002). The Dodo bird verdict is alive and well—Mostly. *Clinical Psychology: Science and Practice, 9*, 2–12. doi:10.1093/clipsy/9.1.2

Maisel, N. C., & Gable, S. L. (2009). The paradox of received support: The importance of responsiveness. *Psychological Science, 20*, 928–932. doi:10.1111/j.1467-9280.2009.02388.x

Manos, R. C., Kanter, J. W., Rusch, L. C., Turner, L. B., Roberts, N. A., & Busch, A. M. (2009). Integrating functional analytic psychotherapy and behavioral activation for the treatment of relationship distress. *Clinical Case Studies, 8*, 122–138. doi:10.1177/1534650109332484

Maslach, C., & Jackson, S. (1981). The measurement of experienced burnout. *Journal of Organizational Behaviour, 2*, 99–113. doi:10.1002/job.4030020205

Oberlander, C. L. (2006). Evaluating the effects of domestic violence on children. In S. N. Sparta & G. P. Koocher (Eds.), *Forensic mental health assessment of children and adolescents* (pp. 149–174). New York, NY: Oxford University Press.

Pole, N., Neylan, T. C., Best, S. R., Orr, S. P., & Marmar, C. R. (2003). Fear-potentiated startle and posttraumatic stress symptoms in urban police officers. *Journal of Traumatic Stress, 16*, 471–479. doi:10.1023/A:1025758411370

Repetti, R. L., Taylor, S., & Seeman, T. (2002). Risky families: Family social environments and the mental and physical health of offspring. *Psychological Bulletin, 128*, 330–366. doi:10.1037/0033-2909.128.2.330

Repetti, R., Wang, S., & Saxbe, D. (2009). Bringing it all back home. *Current Directions in Psychological Science, 18*, 106–111. doi:10.1111/j.1467-8721.2009.01618.x

Reynaud, M., Karila, L., Blecha, L., & Benyamina, A. (2010). Is love passion an addictive disorder? *The American Journal of Drug and Alcohol Abuse, 36*, 261–267. doi:10.3109/00952990.2010.495183

Roberts, N. A., Leonard, R. C., Butler, E. A., Levenson, R. W., & Kanter, J. W. (in press). Job stress and dyadic synchrony in police marriages: A preliminary investigation. *Family Process.*

Roberts, N. A., & Levenson, R. W. (2001). The remains of the workday: Impact of job stress and exhaustion on marital interaction in police couples. *Journal of Marriage and Family*, 63, 1052–1067. doi:10.1111/j.1741-3737.2001.01052.x

Roberts, N. A., Levenson, R. W., & Gross, J. (2008). Cardiovascular costs of emotion suppression cross ethnic lines. *International Journal of Psychophysiology*, 70, 82–87. doi:10.1016/j.ijpsycho.2008.06.003

Robles, T. F., & Kiecolt-Glaser, J. K. (2003). The physiology of marriage: Pathways to health. *Physiology & Behavior*, 79, 409–416. doi:10.1016/S0031-9384(03)00160-4

Rosenfeld, M. J., & Thomas, R. J. (in press). Searching for a mate: The rise of the Internet as a social intermediary. *American Sociological Review*. Retrieved from http://www.stanford.edu/~mrosenfe/Rosenfeld_How_Couples_Meet_Working_Paper.pdf

Rosenzweig, S. (1936). Some implicit common factors in diverse methods of psychotherapy: "At last the Dodo said, 'Everybody has won and all must have prizes.'" *American Journal of Orthopsychiatry*, 6, 412–415. doi:10.1111/j.1939-0025.1936.tb05248.x

Sbarra, D. A., & Hazan, C. (2008). Coregulation, dysregulation, self-regulation: An integrative analysis and empirical agenda for understanding adult attachment, separation, loss, and recovery. *Personality and Social Psychology Review*, 12, 141–167. doi:10.1177/1088868308315702

Selcuk, E., Zayas, V., & Hazan, C. (2010). Beyond satisfaction: The role of attachment in marital functioning. *Journal of Family Theory & Review*, 2, 258–279. doi:10.1111/j.1756-2589.2010.00061.x

Seligman, M. E. (1990). Why is there so much depression today? The waxing of the individual and the waning of the commons. In R. E. Ingram (Ed.), *Contemporary psychological approaches to depression* (pp. 1–9). New York, NY: Plenum Press. doi:10.1007/978-1-4613-0649-8_1

Stanhope, V. (2002). Culture, control, and family involvement: A comparison of psychosocial rehabilitation in India and the United States. *Psychiatric Rehabilitation Journal*, 25, 273–280.

Story, L. B., & Repetti, R. (2006). Daily occupational stressors and marital behavior. *Journal of Family Psychology*, 20, 690–700. doi:10.1037/0893-3200.20.4.690

Twenge, J., Konrath, S., Foster, J., Campbell, W. K., & Bushman, B. (2008). Egos inflating over time: A cross-temporal meta-analysis of the Narcissistic Personality Inventory. *Journal of Personality*, 76, 875–901.

Uchino, B. N., Holt-Lunstad, J., Uno, D., & Flinders, J. B. (2001). Heterogeneity in the social networks of young and older adults: Prediction of mental health and cardiovascular reactivity during acute stress. *Journal of Behavioral Medicine*, 24, 361–382. doi:10.1023/A:1010634902498

Wile, D. B. (1995). *After the fight*. New York, NY: Guilford Press.

Wu, P.-L., & Chiou, W. (2009). More options lead to more searching and worse choices in finding partners for romantic relationships online: An experimental study. *Cyberpsychology & Behavior*, 12, 31–318. doi:10.1089/cpb.2008.0182

INDEX

DeWall, C. N., 222
Diagnostic and Statistical Manual of Mental Disorders, 244
Dialectical behavior therapy (DBT), 240
Diastolic blood pressure (DBP)
　and marital quality, 71, 72
　with social-evaluative threat, 25
　with stress, 20–21
Diathesis–stress model, 4
Dickerson, S. S., 23
Distress, 217–218
Ditzen, B., 80, 81
Divorce. *See also* Romantic loss
　age effects with, 108–109
　continuing ties with ex-partner after, 102–103
　ethnocultural factors with, 106–107
　gender differences with, 103–104
　health outcomes with, 95–96
　and preloss functioning, 99–100
　social support with, 101
Donnellan, M., 133
Drug use, 124
DuBois, D. L., 175, 177
Dupre, M. E., 70
DW (demand–withdraw) cycle, 132–133
Dyadic regulation processes, 130–136

Eaker, E. D., 69
EAR (electronically activated recorder), 154
East Asian cultures
　conflicting cultural scripts for, 202–203
　diversity of social support scripts in, 195
　emotional support preferences in, 194
　emotion expression/suppression in, 199–200
　emotion regulation in, 197–198
　social support in, 192–193
　support seeking in, 194
Eating habits
　in feedback loop, 135
　indirect mutual influences of partner on, 127

and negative states, 125–126
romantic partner emotional reactions to, 129–130
Electronically activated recorder (EAR), 154
Elwert, F., 105–106
Emotion(s). *See also* Positive emotions
　and chronic pain, 221–222
　expression of, 153, 198–201, 240
　with receiving social support, 41
　and relationship quality, 242
　with romantic loss, 95
　of romantic partners, 129–130
　with social pain, 223
　in social relationships, 196–197
　suppression of, 198–201
Emotional support, 194
Emotion regulation
　with chronic pain, 221–222
　in cultural fit, 196–201
　cultural scripts for, 202
　dyadic processes of, 130–136
　partner influences on, 126–130
　and relationship quality, 126, 242
　in romantic relationships, 121–123
　within-individual processes of, 123–124
Empathy, 46–49, 219
Engebretson, T. O., 202
Environmental factors, 6, 224–225
Epigenetics, 194
Epinephrine, 31
Ethnocultural factors, 104–107. *See also* Cultural context
European American cultures
　emotional support preferences in, 194
　emotion expression/suppression in, 198–200
　emotion regulation in, 197–198
　social support in, 192–193
　support seeking in, 194
Evans, G. W., 31–32
Everyday life, 24–25, 191
Ex-partners, 101–103
Expectancy violation, 26
Experience Corps, 227–228
Expressive suppression, 197–198
Externalizing behaviors, 171–172

Kirschbaum, C., 24
Klein, T., 109
Kobrin, F. E., 106
Konrath, S., 44, 45, 46, 47, 49, 50, 52, 53, 241
Korean Americans, 194
Kram, K. E., 180
Kramrei, E., 101

Laboratory studies, 54
Lamm, H., 78
Landis, K. R., 39, 179
Latinas, 195
Lee, H. S., 48–49
Leitten, C. L., 25–26
LeJeune, J. T., 102
LeMare, L., 171
Leonard, K. E., 127
Lepore, S. J., 31–32
Lesbian, gay, bisexual, transgender, queer/questioning (LGBTQ), 177
Levenson, R. W., 71
Lewis, C. S., 182
Lewis, J., 217
Lewis, M., 227
Lewis, M. A., 128
LGBTQ (lesbian, gay, bisexual, transgender, queer/questioning), 177
Life course, 167–168
Life stories, 217
Light, K. C., 70, 81
Lillard, L. A., 106
Limerance, 79
Loneliness
    in childhood, 170–171
    health outcomes with, 8
    and social pain, 223
Longitudinal studies, 30, 34, 40, 43, 44, 45, 47, 51
Love, 78

Mahler, M., 175
Mahoney, A., 101
Main-effect model, 75
Mandara, J., 106–107
Manzoli, L., 97–98, 104
Margolin, G., 68
Marital relationships, 69–75. *See also* Romantic loss

Marital strain, 70n1
Marital strength, 70n1
Markey, C. N., 129
Marriage, 67–83
    affection and touch in, 77–82
    beneficial effects of, 67–68
    future research directions for, 82–83
    as health predictor, 68–77
Martikainen, P., 107
Martin, S., 101
Marwit, S. J., 102
Matthews, K. A., 202
Mauss, I. B., 199
McAdams, D. P., 217
McCarthy, M., 71
McEwen, B. S., 5
Meadows, S. O., 70
Meaning making, 201
Measurement, 4, 50–51
Mediators
    of eating habits, 125–126
    of family relationships, 150–156
    of romantic loss, 96
    of social support, 193–194
Medical conditions
    in childhood, 172–174
    and peer relationships, 181–182
    and stress, 4–6
Men
    divorce effects on, 103–104
    gender identity in, 175–176
    marriage effects on, 67, 68
    with narcissism behaviors, 50
    receiving of social support by, 42
Mentoring relationships
    in adolescence, 177
    in career development, 180
    in childhood, 227–228
Metabolic syndrome, 69, 71–72
Mihalecz, M. C., 102
Military units, 224–225
Mindfulness, 221–222, 240
Minority groups, 203. *See also* Ethnocultural factors
Mittmann, A., 74
Moderators
    of romantic loss, 96, 98–100
    and social-evaluative threat, 23–24
    social relationships as, 7
    social support as, 32, 100–101

ABOUT THE EDITORS

Matthew L. Newman, PhD, is an assistant professor of psychology at Arizona State University (ASU) in the School of Social and Behavioral Sciences and directs the Stress and Social Relationships Laboratory there. He received his doctorate in social psychology from the University of Texas at Austin in 2003, where he also completed 2 years of postdoctoral training in behavioral neuroscience with the Texas Consortium for Behavioral Neuroscience. Prior to joining the ASU faculty in 2007, Dr. Newman served as a visiting professor at Bard College; he has also held faculty positions at the University of Texas and Southwestern University. Dr. Newman is widely published, and his work has appeared in such peer-reviewed professional journals as the *Journal of Personality and Social Psychology*, *Psychological Science*, the *Journal of Adolescence*, *Personality and Social Psychology Bulletin*, *Hormones and Behavior*, and *American Psychologist*. For more information, visit his website: http://www.matt-newman.net.

Nicole A. Roberts, PhD, is an assistant professor of psychology at Arizona State University (ASU) in the School of Social and Behavioral Sciences and directs the Emotion, Culture, and Psychophysiology Laboratory there. She received her doctorate in clinical psychology from the University of California,

Berkeley, in 2003 and completed her clinical internship and postdoctoral training at the Northern California Veterans Administration Health Care System and University of California, Davis, Department of Psychiatry. Prior to joining the ASU faculty in 2006, she held a faculty position at the University of Wisconsin, Milwaukee. Dr. Roberts's research focuses on the study of emotion and on the cultural and biological forces that shape emotional responses, using both observational and psychophysiological measures. Dr. Roberts is widely published, and her work has appeared in peer-reviewed professional journals such as the *Journal of Marriage and Family*; *Family Process*; the *Journal of Cognitive, Affective, and Behavioral Neuroscience*; *Epilepsy and Behavior*; *Neurology*; and *Emotion*. For more information, visit her website: http://www. asuemotionlab.com.